Advance praise for *Touchdown Jesus:*
The Mixing of Sacred and Secular in American History

"Moore mixes wry wit and reflective criticism in examining how tangled the sacred and the secular are in American culture—from Christmas holidays to prayers at football games to the Christian music industry. With a sharp eye for public inconsistencies and popular humbugs, Moore displays his familiar shrewdness in skewering Protestant foolishness. A search for the prophetic stirs in these pages, yet, as a veteran historian of American religion and culture, Moore knows better than to get his hopes up. *Touchdown Jesus* is a clever and rewarding book."
—Leigh E. Schmidt, Professor of Religion, Princeton University

"R. Laurence Moore draws here on the fruit of his extensive career of research to produce a volume that is at once accessible and insightful and that should appeal to a broad audience. His analysis of the interaction of religion in the United States with a wide array of aspects of our allegedly "secular" culture is subtle, provocative, and witty. Scholars, students, churchgoers, and any who are concerned with current debates over the proper relationship between religion and society will find his work invaluable."
—Peter W. Williams, Distinguished Professor of Comparative Religion and American Studies, Miami University, Oxford, Ohio

"R. Laurence Moore's witty and wide-ranging *Touchdown Jesus* portrays religion's often unexpected power in modern America. Here are ancient and modern Puritans, Jerry Falwell and Christian Right activists, women preachers, Catholic newspaper editors, Martin Luther King and civil rights activists, pro- and anti-evolution propagandists, Black Muslims, and Guy Ballard of the "I Am" movement, among many others. Through them, *Touchdown Jesus* vividly explores the popularization of religion in America—sometimes tawdry, frequently uplifting, seldom uninteresting—that has made the United States all but unique among Western democracies in its persistent religious vitality."
—Jon Butler, William Robertson Coe Professor of American Studies and History, Professor of Religious Studies, Yale University

Touchdown Jesus

Touchdown Jesus

*The Mixing of Sacred
and Secular in American History*

R. Laurence Moore

Westminster John Knox Press
LOUISVILLE • LONDON

Book design by Sharon Adams
Cover design by Mark Abrams
Front cover photo: The *Touchdown Jesus* mural overlooking the Notre Dame campus and football stadium in South Bend, Indiana. Photo by Scott Strazzante/Allsport.
Back cover photo: Notre Dame Stadium in South Bend, Indiana. Photo by Tom Hauck/ Allsport.

First edition
Published by Westminster John Knox Press
Louisville, Kentucky

This book is printed on acid-free paper that meets the American National Standards Institute Z39.48 standard. ∞

PRINTED IN THE UNITED STATES OF AMERICA

03 04 05 06 07 08 09 10 11 12 — 10 9 8 7 6 5 4 3 2 1

Library of Congress Cataloging-in-Publication Data

Moore, R. Laurence (Robert Laurence), 1940–
    Touchdown Jesus: the mixing of sacred and secular in American History /
    R. Laurence Moore.
       p. cm.
    Includes index.
    ISBN 0-664-22370-2
    1. United States—Religion. 2. Religion and culture—United States. I. Title.

BL2525 .M673 2003
306.6'0973—dc21   2002192263

For Lauris, always,
and for Walter Parker Moore Jr.

*"With him disappeared unspeakable sunlight, and
the dark, keen, bright strength of the earth."*

e. e. cummings

Contents

Acknowledgments

I was fortunate to write this book surrounded by very good company. Lady Margaret Hall, University of Oxford, welcomed me as the Starr Foundation Fellow during the Michaelmas Term 2001 and the Trinity Term 2002. I am deeply indebted to fellows and staff of that remarkable college and to its then principle, Sir Brian Fall, and his wife, Delmar. Frances Lannon succeeded Sir Brian as principle, and I am grateful to her for many kindnesses, as I am to Gillian Peele. For their unstinting determination to make my stay in England pleasant and instructive, I thank Clive Holmes and Margery Ord, both of Lady Margaret Hall, and Felicity Heal of Jesus College. As for Americans on the Oxford scene, Dan Howe, who was finishing his last year as the Rhodes Professor, and David Hollinger, who was the Harmsworth Professor, were important companions and interlocutors.

In Paris I was also the recipient of many favors. In particular, I mention Viola Sachs, Martin Bruegel, and Michel Wieviorka. Michel associated me with his *Centre d'analyse et d'intervention sociologiques* (CADIS) at the *École des hautes études en science sociales*. Aside from the many conversations I had with him and his wife, Beatrice, beyond the privilege of free entrance into French museums, my connection to CADIS allowed me to ask a few favors of Michel's remarkable assistant, Jacqueline Longerinas.

I was able to present sections of this book in Oxford and also at conferences in Holland and Italy. In Turin I benefited from an agreement of exchange between the great university of that city and my own home institution, Cornell University. Maurizio Vaudagna, Massimo Salvadori, and Edda Saccomani have listened to me with the sustained interest that only close friends can muster.

The same can be said of my colleagues in the history department at Cornell. For over thirty years I have blessed the dumb luck that brought me to Ithaca in 1972. I might have written the same books in another academic home but not with the same pleasure.

As do most authors, I owe the most to my family. My children, Patrick, Alissa, and Greta, have loved me the longest and in one way or another affect everything I do. My wife, Lauris McKee, has tried hard to influence my work from the direction of her own discipline, anthropology. But that is only the beginning of my debt to her. My brother Walter died in an accident before I had started to write this book. I always liked to imagine that his deep religious faith sufficed to cover my sins as well as his own. He was a splendid person and my constant reminder of how religion can shape very remarkable lives.

What Is Different about Religion in the United States

When I was in grade school, my mother on most Sundays took my brother and me to church while my father went to his office. No one, to my knowledge, has ever suggested that services in Presbyterian churches during the 1950s were child-friendly. Maybe they became so later, but I never took my own children to find out. The gravity of the proceedings in the church where I sat doubtlessly shaped whatever serious sides lie in my character. To John Calvin and his descendants, then, I owe an important debt. Nonetheless, I spent those longest hours of my life counting light bulbs in the Protestant-plain chandeliers that hung from the church ceiling. Maybe, when I lost count, I thought about heaven.

Religion became livelier for me, as a young teen, when Billy Graham swept though my hometown of Houston and conducted one of his headline-grabbing crusades in a football stadium near my house. I was born again, and although mid-adolescence distractions took their toll on the intensity of that feeling, I remained religiously active. It was an era when being active in other ways, the ways prompted by one's hormones, really felt like sin. By the time I packed to leave for college, I had looked at most of the varieties of white Christianity my segregated community had to offer—from Unitarianism, through the standard brands of Protestantism, to Roman Catholicism. Then in an undramatic way, with none of the anger that sometimes attaches to apostasy, I lost my faith.

That was not the end of the story. Because I lived in the United States, a nation that sometimes proclaims itself to be "under God," and because I eventually made the study of American culture my career, I did not lose my interest in religion. For a good part of my adult life, I have spent many of my working days trying to understand how and why Americans, in so

1

many different ways, have made religion central to their lives. Possibly thirty years is too long to think about anything, and especially a subject so closed to outside evaluation as people's private relationship with divinity. To know something about religious behavior and belief is not truly to know what God means to your neighbor. No amount of reading, no amount of interviewing, no amount of theory will reveal in a simple transparent way what lies behind a spiritual claim.

That limitation is not a deterrent to investigation. It is an invitation to keep asking questions. My work on American religious behavior, the "habits of the heart" that the astute French observer Alexis de Tocqueville saw as central to American democracy, has left me with no little respect for the small strategies of human creativity that make communal life possible. As payment for the pleasures of my research, I have attempted to aim this book not at other academics who study religion but at general readers who are interested in what the American philosopher William James called "the varieties of religious experience." Those varieties are in significant ways responsible for the unfolding of all the things that constitute American pluralism. American life, for reasons peculiar to its history, has encouraged many public uses of religion. Depending on one's point of view, those uses have yielded good or bad or mixed consequences. One thing is not subject to doubt: Without them, our contemporary public culture would be something very different from what it is.

I am most interested in religion when it is about something else. That is the dominant mantra that recurs in the following chapters. Looking at religion when it is tied into attitudes and practices that we usually call secular may seem odd, but it comes from my conviction that the secular and the sacred are not always easy to separate in American experience. In fact, I don't think that there is any place on earth where one can find a reliably clear line to demarcate these different spheres. Many cultures do not even see a point in trying to distinguish them. Western men and women do because they have learned to think and to write legal codes by learning to differentiate, by drawing lines of distinction between this thing and that thing. Our dualistic logic, which insists on a difference between the sacred and the secular, has been conditioned by politics, a long history that has often pitted St. Augustine's City of God, originally centered in its earthly guises in Rome, against the various European rulers whose realms constituted the City of Man. Cathedrals and monasteries marked the territory of the sacred where people, consecrated by God, held keys to a spiritual kingdom. They were architecturally distinct from the palaces that housed monarchs and from which radiated complex chains of loyalty that organized the powers of earthly government.

A constitutional separation of church and state, a principle that Americans helped etch into political theory, became an enormously important foundation of classic liberalism. Nothing more clearly evokes the difference that contemporary Westerners feel between their own political systems and self-styled Islamic states based on religious law. Nothing, as a result, creates more tension in the contemporary world. Nonetheless, in Western history church and state have regularly overlapped, albeit in different ways. Long before the adoption of the American Constitution and long before Thomas Jefferson spoke of a "wall of separation," kings and cardinals warred over turf, stopping from time to time to negotiate about what things belonged to Caesar and what things to God. Kings cloaked their offices with divine sanction, and men of the church found plenty of opportunity to oversee, and even to direct, nominally princely affairs. The state grew powerful by encroaching upon the church, but the church responded by filling the state bureaucracies with its men. Religion even in the early Christian era was entangled in just about everything—in economics, in social conduct, and in the struggle for worldly influence. Appropriately, I wrote much of this book in Paris near the Palais-Royal, the splendid residence that Cardinal Richelieu built for himself while serving God, but more famously Louis XIII.

When the Reformation challenged settled arrangements in Northern Europe and England in the sixteenth century, many rulers tried harder to restrict the temporal power of men who were supposed to be tending to church affairs. Henry VIII of England set a bold example. He cut ties with Rome, seized the ecclesiastical lands of the Catholic Church along with the tax revenues that went with those estates, and made himself head of the Church of England. Those actions scarcely separated church and state. They merely set new rules for church/state interaction. The temporal power of churchmen continued.

Elsewhere in Europe, although many Protestant rulers gave churches less room to meddle in state affairs, religion retained an influence that reached into all areas of public life. Godly behavior and civic duty were often posed as synonyms. In John Calvin's Geneva, civil authorities cooperated with ministers to ensure religious uniformity. Reformed divines knew what God wanted just as surely as the pope. None of them believed that the encouragement given ordinary men and women to read the Bible in vernacular languages gave people the license to practice any religion that struck their fancy. In areas conquered by the Reformation, heresy remained both a sacred and a secular crime. The patterns persisted in the new settlement of North America. The virtues of the Pilgrims and Puritans who left England in the seventeenth century for the howling wildernesses of Plymouth and Massachusetts Bay were considerable, and any account of the success of the English colonists must begin with them rather than their lazy compatriots in Virginia. They were not, however, religiously tolerant. To Puritans, religious freedom meant the right to form a civil government that conformed to their idea of God's will. God's will demanded that the state compel people to attend rightly constituted churches and to pay for their maintenance. Exile or execution awaited anyone who too publicly proclaimed a different understanding of divine purpose.

As always before, people in seventeenth-century Europe, whether in Catholic or Protestant countries, and in the North American English colonies, whether in the North or the South, made distinctions between religious and secular behavior. Even in John Winthrop's Boston, where Godly duties were law, the religious authority that guided the Puritan mission waned in strength with each passing decade of the seventeenth century. Ministers remained extremely important public figures, but people followed many rules of conduct in daily life that had little to do with the commandments of God enunciated from church pulpits. Remarkably, many successful New England merchants pursued their businesses as if God read their ledgers of profit and loss over their shoulders. But most business procedures were not covered by anything written in the Bible. Government buildings, meeting halls, fashionable homes, shops, and markets—all structures reflecting secular purposes and activities—dominated the American colonial landscape by the end of the seventeenth century.

People's sense of a difference between sacred and secular widened considerably with the religious settlement that followed the American Revolution, or at least the difference took on a new political meaning. The men who drafted the American Constitution introduced a radically new set of principles to separate church and state. It was the first political document in the West that recognized religious differences among people as something that was socially beneficial. This is the basis for a second mantra important to this book. Nation building has so often involved forcing people within a particular set of borders to choose a single identity. The Spanish monarchs Ferdinand and Isabella sent Columbus off on his voyages at precisely the same moment they told Jews who wanted to remain Jews to get out. In today's world Kurds who do not wish to be classed as Arabs have great difficulty finding an unmolested place to live in the Middle East.

There are a thousand variations of this story, and some of them form part of American history. Yet in the United States the expansion of equality has always involved the erasure of difficulties attached to being different. Religion has been a constitutionally privileged form of difference, and religious pluralism has played an important role in advancing the struggles of many Americans held back because of their race, or ethnicity, or sex, or national origins. The acceptance of religious diversity as a normal condition has been crucial not only in allowing Americans to be different in ways other than religion but also in allowing them, when they chose, to step beyond whatever made them different and to form social and political alliances with others. American freedom at its best is the freedom to have multiple identities.

American freedom has not always been at its best. The famous preamble of the American Constitution disassociated the new national government from any ascribed burden to carry out God's will. "We the people of the United States" acted not as agents of God but on their own behalf to "provide for the common defense, promote the general welfare, and to secure the blessings of liberty to ourselves and our posterity." Nothing more clearly signaled the intention of America's founders to end religious discrimination than their inserting in the Constitution's Sixth Article the principle that there would be no religious test for public office. The president of the United States might profess any of the extant varieties of Christianity or none of them. The president could be a Jew, a Muslim, or a nonbeliever. A person's religious identification was a private choice and had no bearing on citizenship.

Yet we all know that the "no religious test clause" of the Constitution has not in practice admitted as much variety in American political leadership as the language invited. Most of our presidents and vice presidents have belonged to Protestant churches. Not all Americans have embraced the notion that religious pluralism is a good thing. Until the middle of the twentieth century, the Constitution, with the famous religious clauses of the First Amendment ("Congress shall make no law respecting an establishment of religion nor prohibiting the free exercise thereof") applied only to actions of the federal government, leaving the individual states free to create theocracies if they chose.

Actually, all of the American states by the middle of the nineteenth century had adopted written constitutions that followed the formula of church/state separation enunciated in the Constitution. That did not, however, settle a much more significant ambiguity that lay in the work of the founders, one that among other things has prompted some Americans to insist from time to time that the founders meant to establish a Christian nation. What is most certainly true, despite their insistence on a secular state, is that the founders wanted a religious nation. Their intention was never to banish religion to private houses of worship or to silence religious voices in discussions of public issues. Unlike other revolutionary governments that have appeared in world history, beginning in France the same year the Constitution went into effect, the American Constitution makers harbored no grudge against religion. Clerics were not blamed for siding with oppressive rulers and hunted down for execution. Nor was religious faith charged with diverting people's attention away from unjust economic conditions that kept most of them poor.

The American founding philosophy regarded religion as the foundation of all human happiness and virtue. It was absolutely essential to the success of the proposed democratic republic. The founders made no secret of the fact that they wanted religion to be about something else and to affect many things of general public importance. People might identify with any number of sects or denominations, but what all of the faiths taught about ethical behavior laid the basis for a common American citizenship, what some have called civil religion. This remarkable joining of assumptions—a secular state indifferent in formal ways to all religious institutions but dependent for its survival on their health—was what gave American religious affairs a distinctive cast, one that permitted both in strict legal terms and in the practice of daily life a great deal of interaction between the religious and the secular.

Americans, by setting up voluntary churches—that is, religious institutions supported by people who chose to join them—placed religion in the marketplace and trusted Adam Smith's "invisible hand" to assure a just allocation of its blessings. This arrangement allowed religion to have an enormous influence on culture and public life. Knowing this, we can understand why Benjamin Franklin, a very free spirit with respect to religious questions, can exemplify something we call the Protestant ethic. We can understand why many immigrants, who came to the United States seeking a better standard of life, have responded to their adopted home as a "promised land." We can understand why some politicians in both major political parties, politicians who vehemently support the principle of church/state separation, expect faith-based charities to solve the social problems of drug addiction and criminal recidivism.

We might usefully consider the placement of the slogan "In God We Trust" on all American currency as a central paradigm in explaining how Americans have used religion to imagine themselves as a nation and as a culture. Our legal tender brings together the City of God and the City of Man. If religion can be about money, it can be about anything. All Americans, however high or low they imagine Jefferson's wall of separation to be, carry in their purses or their wallets the evidence that religion remains a potent force in American culture.

Many pundits argue that Americans are a more secular people than they were a century ago because while they may go to church they have so many new diverting secular options to pursue. Perhaps, but it is far from clear that the sacred and secular are less intermingled. A century ago we didn't have Christian stores in shopping malls selling rock music, diet books, and T-shirts. After one hundred fifty years of Darwinian science, a succession of scientific triumphs that have enabled human beings to create life in a laboratory, a sexual revolution, and a generation reared without school prayer, nine out of ten Americans say that they believe in God. Polls telling us this and also that the vast majority of Americans regard religion as very important in their lives should not mislead us into thinking that Americans are somehow more spiritual than people of other nations. On the other hand, these polls suggest that American culture has given people many offhanded, though not necessarily trivial, options to express belief in God. A lot of Americans who know how to use computers and every other implement of modern technology also believe in angels.

Anyone inclined to argue that the quality of the religious lives Americans profess to lead has declined must ask: compared to what standard? Why should we think that farmers and Americans living in small towns in the nineteenth century gave more thought to divine purpose than Americans today who practice Zen meditation or who find something personally important to them in the Church of Scientology? Can lamentations about the superficiality of American's religious commitments credibly imply that the quality of our purportedly secular lives has risen? I find it difficult to watch American television, during the day or during prime time, and say to myself that televangelists bear special blame for having trivialized our culture. The evidence of trivialization is so much stronger elsewhere and in any case can be found abundantly in any period of American history. Foreign critics of the United States have always cited its religious behavior as evidence of what bad things can happen in an overly democratized society. Jim and Tammy Bakker provided nothing particularly novel in that category. I have not avoided making judgments in the pages that follow. But I have intentionally sidestepped the temptation to make estimates of decline and progress.

A better complaint to make about American religion than its shallowness is its very failure to try to maintain a sharp distinction between the sacred and the secular, a distinction that might give churches a vista from which to criticize the world around them. Sometimes a sharp churchly assertion that God wants more than a political compromise can push a nation toward greater social justice. American churches have supplied plenty of social critics and social reformers but very few prophets. Religious leaders and political leaders more often than not go about their business doing similar things and extolling the same virtues. As part of the free enterprise system, American religious leaders, pragmatists to the core, measure their highest goals by the expansion of their membership roles and the amount of money they raise. Americans, religious and secular, display a mighty confidence in growth as a sign of health.

So how do we begin this story? Some years ago, when I was starting to write something else, my young son, Patrick, about seven years old, was playing at our house with a friend, David. He asked David when his family would put up a Christmas tree. David replied that his family was Jewish and did not celebrate Christmas. Patrick cast a puzzled look at me and, knowing at least that we weren't Jewish, asked, "What are we, Daddy? Are we British?" I laughed at the question, although it occurred to me later that it said a lot about how religion in American is linked to identity formation, often in accidental ways. So did the whole exchange. David, whose parents I knew regarded themselves as secular (i.e., mostly nonobservant) Jews, understood the meaning of being Jewish in America as in part not having a Christmas tree. Being British had no explicit religious meaning to Patrick, but it defined well enough the kind of church he would have attended had his parents been practicing Christians. It was David, not Patrick, who recognized in Christmas a religious significance, although he could scarcely have specified of what sort. What mattered was that he stood apart from it. Meanwhile, Patrick learned, though not from his parents, that what he looked forward to as a day of gifts and the effective beginning of the ski season defined him in some religious way, not because he went to church but because it linked him to beliefs and hence to the culture of his grandparents and cousins.

That story already contains a number of elements suggesting how religion is always about something else and how it affects identity. We begin in chapter 1 to explore the meaning of the public displays of religion in the United States, present and past. These include the symbols of Christmas. Why do these displays matter? How do they unite Americans? How do they divide Americans? As in the rest of the book, the aim is to give historical perspective to the way religion operates in American culture at the beginning of the twenty-first century. A lot has changed since the American Constitution was adopted. But a lot has not changed. Our present-day quarrels about how to interpret the religious clauses of the First Amendment might be more fruitful if we understood better how history has shaped those quarrels. What is crucially at stake in our commitment to church/state separation, and what makes American experience different from the experience of Northern Ireland or much of the Middle East, is the notion that government should never do anything to make religion a point of political and social division. The state, any state, whatever it does, will at times offend someone's religious conscience. But when the state deliberately contributes to the hostility that so often accompanies different religious beliefs and practices, it has violated the principle of church/state separation that matters most. That principle is in a vital way about something else. It is about the American concept of liberty.

Chapter One

Touchdown Jesus and Other Controversies about the Public Display of Religion

A t Notre Dame, America's best-known Catholic university, one side of the library faces the football stadium and is covered with a large mosaic mural of Christ. It is known affectionately as "Touchdown Jesus" because Jesus has his arms raised as if signaling a touchdown. No one thinks that the mural was placed where it is to help Notre Dame win football games. In fact, seats added to the stadium now block the view. But surely thousands of Catholic football fans, with their very human hearts, once looked affectionately toward the library whenever a home game was going Notre Dame's way. Or if it wasn't, a Notre Dame quarterback could always try the "Hail Mary" pass, a last-ditch play to score a winning touchdown in the game's closing seconds. Religion is in the lexicon of American football, a fact that suggests how easily religious Americans can entwine the sacred with the secular. Knute Rockne, Notre Dame's famous football coach of the 1920s, put the matter clearly: "Outside of the Church the best thing we've got is good, clean football."

We are not just talking about Catholic Americans. Although American Protestants sniff at "Touchdown Jesus" or at players who cross themselves before attempting a field goal as Catholic superstition, they have their own ways of trying to put God on their side at a football game. Consider, for example, the flap about the legal fate of prayer at the opening of high school football games. The small town of Santa Fe, Texas, lies forty miles southeast of Houston. In the mid-1990s, it was composed of some ten thousand residents, including many white Baptists who once were the most vehemently opposed of all religious groups to any practice that burdened churches with worldly concerns. The success of the high school football team was a community passion, and before each game the student council chaplain said a prayer over the public address system. Most people in the stadiums bowed their heads. The ritual was disrupted when in 1995 several families representing Catholic and Mormon students filed suit, claiming that the practice violated the "no religious establishment clause" of the Constitution's First Amendment. *Santa Fe v. Doe* reached the Supreme Court in 2000, and by a 6–3 vote it sided with the petitioners, proscribing a practice that undoubtedly had the backing of most of the people who lived in Santa Fe.

The prayerful opening of American football games was once common in high school and college contests. Although the practice had disappeared in many parts of the country, the Texas case that reached the Supreme Court made clear that it was far from dead everywhere. In Texas and across much of the South, parents and students protested the Court's action. Groups that were formed to encourage "spontaneous prayer" before games proudly named themselves "We Still Pray" and "No Pray/ No Play." In Hattiesburg, Mississippi, forty-five hundred high school football fans joined hands in the local stadium and recited the Lord's Prayer. George W. Bush, then the governor of Texas, agreed with the overwhelming majority of voters (94 percent) in the Texas Republican primary who favored a nonbinding resolution backing student-initiated prayer at school sporting events.

Clearly a substantial number of Americans are nostalgic, in some cases fiercely defensive, about this particular form of public piety. And many others, while they may not feel strongly about prayer over the public address system, are pleased to see their gridiron heroes, professional and amateur, pray together in the locker room or kneel with bowed heads after scoring a touchdown. One wonders whether these same Americans would be equally comfortable if they were asked to pray before a bullfight or before a horse race. Or would they not perhaps think that it is wrong to implicate God in some public spectacles?

In the United States, the ways in which religious rituals have been attached to secular events have not followed a predictable logic. Prayer has not intruded into very many sporting events. Charles Kimball, a Texas Baptist minister who agreed with the Supreme Court in the Santa Fe dispute, wondered why football fans showed no concern about the "exclusion" of God from high school soccer games, or baseball games, or golf matches. In any case, Kimball noted, God does not need a prayer for permission to go where God wants to go. We might say that many sports disqualify themselves as venues for religious meditation because their primary purpose is to draw blood and to encourage gambling. But that is precisely what American football does. It is a game of intentionally brutal contact that is bound to result in bodily harm. And although betting windows are not allowed in football stadiums as they are at racetracks, football, both college and professional, generates a staggering amount of gambling. Professional odds makers take more money from football fans each year than is given to all of America's houses of worship.

Invoking God in Public Forums and in Public Schools

Many things in the American past might lead us to expect that most people would protest any action that purported to impart religious meaning to a recreational diversion. After all, Americans are supposed to be the world's hardest workers. They are a people who, because they make work synonymous with their sense of self-worth, do not allow themselves many holidays. The Puritan notion that idle play is Satan's way to ensnare people's souls into eternal damnation may be dead. But strong feelings about the morality of hard work are buried deep in the bones of many Americans. That attitude suggests a quick answer to the question of why so many Americans want to pray at football games: It takes the guilt away. A quick prayer transforms football into a healthy diversion and a moral surrogate for work.

This thought is not so much wrong as it is peripheral to what is a much larger issue in American life and history. Many Americans want to maintain religion as an important part of public, secular life because they believe that God blesses America. The Constitution posed a problem for them. In taking away an established church, it robbed them of a script for keeping religion in the public eye. They had to wing it. They had to invent ways to acknowledge their debt, for they believed that if Americans failed in that duty, the country would decline. The United States built into its past and present a powerful story about itself as a modern promised land.

Yet we are not dealing with unanimous national sentiment. Many people think that it is improper to deal religion into any public occasion sponsored in any way by any branch of government. The conflicting views have made public religious rituals a cause of discord among Americans. Probably no other country in the world has found so many reasons to argue about the appropriateness of religious displays at many different kinds of public events. Some Americans seem to think they are always appropriate, even if they blatantly favor one religion over another. Others believe they are never appropriate, even if they bend over backwards to be nonsectarian. Sometimes prayer becomes customary. Sometimes it does not. The patterns shift, with or without court interventions.

For over three decades the center of the storm has been the issue of prayer in public schools, not in their football stadiums but in their class-rooms. In 1962 the Supreme Court handed down a decision in a case that a group of New York parents had brought against the state's Board of Regents. The issue was whether the Constitution permitted public school districts to authorize prayer as part of the school day. School prayer had had a tangled history. A number of states had never permitted it, and other states, including New York, required it. What was interesting about the New York case was that the so-called Regents' Prayer was a thoroughly innocuous invocation of divinity. It read: "Almighty God, We acknowl-edge our dependence upon Thee, and we beg Thy blessings upon us, our parents, our teachers, and our Country." Unlike the Lord's Prayer, which some school districts in the United States used, the words tried to sever any association with a particular religious tradition. Still it was prayer, hence religious. Even though school children could choose not to take part in the ceremony, the Supreme Court, in *Engle v. Vitale*, said that it violated the "no religious establishment clause" of the First Amendment to the Constitution.

The almost unanimous decision, supported by many religious groups, has splintered public opinion. Parents who had never given much thought to school prayer have suddenly become strident partisans on one side or the other. Americans who vociferously support school prayer, probably more of them today than in 1962 when the Supreme Court struck down the practice, hurl epithets at Americans who see school prayer destroy-ing the fabric of church/state separation. Sometimes a cool head suggests that the issue is way overblown. Few listen. Those who support *Engle v. Vitale*, and the Court's decision a year later in *Abington Township v. Schempp*, which added Bible reading in public schools to the Constitution's list of banned practices, insist that religion is fine in its place but that place is not in any institution that receives financial support from the govern-ment. Never mind that prayer is used to open sessions of Congress and of the Supreme Court itself. As noted, in examining the role of religion in public life, we should not expect consistency.

What the Founders Thought (As Best We Know)

We will come back to prayer and other contemporary disputes. However, to understand why controversy about religion in public assemblies exists at all, we need to go back to the beginning. The godless Constitution intended no antipathy toward religion. Quite the contrary. Some of the most famous men associated with the Revolutionary and Constitutional eras—Thomas Jefferson, Benjamin Franklin, James Madison—did not belong to churches. They held theological views that were in the late eighteenth century known as Deism. Deists regarded Jesus as a great moral teacher but not as God. They found the evidence for God's existence in the orderly workings of nature, the machine-like perfection of the natural order, rather than in the Bible. Other Revolutionary leaders held more conventional religious views. Although we do not know much about the religious attitudes of everyone who was present in Philadelphia to draft the Constitution, what we do know suggests that most of them belonged to Christian churches and attended them. We also know that, whether they were Deist or Congregational or Episcopalian, or not much of anything, they shared an important assumption: Religion was the foundation of virtue.

The people who separated the business of religion from the business of government posited religion as an essential foundation of civil society. This fact more than anything else explains why later Americans would never agree about whether religious exercises belonged in public assemblies. The disagreement was apparent even before the Constitution was ratified. Clerics who wanted to find ways to make up for the Constitution's omission of God and religious tests called upon national leaders to rewrite the document. To them the nation was in a crisis caused by lack of attention to God. Most Americans in 1787 neither belonged to nor regularly attended any house of worship. Church membership varied from place to place but stood somewhere around 10 percent of the total population.

Given the lethargic support that Americans rendered to churches in an era when churches still received tax support in many of the former English colonies, the decision to relieve the national government of any responsibility to promote religion looked like a risky gamble. It was as if a group of leaders agreed that public education was vitally important to the health of the state yet at the same time barred the state from contributing money to build schools. We should not be surprised, then, that many of the nation's first political leaders viewed certain kinds of religious expression not only as appropriate in the halls of government but also in almost any public ceremony that drew large numbers of Americans together.

George Washington took a middle road. When he rose to take the first oath of office administered to an American president, he chose to add the words "so help me God" to the secular words prescribed in the Constitution. (Those words are: "I do solemnly swear [or affirm] that I will faithfully execute the office of the President of the United States, and will to the best of my ability preserve, protect, and defend the Constitution of the United States.") In addition, he spoke the oath with his right hand placed on a Bible and made sure that a minister was present to bless the event. At the same time, by including these sacred rituals in what was supposed to be the secular investiture of a national leader, rituals that have been observed by all subsequent American presidents, Washington made no commitment to act as God's agent. He simply thought it useful (and useful is the precise word) for Americans to remember God on important public occasions. Washington set aside the strictest interpretation of how church and state might be separated, because like many others he hoped that the private religious views of Americans would coalesce in public life into a loose sort of civil religion. The government would not sponsor it with money but would lend it some formal encouragement.

Other people in the early republic held stricter views about church/ state separation than Washington, but none of the ones elected to public office were prepared to banish God from their public speeches, at least those that had ceremonial importance. Consider, for example, Thomas Jefferson. In his famous letter to a group of Baptists in Danbury, Connecticut, he spoke of the need to build "a wall of separation between church and state." That is a strong metaphor. Later, although the phrase was not in the Constitution or any piece of legislation, many American jurists used it to gloss the meaning of the First Amendment. Jefferson mostly meant what he said and regarded his own religious views as private and not relevant to the performance of his presidential duties. Yet Jefferson devoted a paragraph to divine providence in both of his inaugural addresses. So also did James Madison, who held even stricter views than Jefferson about maintaining well-defined boundaries between government and religion. Unlike many New England clerics, he did not believe that the godless Constitution he had helped to write was responsible for the British burning of the White House during the War of 1812. He did not regard the United States as a modern chosen nation. But in his first inaugural address delivered on March 4, 1809, he said, "My confidence will under every difficulty be best placed . . . in the guardianship and guidance of that Almighty Being whose power regulates the destiny of nations, whose blessings have been so conspicuously dispensed to this rising Republic."

What happened next is very important. Without adding God to the Constitution, without national leaders retreating any more than has been indicated from church/state separation, and with all the states but two giving religion no tax support, Americans started going to churches in record numbers. That fact seemed to confirm that the founders had read the right lesson from history. It told them that whenever states had established an official religion or in any other way made a religious practice mandatory, then people who took religion seriously began to quarrel. Those men and women who endorsed what the state mandated as the proper faith fought with those who dissented. The result was civil disorder and a corrupt religion that drove people away from churches. Influenced by the rationalist philosophies of the late eighteenth century, the founders were convinced that if government retired from the business of enforcing or seeming to care about religious orthodoxy, religion would prosper. Moreover, religious differences, maintained in private, would in public be subordinated to the larger national concern of sustaining moral conduct in the young republic. Jefferson anticipated that within several decades most Americans would be Christians in ethical terms, but no longer much concerned with whether Christ was God, whether he was born of a virgin, or whether he had risen from the dead. If not Deists, they would be Unitarians, the most rational of the then existing forms of Christianity.

In fact, the expansion of religious activity in America took forms that no one had expected. Despite Jefferson, Deism disappeared and Unitarians survived as a tiny denomination that scarcely mattered to anyone who lived outside a fifty-mile radius of Boston. In 1850 the largest single religious denomination in the United States was Roman Catholicism. Methodists and Baptists that had been small sects at the time of the American Revolution and the professed faith of only a few of the drafters of the American Constitution became the two largest Protestant denominations. The Protestant churches that had been most important during the colonial period—Presbyterians, Congregationalists, and Episcopalians (formerly Anglicans)—watched their relative numbers decline, although they retained the allegiance of many of the country's social and political elite. What was most striking about the religious landscape of America a half-century after the nation had begun was that religious divisions had multiplied rather than diminished. Some arose from schisms. Some came from Europe. Some were homegrown novelties. As one European churchman remarked, America became a "motley sampler" of church history.

Whether all the different religions had kept Americans virtuous or had united them in common civic commitments was a question that aroused considerable anxiety. And rightly so. The only certain thing was that religion, without any government sponsorship, was very visible in American public life. The energies that had drawn more and more Americans into organized religions, at the same time dividing them, were the forces of market competition. Americans who wanted to build churches had to drum up business. They had to find ways to sell their product and to engage in what would later be called product differentiation. Religious leaders called this activity proselytizing, and many of them became extremely good at it. Their efforts placed religion in the center of America's marketplace of culture and guaranteed that much about American religious life was enacted in public rather than within the church walls of individual denominations. From the beginning, American republican religion was closely related to the secular world of politics, commerce, and even entertainment. It was very much about something else.

Protestant Revivals and the Public Performance of Religion

The operation of the religious marketplace took some specific forms. Revivals, those sometimes riotous assemblies that became an engine of proselytizing, at least among many Protestants, were in the early nineteenth century the most important. Religious revivals were not American inventions. They began in Germany almost simultaneously with the Reformation itself. England and Scotland provided many prototypes for what later would be seen as peculiarly American religious behavior. In the eighteenth-century English colonies, revival fever first gained significance through the preaching of George Whitefield, a Church of England cleric who was a good friend of John and Charles Wesley, the founders of English Methodism. Whitefield's innovations sparked criticism on both sides of the Atlantic, but they provided one important way for American religion to move beyond the private space of churches into the public sphere.

From Whitefield we can track a process that has lasted until the present day. In his several preaching tours up and down the American colonies, he popularized a dramatic, emotional preaching style that focused his listeners on the state of their souls. Christian conversion, in the communities he touched, became something urgent, a matter for instant decision, rather than something that took years of prayerful reflection and preparation. Whitefield's public performances drew crowds far too large for any church building to hold. By taking the pulpit into the open fields and into the streets of colonial cities, he changed the scale of religion as well as its mission. He told ministers that they had much more to do than write sermons and wait for crowds to show up and listen. They needed to bring religion to people who had not paid much attention to the good news of the Christian faith. Whitefield was America's first religious entrepreneur—and its first religious celebrity.

He also formed an unlikely partnership with Benjamin Franklin, one of America's first important entrepreneurs of printed material. The partnership was unlikely because Franklin was not a man who worried much about the state of his immortal soul. He had little use for the ministers of Philadelphia, where he lived after fleeing the Puritan stronghold of Boston. Yet Franklin held Whitefield in high esteem because, in Franklin's opinion, Whitefield understood that the point of religion was not to bore people with dry sermons explicating fine points of theology but to inspire them to do good deeds. Franklin did not care whether the American colonials went to heaven, but he did want them to behave virtuously in this life. Franklin estimated that Whitefield's voice could carry outdoors to an audience of twenty-five thousand. He observed that people hung on Whitefield's words and opened their pocketbooks when he appealed to their charity. Whitefield's religion, as Franklin understood it, was a message for social improvement. He was delighted, then, to publish Whitefield's sermons.

Whitefield's performances, and those of other colonial ministers who were caught up by the revival spirit, had many critics. The Great Awakening, which is a name that historians have given to this period of the mid-eighteenth century, meant trouble for dull sermonizers whose churches were emptied whenever Whitefield or some other itinerant spellbinder came into town. Their didactic, very long sermons drew on the knowledge they had gained studying at Cambridge back in England or at the young colonial colleges of Harvard, Yale, Princeton, and William and Mary. Whitefield was well educated and his sermons were by no means short. The difference was that he understood theater, not the theater of the Catholic mass but the theater created by professional stage actors. Protestant moralists who pursued a long-standing quarrel with secular theater rushed forward to say that the revivals were more entertainment than sacred devotion. They began a losing war to prevent them from becoming a normal part of religious life.

Here were the dangers that they cited. Whitefield carried religion into places that transformed it into something else. In speaking to people who had no necessary respect for his calling or his message, he risked making religion a subject of ridicule. To compromise the message of religion in order to give it a large audience debased it and trivialized it. Church services belonged in churches, and not in city streets where scoffers and the least virtuous members of the community might form part of the crowd. The nineteenth century had a word for such a crowd. It was a "promiscuous assembly," that is, a large gathering of men and women who did not know one another, who came from different social classes, who were of various ages, and whose virtue could not be taken for granted. Revivalists were the first to bring such crowds together for religious meetings, and the critics warned that what they did threatened to sully the content and authority of religion. They did not want religion to be about something else.

Charles Finney and the Revivals of the Early Nineteenth Century

The high tide of colonial revivalism had ebbed by the time of the American Revolution. The passing of itinerant pastors from the scene pleased defenders of the old ways, but their knowledge that not many Americans were going to church tempered the delight. It got worse for them. After 1800, American church membership surged upward following a renewed wave of revivalism. This time it became a permanent part of the religious landscape.

At the beginning of the nineteenth century the biggest explosion of revivalism came at Cane Ridge, Kentucky, a place on America's expanding frontier. It is difficult to make out exactly what happened there. If the accounts we have of the Cane Ridge meetings are even roughly accurate, then just about every living person in Kentucky, along with their horses and hound dogs, traveled to them. Over a five-day period they heard dozen of preachers who represented almost as many Protestant traditions. The accounts tell us that their words, or the spirit of God acting through them, had a startling effect. Men, women, and children fell onto the ground in religious swoons. They cried, they shouted, they laughed hysterically. Their bodies shook and gyrated. Some men fell on all fours and chased the devil up trees. One has got to think that there were more than a few people present who just sat back and could not believe what they were seeing.

We can follow any number of stories that illustrate the fallout from Cane Ridge. A new sort of cleric appeared in American religious history—the minister without a college degree, who spoke the language of ordinary Americans, and who seemed in retrospect to typify the era of Jacksonian democracy. The most famous representatives of this new clerical type were the Methodist circuit riders, who carried the gospel message of Christianity to barely settled areas of the American frontier. After them, the individual who had the most impact on shaping the course of American revivalism was Charles Grandison Finney. Finney grew up in western New York State and intended to become a lawyer. But God had another plan for him. Sitting in his lawyer's office, he felt himself filled with "waves of liquid love." God's spirit moved in him, and the religious skepticism he had maintained up to that moment evaporated. To a bewildered client who had brought a case to Finney, he explained that he could not plead his cause. His life henceforth was to plead the cause of the Lord.

To plead for the Lord, Finney needed to be ordained as a Presbyterian minister. Presbyterians demanded a higher level of education for their ministers than the rapidly growing Baptist and Methodist denominations. Finney's examiners found his grasp of Presbyterian doctrine spotty, and urged him to attend Princeton, an institution that was then and for a long time afterwards associated with conservative Presbyterian belief. Finney demurred, suggesting that the spirit of God moving in a person was a more important qualification for preaching than a college education. To conservatives this was a dangerous doctrine. Somehow Finney's persistence wore his examiners down, and they made an exception for him. Without going to Princeton, Finney got his license to preach. No one in his generation did so more effectively.

Finney recognized the validity of some of the charges made by the critics of revivalism. He did not wish to repeat the excesses of Cane Ridge or in any other way to contribute to the disorder of American society. He thought that ministers ought to be able to read and write and to have studied the Bible. He was particularly careful not to do anything that undermined ministerial authority. Before he preached anywhere, he sought an invitation from the local clergy. Wherever possible he conducted his meeting in their churches. He needed these partnerships with pastors who, unlike him, did not move from place to place. Unless their churches received new members as a result of his preaching, he could not count his revival a success.

Finney's sermons were emotional. He believed that conversion manifested itself in unusual behavior. He championed "new measures" that were designed to break down the calm sobriety that sinners often used to mask the darkness of their souls. But Finney's great achievement was to impose orderly organization on revivals. He orchestrated his meetings so that he, not sinners rolling in the church aisles, controlled the proceedings from beginning to end. He brought potential converts to the front of the church and placed them on an "anxious bench," apart from the rest of the congregation and under his eye. Accounts of his revival meetings suggest that he focused the drama of the meeting on one or two individuals and never allowed an undisciplined wave of emotion to sweep away the self-control of the assembly. Finney claimed that God told him what to say whenever he preached and that he did not need to write down sermons in advance. Yet his performances were not at all spontaneous. Finney knew what he wanted to say and how he wanted to say it. He even wrote a manual for other preachers instructing them on how to make their sermon delivery more effective. Like Whitefield before him, he recognized that the techniques needed for preaching resembled the techniques of the stage actor.

His critics remained unconvinced. They still worried about the public exposure of religion, the carrying of the Christian message into "promiscuous assemblies." Finney knew that many of the people who attended his meetings came in search of little more than amusement. They stood in the back and snickered. Their behavior and the emotional responses of those who experienced conversion made religion a target of parody. Frances Trollope, an Englishwoman who spent several unhappy years in Cincinnati, commented that "the coarsest comedy ever written would be a less detestable exhibition for the eyes of youth" than the sight of "violent hysterics and convulsions seizing young girls who fell on their faces exclaiming 'Oh Lord!' 'Oh Lord Jesus!' 'Help me, Jesus!' and the like."

Yet despite the critics, the revivals suggested a solution to a number of large problems attendant to the growing pains of a young nation. They were a way of organizing people for action. Men and women who did not know one another came together and experienced a collective energy. They were both instructed and entertained. Those who managed the assemblies unleashed emotion and also controlled it. Revivalists, far more than the leaders of any European established church at that time, knew how to make religion a part of the daily life of ordinary people. More than anything else until the formation of political parties in the 1830s, revivals ushered the United States into an age of participatory democracy.

Revivals as a Cultural Model

There is no reliable way to judge claims about how many Americans were securely converted to a deep religious faith as a result of early-nineteenth-century revivals. If one believes that a decision to join a church measures increased religious commitment, then evidence favors extravagant claims made by the revivalists. Throughout the nineteenth century those American Protestant religions that embraced revivalism were the ones that grew the fastest. Those that did not declined. Baptists, Methodists, and some branches of Presbyterians raced ahead of Congregationalists, Episcopalians, and Unitarians. The success and spread of American

Mormonism after the 1830s would have been unthinkable without the proselytizing skills developed by the Latter-day Saints. Without revivalism, the black slaves of the American South would not have become Christian. Roman Catholicism was the only large American Christian faith whose growth did not owe to revivalism.

Revivalism did more than reshape the denominational map of American Protestantism. Finney and other revival ministers taught Americans that the God who blessed America was a God who could be roused to improve the nation. God could be roused to fight drunkenness. God could be roused to turn drifters into disciplined workers. God could be roused to trample out God's vengeance where the grapes of wrath are stored. That is, God could be roused to help Americans make their democratic experiment work. Revival meetings showed Americans how they could organize themselves for effective community action. From descriptions of crowded meetings left by nineteenth-century observers, one cannot always tell whether what is being described is a religious revival or a political rally. There was a good reason for that. When American political parties began in the 1830s to assume the forms that we recognize today, the leaders of those parties had the revivals as models to copy. They orchestrated crowd behavior to generate enthusiasm for a cause.

Revivalists held their meeting in places other than churches. That alone made them difficult to distinguish from political rallies that made a generous use of prayer. Revivalists, promoting religion as a public resource, taught secular politicians and reformers to promote whatever cause they espoused as one favored by God. Revivalists boasted that they filled the churches at the same time they emptied the saloons. The results of a successful revival included better social order, disciplined workers, and a lower rate of crime. As we will see in subsequent chapters, any number of groups organized to promote secular purposes assumed that religion was a natural ally. The many reform organizations formed in antebellum America, including those that combated the evil of slavery, were only the beginning.

The critics of the revivals and of their democratic cultural style had no complaint about a more orderly America, if that in fact was the effect of churchgoing. What worried them was the watering down of faith. What happens to religion, they asked, when it justifies itself by the social benefits it confers rather than by its ability to bring people humbly before their God? The same concern is just as valid today, for stressing the social benefits of religion requires inventing public expressions of religion that gave as little offense as possible. If you want religion to serve the cause of family values, you must try to imagine a religion that appeals equally to Christians and Jews and maybe even Muslims. Earlier expressions of public religion were less accommodating to non-Christian, in fact to non-Protestant faiths, but there had always been an effort to give public religion a nonsectarian character. Americans liked to think that because they did not have an established church, they did not display religion in ways that were offensive. Unlike in England where one church had a monopoly, American supporters of public religion looked for formulas that would serve everyone. They failed, and there was a price to pay. Their search for a nonsectarian creed turned their attention away from theology. The critics again made the most of that deficiency. They wondered aloud why any God would bless a country when the prayers offered to God in public assemblies had so little robustness.

Even so we should not wonder that revivalists in American life became famous. Dwight Moody followed Charles Finney and made music an integral part of the show. After Moody, Billy Sunday left the game of baseball and made his career on the revival circuit. Later, Americans witnessed the enormous drawing power of Billy Graham, Oral Roberts, Pat Robertson, and Jim and Tammy Bakker. All of them learned that their religion played best in secular venues, large theaters and sports stadiums. Their style both influenced and was influenced by popular entertainments. When radio and television came along, they were prepared to make skillful use of mass media.

Giving Religion a Secular Purpose

With this background in mind, we can return to the issue of school prayer and Bible reading. They illustrate the drive to join religion to a secular purpose with exceptional clarity. When individual states first began to organize public schools, which they distinguished from religious schools, their promoters agreed that even in these mostly secular settings children ought to learn something about religion. A majority of state leaders also believed that classroom religion had to be nonsectarian, that is, it could not appear to endorse the practices or the tenets of a particular religious denomination. Massachusetts led the way, and in the 1820s passed a law that mandated this nonsectarian proviso. But what did it mean not to favor one religion over another? Horace Mann, the famous superintendent of Massachusetts's schools during the 1840s, was a Unitarian. To him, nonsectarian religion permitted the use of biblical passages in schoolbooks designed to teach children how to read. The readers compiled by Reverend William

McGuffey were the most famous. Nonsectarian religion, according to Mann, also allowed teachers to read passages from the Bible at the start of the school day, although they could not make comments about what they read. The Bible used in these exercises was the King James Version, one of the finest literary achievements of the English reformation.

Opposition was predictable, and it came from two quarters. The first chorus of negative voices rose from Protestant ministers representing Calvinist churches that had up until the 1830s comprised the religious establishment of Massachusetts. They asked, not unreasonably, how religion could do any possible good if it were stripped of all doctrinal content. Children, they argued, already knew before they came to school that some kind of God existed. What schools ought to promulgate was information about the right sort of God. Vague and imprecise religious teachings, which in their minds was precisely what Mann's Unitarian views amounted to, harmed children by suggesting to them that one religion was as good as the next.

The second, and more important, opponents were Roman Catholics. In the 1840s Ireland, devastated by a potato famine and years of English misrule, was sending a large number of immigrants to the United States, and these immigrants settled mostly in cities along the Atlantic coast. Boston's and New York City's Catholic population soared as a result. The Irish Catholic clergy proved to be an assertive bunch, and they were not happy with the direction that American public schools were taking. They agreed with Horace Mann and other Protestant educational leaders in the view that religion ought to be part of the school day. But they were outraged by the practice of reading from a Protestant Bible. How could that be nonsectarian? And even if the English Catholic translation of the Bible, the so-called Douay-Rheims Version, were substituted for the King James Bible, Catholics regarded reading from the Bible without clerical guidance as dangerous. What were schoolchildren going to make of a difficult book unless someone who was versed in true religion explained to them what the language meant? What Mann proposed was Protestant error. It was sectarian. It was unacceptable.

For the rest of the nineteenth century, controversies about religion in the schools centered on whether and how to include Bible reading in the school day. Prayer often complicated the arguments, although only in the twentieth century did prayer become as common in public schools as Bible reading. Many school districts settled the problem of Bible reading by eliminating the practice. The supreme courts in a few midwestern states declared that it violated the provisions of their state constitutions.

One of the least useful myths about America is the one holding that until the Supreme Court of the United States acted to proscribe religious exercises, schools everywhere in the United States began the day with Bible reading and prayer.

Even so, many nineteenth-century public school districts, especially those in the Northeast, wanted to open the school day with a religious exercise, one that most people would accept as nonsectarian. Since religious diversity was increasing, especially after the American Civil War, when large numbers of Jewish immigrants arrived in the United States, the complexity of finding magic words that sounded both religious and nonsectarian increased. The only possible solution was to saddle classroom religion with an explicitly secular purpose. The New York State Regents' Prayer, which the United States Supreme Court declared unconstitutional in 1962, perfectly illustrated what happened. The prayer did not pretend to tell schoolchildren anything serious about religion. Its purpose was to make children respect authority. Justice William Brennan, in his lengthy concurring opinion in the *Abington* case, noted that among the claimed secular aims of Bible reading were fostering harmony and tolerance among pupils, enhancing the authority of teachers and inspiring better discipline. Those announced aims did not in his mind save the practice as constitutionally acceptable, but they indicated how many educators had tried to get it by the Court. With similar hopes, defenders of prayer at high school football games cited the positive effect of prayers on the "fair play and sportsmanlike behavior of both players and spectators."

Those who support the return of school prayer have been horrified by recent court decisions that threaten to take God out of the Pledge of Allegiance to the American flag. The Pledge of Allegiance remains in most public schools as the only ceremony where God receives a mention, even if that mention was an afterthought. Schoolchildren recited the pledge for years without the phrase "under God." In the 1950s, Congress revised the pledge to include the phrase, because Americans were fighting the Cold War. National legislators wanted to distinguish the secular American state, friendly to religion, from the secular Soviet state, hostile to religion. As a gesture toward preserving the public display of religion, the modification was a small one, no more a breach in the wall of separation than George Washington's inaugural oath. Yet almost a half century later the phrase "under God" has started controversy.

To an alien visitor from Mars, with only a few days to spend in the United States, the controversy might seem to be about the wrong thing. If the health of religion in the United States depends on two words inserted into the Pledge of Allegiance, then American religion is surely running on empty. On the other hand, secularists who think that the same two words endanger the American republic are ignoring the many ways that religion is already embedded in American culture. If Thomas Jefferson and James Madison could call upon public religion, then contemporary defenders of church/state separation might usefully save their complaints for larger breeches in the wall of separation.

Or maybe the issue is not trivial at all. Shortly before the United States entered World War II, the Supreme Court heard a complaint from Jehovah's Witnesses whose children were suspended from school for refusing to pledge allegiance to the American flag, even before the phrase "under God" had been added. They claimed that saluting a secular icon was blasphemous. The Court heard the same complaint twice. In its first decision, *Minersville School District v. Gobitis* (1940), Justice Felix Frankfurter spoke for the 8–1 majority in holding against the Witnesses. Frankfurter said that the state's secular need to create national unity nullified any claim of constitutional violation. Besides, the First Amendment protections of religious freedom did not then apply to laws passed by states. Several years later, the Court, in *West Virginia Board of Education v. Barnette* (1943), changed its mind and held that the children of Jehovah's Witnesses might be exempted from the pledge ritual. The general practice continued, however. With respect to the present controversy, the Supreme Court will likely accept the pledge, with the phrase "under God," as a useful custom that does not violate the Constitution. It invites young Americans to reflect on the meaning of citizenship.

As a ceremony of civil religion, the pledge is supposed to teach everyone who recites it that even if the United States is not God's chosen nation, it must imagine that the actions it takes, either domestically or in foreign affairs, are subject to God's judgments. Abraham Lincoln, one of the least conventionally religious of all American presidents, accepted that idea. It is the text of his powerful second inaugural address that pled for the reconciliation of the nation:

> Fondly do we hope, fervently do we pray, that this mighty scourge of war may speedily pass away. Yet if God wills that it continue until all the wealth piled by the bondsman's two hundred and fifty years of unrequited toil shall be sunk, and until every drop of blood drawn with the lash shall be paid by another drawn with the sword, as was said three thousand years ago, so still it must be said "the judgments of the Lord are true and righteous altogether."

Christmas: The Ultimate Secular Holiday

To end this discussion of the blending of the sacred into the secular in American life, we turn to the most visible example: the selling of Christmas. We begin with a question. How is it possible that at the start of the twenty-first century, with seemingly everyone sensitive to issues of religious pluralism, and relatively few people declaring publicly any longer that America is a Christian nation, that a day which explicitly sets one of the world's religions above all others is a national holiday? Is not the public recognition given to Christmas a far greater violation of church/state separation than school prayer? Some other countries that profess to be secular, India for example, solve the problem of treating religions equally by declaring days off for all religious traditions. But the United States does not have many holidays. With the exception of the highly secularized national day of Thanksgiving, Christmas is the only religious holiday that gets national recognition, and with surprisingly little complaint.

The answer lies in what happens during the Christmas season. If you can forget about the name, the pretense that the public celebration of Christmas is not religious makes some sense. No one believes that Christ was born on December 25 in the year zero. Christmas gained a place on the religious calendar of the Catholic Church only because it was a useful way to wean people away from the pagan festivals associated with the winter solstice. The first Protestants thought that the holiday was pagan and eliminated its observance along with all the other "phony" religious holidays countenanced by Roman Catholics. Protestants kept Easter, but Easter always fell on Sunday, which was already, albeit somewhat illegitimately, an official day for Americans to rest. (When American post offices, after a long controversy, decided to close on Sunday, officials gave a secular reason, the need for a day off for postal workers. Courts allowed Sunday closing laws for businesses to continue only because they too were framed with a secular rationale.)

Christmas gradually eased its way back into Protestant American life in the early decades of the nineteenth century through association with the practice of gift giving. American commerce saw a way to make money. American gift giving recalled less the visit of the three magi to the Christ child than the visit of St. Nicholas (later the jolly American Santa Claus) given immortality in 1822 by Clement Moore's famous poem. The department stores of the late nineteenth and early twentieth century, beginning with Wanamaker's in Philadelphia and Macy's in New York City, transformed Christmas in America into an economic necessity. American prosperity from year to year stands or falls on the success of sales during the holiday season. No imaginable Supreme Court is going to create obstacles to this consumer juggernaut. Nor is any Jewish group or Islamic group likely to finance a test case to bring down Christmas. They too are merchants.

What the Supreme Court has instead done through a series of decisions is to enhance the secular disguise of Christmas. It has ruled unconstitutional the practice of setting up a nativity scene on public property, unless it is surrounded by Frosty the Snowman, Rudolph the Red-Nosed Reindeer, and perhaps a menorah. It remains okay, or kosher, for the president of the United States to light a "national" Christmas tree in Washington, even one with a star that refers to the Star of Bethlehem. Singing Christmas carols on public property has to be accompanied by the songs of Hanukkah and secular songs of the season. To people who say every year that it is time to put Christ back in Christmas, there are two possible answers. The first is that he has never been there, so no model exists for putting him back. The second answer is also a warning—if Christ ever were allowed to dominate the public celebration of Christmas, the national holiday would have to be scrapped.

What we seem to have in Christmas is a successful cultural compromise, a blend of sacred and secular that allows almost everyone to get something from it. Many people are convinced that there are fewer and fewer such successful compromises left in the American "public square." Since the 1960s some politicians have warned Americans that they are engaged in a great culture war, one that pits religion and goodness against atheism and immorality. The truth is that the quarrels of recent years are not between religion and no religion, but among religious Americans who disagree about the proper way to display religion in public. Despite the prominence that pollsters and journalists give to religious politics, America may be seeing a small trend back to pietist-style religions that regard worship as something private, something that is only about religion. That is a disputable claim. But it is well to remember in any case that the people who oppose the public display of religion are not necessarily secular humanists. They are religious men and women who wonder whether their God is well served by presidents who take their oath of office with their hand on a Bible and refer to God in their inaugural addresses. They, not militant atheists, are most likely to be bothered by the mixture of God and mammon on American currency.

Actually, religion remains a prominent part of American public life, something that strikes many Europeans as strange and distinctly American. So long as most Americans claim to be religious, and so long as they have democratically elected politicians to represent them, God is not going to disappear from public ceremonies. The people who objected to religious revivals in the first part of the nineteenth century and the "promiscuous assemblies" they gathered were the forbearers of the people who now object to public school prayer and prayer to open a football game. They have won some court battles, and they have succeeded in making public religion less Protestant. They have not, however, stopped the intermingling of American religions with general cultural practices. Other religions besides those that were most in evidence in the early American republic now make claims on the public square.

In the next chapter we will explore the validity of the claim that the United States has been until very recently a Protestant nation. The argument of the chapter will challenge that idea, but not by counting the number of people who claim to be Protestant and setting that number against the number of people who claim to be Catholic or Jewish or something else. We will look for clues in the institutions of popular culture where different religious identities reinforced other kinds of identities and competed to affect the tenor of American life. The underlying question is: What would the United States look like if it truly had always been a Protestant nation? The answer is that it would be something very different from what it is.

Chapter Two

Post-Protestant Culture:
Was There Ever Anything Else?

George Bancroft, the great nineteenth-century historian, gave Americans a beautifully written and stirring account of the birth of their nation. The multivolume *History of the United States* was unabashedly triumphant in its perspective, and no subsequent patriotic account of American freedom has really touched it in its persuasiveness and, up to a point, in its accuracy. What Bancroft lacked was a generous sense of American diversity. This deficit was significant, for it was this unfortunate legacy that future American historians most reliably imitated. Bancroft's account of the period of colonization (contained in the first three volumes published between 1834 and 1840) could not ignore the fact that Spanish and French colonists had gotten to the New World first. They had preceded the English colonists in crossing the Atlantic by over a century. They built impressive settlements on top of the destroyed cultures of the native inhabitants. But Bancroft saw nothing of lasting significance in any of this. The English colonists, whose cause he celebrated, took over from the French and the Spanish. European Catholics, in Bancroft's view, were not able to do much more with the area that became the United States than the people they displaced. Providence had reserved that part of North America for a prepared people, an English people, a Protestant people.

Thus, Bancroft branded America a Protestant nation. He did so in the 1840s when the colonial Puritan influence was very much on the decline and when Catholics had become the largest group of immigrants into the country. Nonetheless, his view of things lasted for a long time. Only in the last half of the twentieth century, largely in response to the election of John Kennedy as president and an enormous wave of new immigration into the United States that began in the 1960s, did pundits start talking about post-Protestant American culture. Before that, any account of the United States assumed that the only noteworthy events in the American past derived from the actions of Protestant elites. Non-Protestants in North America, from Massasoit to Antonio Lopez de Santa Anna to Al Smith, were written into American history as losers.

This version of the past makes sense only if you take a very narrow view of culture and are content with loose definitions of religious categories. What, for example, do we actually mean by the word *Protestant*. Does it mean anything more than Christian, but non-Catholic? We can label as Protestant all Christian religions in Europe that during the sixteenth century severed their ties with Rome, turned the clergy out of monasteries, and rejected the doctrine of transubstantiation. But what do we do with religious groups, the most notable being Anabaptists, who insist that they did these things prior to 1517, the conventional date in history that marks the onset of the Reformation? There are other complications. Not all churches linked to the Protestant Reformation owed much either to John Calvin or to Martin Luther.

How in particular do we classify the "reformed" Church of England? English Puritans regarded the Church of England as more Roman Catholic than Calvinist Protestant. They were right in many ways, and their judgment continues to ring true about High Church American Episcopalians. Methodists, who sprang from the Anglican Church, are normally deemed Protestant, although they discarded Luther's central rallying cry "by faith alone" along with Calvin's emphasis on predestination. American Methodists do not like the pope, but is that enough to put them in the same family as Presbyterians? And how do we classify all those American religions that sprang into institutional life during the nineteenth century? Are Unitarians and Universalists Protestant? Shakers, Swedenborgians, and Spiritualists? Latter-day Saints? Christian Scientists? Seventh-Day Adventists and Jehovah's Witnesses? They are not Catholics but neither are Hindus.

Maybe it is sufficient to know that more Americans identified themselves as Protestant than with any other religious label during the nineteenth and twentieth centuries. More significant, they did so even if they belonged to no church. Catholic and Protestant were powerful polarities that had developed in the European imagination during ugly religious wars. They were then carried to the English colonies of North America. Catholics, taught by nineteenth-century popes who regarded the United States almost as a pagan nation, believed in Catholic/Protestant dualism as fiercely as Protestants. Nonetheless, when you use the word Protestant you are already talking about religious pluralism. American Protestants were plural in the eighteenth century, and they became more so in the nineteenth and twentieth centuries. Moreover, Irish Catholics and Italian Catholics crossed the Atlantic and discovered with a lot of other ethnic Catholics that they too were plural. Their church was not universal at all.

Religion as a Culture Type

People who referred to America as a Protestant nation were not thinking primarily about religious doctrines. They were thinking about Protestant and Catholic as cultural types, as people with different values and world-views. To know somebody's religious identification, you did not have to follow him or her to church. You could watch what people did when they were not worshiping. The German sociologist Max Weber, in his classic study *The Protestant Ethic and the Spirit of Capitalism*, was able to turn Benjamin Franklin into a convincing Protestant because he worked hard. He drew up rules of self-discipline designed to smother every natural urge of his body. That for Weber was Protestant behavior even though Franklin's religious convictions were as distant from Calvinism as Calvinism was from Catholicism.

Cultural categories based on religion have given us an impressive range of exaggerated stereotypes. The broadest caricatures turn Protestants into sexually uptight individuals who are suspicious of all forms of merrymaking. They walk as stiffly as people just released from a straightjacket. They plan ahead, are sympathetic to all reforms that preach moderation, and make sure everything is closed on Sunday. Catholics, in contrast, even if they have not been to mass in thirty years, are supposed to have a flair for the dramatic. They do not expect to be damned for lustful, intemperate acts, and place loyalty to their large families above individualism and the desire for self-improvement. They define relaxation as having fun.

Overstatement is inherent in all stereotypes. Any listing of general qualities will inadequately describe most individual Protestants and most individual Catholics. Yet thinking in cultural terms can be useful. Is not culture about the practices that make us different? Class, national origin, and a dozen other circumstances also shape how people behave in their secular lives. But religion has been in this respect of crucial importance in the United States. People used it to define themselves into groups that shared codes of behavior.

For example, advice manuals that abounded in nineteenth-century America point to many of the traits people have in mind when they claim that Protestant values defined most of America's early history. These manuals, although aimed at diverse audiences, addressed young men and women whose hormones put them in the highest risk category of people likely to go astray. Reading the advice given to them almost confirms H. L. Mencken's definition of Puritanism as the "haunting fear that someone, somewhere, may be happy." One can perhaps understand the demand for abstinence from any kind of sexual contact between unmarried boys and girls. Protestants were not the only ones who set their face against fornication. What is perhaps less understandable is the discouragement that advice manuals gave to sexual pleasure within marriage. One might plausibly argue that some Protestant moralists wanted to extend the sexual renunciations of the Catholic priesthood to everyone. Like Benjamin Franklin before he went to Paris, they recommended a parsimonious use of "venery." Sexual energy was similar to money. It needed to be carefully saved and spent with a temperance bordering on abstinence.

The plethora of advice manuals in nineteenth-century America is open to a number of possibly conflicting interpretations. Maybe they correctly stated how most people who called themselves Protestant behaved, but that is doubtful. Obviously if most people did what they were advised to do, so many manuals would have been unnecessary. In part, then, they were written to persuade people to do things they were not doing. Nonetheless, Protestant guides to behavior, like Protestant revivals, promoted a code of conduct that in the first half of the nineteenth century defined a Protestant middle class. They also affected the way that many native-born Protestant workers thought of themselves. A belief in sobriety, and often its practice, was a badge of respectability. Those who wore it announced to the community that they were men and women of standing or that they were bright young men who would skimp and save to make their fortunes. They also announced, or so they thought, that they were not Catholic.

To be sure, we have plenty of evidence that the ministers who tried to sell the strictest forms of Protestant self-discipline were running against the tide. In American towns and cities, many of the people who belonged to the various roughly Protestant churches went to the theater against the advice of clergy. They drank enough to keep tavern owners in business. They enjoyed sex. What made them cultural Protestants was their guilt.

Catholic Rules

Meanwhile, immigrants into the United States, who after 1840 were mostly Catholic and mostly working class, were learning to enjoy some aspects of American life with a much freer conscience. Roman

Catholics had their own advice manuals, as strict in some ways as anything Protestants wrote. American Protestant leaders blamed Catholics for developments in America that they did not like. They knew that nineteenth-century popes disapproved of republican governments and militantly opposed the American way of separating church and state. The alleged inability of Catholics to become good citizens gave Protestant mobs encouragement to burn convents and Catholic churches. Yet after his famous visit to the United States in 1831, Alexis de Tocqueville, a Frenchman and also a Catholic, suggested that American Catholics were more naturally inclined toward egalitarian democracy than any other group in America. That was partly because they were poor. But it was also because the Catholic Church was the only religious denomination in America that encouraged the very rich and the very poor to pray together. Tocqueville noted that "the priest alone rises above the flock—and all else—the wise and ignorant, the man of genius and the vulgar now are on the same level." American Catholics were prepared to make a substantial contribution to American political life.

And to American culture. For Protestants who looked upon all foreigners with suspicion, the contributions degraded the American Way. They were signs of moral decline and corrupt political leadership. Historians have often missed the Catholic importance in nineteenth-century American culture because they looked for it at the wrong end of the social scale. They too easily assumed that any really significant Catholic who popped up in American cultural history was in no significant way Catholic. He was either a lapsed Catholic or someone who had learned to behave like a Protestant. The equation of cultural influence with successful assimilation of Protestant standards is powerful but misleading. What we need to recognize is that nineteenth-century American culture was every bit as much a product of Catholic (and then Jewish) immigrants as of Protestant elite groups. In fact, what we today call popular culture, if we use the advice manuals to demarcate Protestant norms, was barely Protestant at all. As we will see presently and more fully in the next chapter, Catholics forced Protestants to change their minds and their behavior.

Mathew Carey and American Readers

What happens when one grows up in a religious tradition? How do the experiences not just of church, but also of family and community, affect what someone does later in life? The suggestion in this chapter is that growing up Catholic, or Jewish, was different from growing up

Protestant. Even with the enormous differences within those traditions, the people who called themselves Protestant or Catholic or Jew have touched the broader landscape of American culture in different ways. The differences are only in part predicated on religious doctrines.

The subject is a large one. We can best approach it through specific examples. Mathew Carey, James Gordon Bennett, and Tony Pastor are three nineteenth-century American Catholics who played a significant role in shaping American popular culture. Historians have not ignored their careers, but they have ignored their Catholicism. It is not always correct to say that Catholic morality more easily than Protestant morality found something worthy in the play and idle amusements enjoyed by ordinary men and women. But in the careers of these three men, careers that depended on the patronage of immigrant, largely working-class audiences, the distinction carries some significance.

Mathew Carey was an innovative bookseller, publisher, editor, author, polemicist, and outspoken Catholic layman. He was born in Dublin in 1760, the son of moderately prosperous parents. Before he was twenty, he had set his sights on a trade in printing. At the age of twenty-one, he penned an anonymous pamphlet calling for the immediate repeal of England's penal code against Catholics. It was sufficiently politically charged to prompt his parents to pack him off to France for a spell. In Paris he worked briefly for Benjamin Franklin, who was enjoying his status as a Gallic hero. Carey made a more durable contact with the Catholic American hero, the Marquis de Lafayette, who aided the former English colonists in their revolution. He returned to Dublin, was jailed for writing incendiary tracts against British rule, and in 1784 left Ireland for good. He was twenty-four when he arrived in his new home of Philadelphia, three years before the writing of the American Constitution.

With money advanced by Lafayette, Carey started a newspaper. But he soon launched a bookselling and publishing firm. It was named "Mathew Carey" until 1817, then "Mathew Carey and Son" until 1824, and then, following Carey's retirement from the business, "Carey and Lea." It was the largest publishing and distributing book firm in America in the first decades of the nineteenth century. Carey succeeded through innovation. He entered an industry that operated primarily in a local market and transformed it into a national operation. His book-publishing enterprise depended on a traveling network of booksellers (not so different from Methodist circuit riders) who worked on commission, and who scoured their designated routes in search of subscribers. These sellers reported to Carey the emerging taste of the reading public, and Carey printed books to suit their taste.

Finding ways to gauge the likes and dislikes of readers was the key. Notions of what people ought to read did not hamper Carey's decisions. Every early publishing firm depended on a stock of steady sellers. One steady seller remained the Bible, and Carey published many of them. He printed Protestant Bibles and in 1790 the first American edition of the English Catholic Bible—the so-called Douay-Rheims Bible. But Carey also knew that American readers in the early nineteenth century were buying fewer devotional tracts and looking for more entertaining print material. Carey printed novels, which Protestants were not supposed to read because they inflamed the imagination. Fiction supposedly led away from the path of moral duty. Protestant women read novels anyway. Carey was the fortunate publisher of Susannah Rowson's *Charlotte Temple*, a book that no one reads today but that caused a sensation in its time. *Charlotte Temple* was a tale of seduction that outstripped in sales all other fictional work in the first decades of the nineteenth century. The woman who "fell" in the story was good; the man who "ruined" her, a cad. Conventional morality required that she die anyway, but not before readers took secret pleasure in the sexual intrigue. The Harper brothers, good Methodists who started their own successful publishing firm a bit later than Carey, would not have touched this book.

Carey took some of his relaxed attitude about reader taste from one of his circuit-riding booksellers, the colorful Mason Locke Weems, or Parson Weems as he was better known to early American readers. Weems was a Protestant, in fact an ordained minister of the Protestant Episcopal Church, and the author of a number of moral tracts in addition to his famous *Life of Washington*. He will figure more prominently in our next chapter. Out in the countryside trying to find subscribers for Carey's books, Weems pled with Carey to "stop crushing me to earth by ten thousand puritanical books." Carey did not need the advice again.

The profit motive was not all consuming to Carey. He professed an interest in the moral behavior of his compatriots and convinced himself that his business improved the moral standards of his readers. As his autobiography made clear, he believed in thrift, savings, and temperance. So did many other American Catholics, even if Protestant ministers imagined that these virtues belonged only to their faith. What Carey did not share with Protestant moralists was their alarm at the proliferation of commercial urban entertainments in America. The cheaper varieties gained popularity among working-class people and immigrants. Carey saw no moral dangers in novels, and he loved theater. Plays had been a focus of Protestant disapproval since the Puritan Oliver Cromwell had banned them during the period of his protectorate over England (1653–58). The Stuart monarchs, once restored to the throne, opened the playhouses again. The Restoration playwrights took their revenge on the Puritans by staging hilarious comedies that centered on sex. To American Protestants, stage bawdiness was not the problem. The problem was that the theater transported people into a realm of falsehood. It made reality insubstantial. Actors and actresses threw the idea of steady character to the winds, and plunged themselves into a different role every night on stage. Protestant moralists kept the theater under a moral cloud for much of the early nineteenth century. Carey regarded these fears as nonsense. Some morally wicked plays might deserve censure, but the theater did not in and of itself pose danger. In Catholicism, theatricality was an aid to faith.

Carey was a member of St. Mary's Catholic Church in Philadelphia. In the early 1820s he took the side of a popular priest, a man named William Hogan, against Philadelphia's Catholic bishop, who had sacked Hogan for disobedience. Protestants imagined that since Catholics truckled under to the authority of their church, they could not become loyal citizens of the United States. Carey showed them a different reality. In an open pamphlet warfare, Carey accused his bishop of harboring "arbitrary notions of Episcopal authority," a fault attributable to the fact that he had only been in the country for a "few days" and had not learned its "manners and customs." In taking this stand, Carey had not suddenly become a Protestant. He had learned to resist arbitrary authority in Catholic Ireland fighting against the Protestant English. The experience made him perfectly comfortable with the republican democracy he found in the United States.

Carey championed the cause of the Irish immigrant in a period just before anti-immigrant prejudices became a potent political force in the United States. When he died in 1839 from injuries suffered in a carriage accident, he received one of the largest public funerals in Philadelphia's history. Carey never made much of the hostility that his fellow Philadelphians harbored toward Catholics. In 1844, a few years after his death, Philadelphia was torn apart by riots between Catholic immigrants and native-born wage earners. The American Protestant leaders who encouraged these riots regarded Catholicism as alien to American ideals. Carey's successful career had not changed that fact. His business did effect change of another sort. The print material published by his company demonstrated that the stricture contained in Protestant advice manuals would not, unchallenged, determine the direction in which popular democratic taste was moving.

James Gordon Bennett and the Cheap American Newspaper

James Gordon Bennett, the founder and editor of the path-breaking *New York Herald*, had even less use than Carey for the cultural warnings of Protestant clerics. He fought them, although in the process he also ran into trouble with the leaders of his own church. Bennett's story began in Scotland in 1795. His father, a prosperous farmer, worked hard to keep his sons within the Catholic faith. In Scotland Catholics had almost disappeared with Mary Queen of Scots. At age fifteen, James entered the Catholic seminary in Aberdeen to study for the priesthood. He left four years later, not a priest, but with an education far better than what was common for young men who grew up in the United States. He studied Greek, Latin, French, logic, science, secular history, and church history. Out of that Catholic background emerged an independent mind. Bennett never left the church, but he concluded that Catholicism incorporated many "ridiculous superstitions."

In 1819, now twenty-four, Bennett immigrated to North America— first to Canada, which he left quickly because of his dislike of things British, then to Boston, which was too Puritan for him, and then for a few years to Charleston, South Carolina, where he worked for a newspaper. He liked Charleston and the South, and tolerated slavery, the region's peculiar institution. Later in his career he became a fierce foe of abolitionism. In 1823 he decamped once again, this time to New York City. There he stayed, working for several pro-Jacksonian newspapers until in 1835 he founded his own important newspaper, the *New York Herald*.

It was not America's first penny newspaper. That was Benjamin Day's *New York Sun* ("it shines for all") founded two years previously. But Bennett's paper was the most important of the genre. The *Herald* gained more readers than any other newspaper. It revolutionized American journalism by its break with political party affiliation, by its means of distribution, by its news reportage, and especially by the way it defined the news. Although probably best remembered for its coverage of sensational crime stories, the *Herald* hired skilled reporters in all departments. It covered Wall Street, it covered sports, it covered religion, and it covered local and national politics. Bennett sent staff abroad to gather news from around the world. Not everyone in New York City read the *Herald*, but it contained material to interest a large number of people, including the city's swelling immigrant population. The *Herald* made Bennett famous. It made him rich. And it made him the enemy of elite groups who equated Bennett's journalism with bad morals.

"An editor," according to Bennett, "must always be with the people, think with them, feel with them, and he need fear nothing." Bennett emphasized crime reporting and scandal because these subjects interested readers. For the same reason the *Herald* reported the results of horse races, cockfights, and bare-knuckle fights. Most of the Protestant clergy condemned spectator sports because of their association with gambling and drinking. Bennett's answer to them was simple. The pleasures of ordinary people deserved respect. Bennett deplored immorality, but he also deplored people who set the boundaries of moral behavior too narrowly. He set the stage for a "culture war" that he relished.

In 1840 an influential group of New Yorkers, Protestant clergy, social leaders, and rival editors, launched a movement to destroy the *Herald*. Even New York City's outspoken Catholic archbishop, John Hughes, joined their crusade, for he thought that Bennett was hostile to all religion. Bennett had certainly seized opportunities to criticize the Catholic Church. In defending New York's emerging public school system against complaints made by Archbishop Hughes, Bennett editorialized that the archbishop "had shown himself utterly deficient in honesty and common sense"—blinded to all facts, save the dogmas and "drivelings of the Catholic church in the last stage of decrepitude." Such outspokenness left Bennett with few allies among the social elite of New York. The party of "holy allies" accused him of printing "salacious stories, of using indelicate language, and of blasphemy."

Bennett defended himself as a moralist and a friend of religion. He seemed irreligious only because he did not like the clergy of any religion who took authoritarian views toward activities enjoyed by their parishioners. He considered himself a good Catholic. The church finally learned to value his accomplishments. He was married in St. Peter's Catholic Church in New York City. When he died in 1872, some thought was given to a mass at St. Patrick's with Archbishop John McClosky officiating. (Bennett had outlived Archbishop Hughes.) That was not done. The funeral was in Bennett's home, and he was buried in Greenwood Cemetery in Brooklyn. Even so, Archbishop McClosky administered the last rites and the vicar general of the Roman Catholic diocese presided at the services. Bennett's sin, if that is what we are talking about, was to celebrate the cultural tastes of American democracy.

Tocqueville, when he wrote about American egalitarian democracy, had not been as enthusiastic. Time and again, the *Herald* exhibited the disdain for learning that Tocqueville feared would overtake European society if it followed too closely the American example. But whether or not Bennett had served his own church well or had raised the intellectual level of Americans, he had made himself a hero to many of New York's immigrant Catholics. His *Herald* was for them a contact with the American community beyond their own parochial neighborhoods and beyond their churches. Reading the *Herald* was not the worst way of becoming American even if we might wish there had been better ways. We may be grateful that Bennett furnished an alternative to Protestant advice manuals. In battling for American democratic commercial culture against the opposition of Protestant tastemakers, he clearly won the war. Yet Bennett was tolerant of slavery and outspokenly anti-Semitic. Those attitudes too had a democratic audience.

Tony Pastor and Working-Class Audiences

Catholic immigrant audiences played a critical role in shaping popular commercial culture in nineteenth-century America. What they liked determined what succeeded and what failed. Tony Pastor, our third example, knew that. Pastor was born in New York City in the 1830s, the son of a violinist of Italian descent. He rose to become in the decades following the Civil War America's most famous and successful theatrical manager. Tony Pastor's Variety Show, which he founded in 1865, settled into an "Opera House" that Pastor built on the Bowery. Opera House in the nineteenth century meant not Lincoln Center but a theater that staged a wide variety of popular entertainments. Pastor's intention was to move variety theater out of "concert saloons," which were boisterous male haunts that encouraged heavy drinking, into a venue resembling "legitimate theater." The adjective "legitimate" suggested that respectable women could attend performances with their children without endangering the family's reputation. By the time Pastor reached the twilight of his career, having moved his theater progressively up town until it reached Union Square, he had become one of the two or three most important people who founded American vaudeville.

In the 1890s Benjamin Keith and Edward Albee opened the Union Square Theater in New York City and soon became the dominant booking agents for touring acts of American vaudeville. With a squeaky clean reputation—no profanity and no sexual innuendos—their shows, dubbed the Sunday School wing of American vaudeville, made a great deal of money. What Keith and Albee accomplished built on the achievements of Pastor, who prohibited smoking, drinking, and unattached women in his auditorium. Probably P. T. Barnum deserves credit for having invented family entertainment in America. His famous museum in New York City, popular long before Barnum entered the circus business, was part edifying display, part popular theater, and part hokum. Tony Pastor's contribution was to take family entertainment into venues where it had not been common. He made it popular with audiences who were not accustomed to spending an evening out and staying sober.

Pastor recognized the commercial advantages of cleansing popular culture of moral stigmas. The ones he worried about were not the ones enumerated by Puritanism. Unlike Bennett, he worried about what his own church thought of his entertainments. He was a devout Catholic who kept a poor box in his theater lobby and hung a crucifix on the wall of his office. One account claims that he constructed a small devotional shrine backstage where he repaired each evening after the show and after checking the box-office receipts. Pastor was unable to convince everyone that variety theater was a safe venue for God-fearing Americans. Variety theater remained on a list of dangerous pleasures as something that many Protestant church leaders regarded as only slightly better than saloons and brothels. Tony Pastor's trust in American democratic culture was greater than theirs. He imposed moral behavior on his audiences, but that did not mean he disapproved of smoking and drinking. On certain occasions he did both. He would travel a long way to see a prizefight, for he did not regard betting as a certain path to debauchery.

The audiences in New York City who patronized Pastor's theater and similar businesses were heavily made up of immigrants and therefore heavily made up of Catholics. During the years of Pastor's ascendancy Irish Americans were the largest part of the audiences. They also supplied many of the performers for variety theater. It did not matter in this case that Pastor was Italian. His bill of attractions always included Irish entertainers. William Scanlan, Pat Rooney, and P. C. Foy were the most famous. In the early 1880s Pastor booked for his stage two pious Irish Catholic performers, Jerry and Nellie Cohan. Their family group included a son, George M., born on the Fourth of July, 1878. Cohan's name was to become a legend in American show business. It is impossible to imagine American popular culture as it developed in the twentieth century—whether the stage, or music, or movies—without the contribution of American Catholics. They were the first untroubled consumers of urban commercial culture in America. They patronized every form of cheap entertainment. They read the dime novels and the sensational penny press. They attended prizefights and horse races. They filled the opera houses for variety theater and crowded into the first nickelodeons.

All of these forms of entertainment began under a moral cloud, in part because moralists disdained the manners of immigrant audiences who made them successful. Those audiences changed the face of American culture. As we will see in the next chapter, it was the Protestant leaders who retreated, although they invented their own form of commercial culture in the process.

The New Jewish American

By the end of the nineteenth century two groups other than Catholics were making distinctive contributions to American popular culture— African Americans, who are also the subject of a separate chapter, and immigrant Jews. Historians have in general paid more attention to the Jewish influence on American culture than the Catholic contribution. That is probably because Jews, sooner than Catholics, made important contributions to American high culture as well. But in the late nineteenth century, Jewish immigrants were typically poor. Protestant leaders did not like them any better than Catholics.

The first large groups of Jews arrived in the United States in the early nineteenth century from German-speaking areas of central Europe. They embraced Reform Judaism, praised the Constitution and its separation of church and state, and proclaimed America their Zion. The later and larger wave of Jewish immigration that came through Ellis Island from Russia and Eastern Europe starting in the 1870s was more culturally distinct. They spoke Yiddish, dressed in strange clothes, and if they were religiously observant clung to Orthodoxy. Christians, including Irish Catholics, wondered whether such people could be assimilated into American life. They had to be. Almost uniquely among the immigrants who chose to come to America in the nineteenth century, they had no homeland to return to. Anti-Semitism increased in the United States. Jews faced discrimination almost everywhere they turned. Still, not being able to book a hotel in Saratoga Springs was not as bad as a pogrom.

Yiddish-speaking Jews brought from Russia and Eastern Europe their own forms of culture adaptable to American urban life. The Jewish religion lacked the drama associated with the Catholic mass. Jewish synagogues on the lower east side of Manhattan were cramped places of worship that most Jews never attended. What mattered was Jewish daily life, which on the streets and in the home was rich in performance. In the seder dinners remembering Passover, Jewish children learned to imagine, participate in, and act out the Jewish flight from Egypt. Yiddish theater flourished in the Jewish neighborhoods of New York in the late nineteenth century. It was a secular institution with deep roots in the communal religious life of the East European shtetl.

Jewish performers had become headline acts of vaudeville by the early twentieth century. Jewish musicians virtually alone created the famous fictional street, Tin Pan Alley. Many of the most popular voices in early radio were Jewish, even if their names were changed from Benjamin Kubelsky to Jack Benny or from Nathan Birnbaum to George Burns. Hollywood represented the most famous Jewish contribution to American popular culture. Jewish entrepreneurs who never learned English very well spotted a commercial opportunity in the wide popularity of the nickelodeons among immigrant Americans. Samuel L. Rothafel made his nickname "Roxy" synonymous with the great movie palaces that rose in American cities in the second decade of the twentieth century. These attracted Americans from all social classes. Marcus Loew, Adolph Zukor, Carl Laemmle, and William Fox went to California and built the movie industry. A group of immigrants who by all standard observations stood way outside the mainstream of American life created the industry that more than any other thing represented the United States to the rest of the world.

In the early part of the twentieth century Protestants were still trying to rein things in. From the very beginning they lodged moral complaints against movies. The charges were numerous. Movies drew young people into darkened, unchaperoned environments where they sat for hours in mixed company. The invitation to sexual play was strong, even without images of scantily clad women who appeared in many short film clips. When the movies began to tell stories, the stories often revolved around sexual themes. That was especially true during the early years of Hollywood film production. The Protestant clergy in cities and towns led strident campaigns to censor the movies. Pressure mounted to such a level that in 1922 Hollywood executives appointed William Harrison Hays, known as Will, to run their trade association. He was supposed to police the morals of the Hollywood studios. Like the General Council of Women's Clubs and the Federal Council of Churches, he condemned smut. Hays was a Presbyterian and a prominent elder in his church.

The collective efforts failed to change very much. Nor did any of the subsequent mobilizations of Protestant sentiment, often led by newly enfranchised women, make movies pure during the 1920s. Audiences apparently liked what they saw. Oddly, and this fact speaks volumes about who was running popular culture in twentieth-century America, the Catholic Church forced the movies to change their ways. It placed a moral code on Hollywood. Martin Quigley, the Catholic publisher of the *Motion Picture Herald*, started the crusade. He turned to friends in the Catholic hierarchy, including Cardinal Mundelein of Chicago. He also spoke with Joseph I. Breen, a lay Catholic whom Will Hays had installed in Hollywood in the early 1930s, to clean up movie scripts. Nothing much happened until in 1933 the Catholic Church organized its famous and effective Legion of Decency. The Legion inaugurated a system of ratings—A for morally unobjectionable, B for morally objectionable in part, and C for condemned. All American Catholics knew about the ratings and knew that they were expected to boycott C films. Not every Catholic obeyed, but enough did to bring strong economic pressure on the film industry.

In part to make sure that films did not receive a C rating, Hays's office in 1934 set up the Production Code Association, headed by Breen. It proved to be a review council with real authority to police the morals of Hollywood productions. After 1934 any picture that did not carry the Production Code Seal was doomed to limited distribution. Another Catholic, Father Daniel Lord, a professor at Catholic St. Louis University, wrote the code that set forth guidelines for how films should treat such morally difficult subjects as divorce, adultery, prostitution, violence, and crime. It also enumerated subjects that movies could not treat at all—abortion, incest, miscegenation, homosexuality, birth control, or anything demeaning religion or the clergy.

Never before in the history of American commercial culture had the entrepreneurs of an entertainment industry bowed to pressure to encode explicit restrictions. And it was not the Protestants, despite their steady efforts for over a century to publicize the moral defects of popular culture, who won the victory. A Jewish industry, hemmed in by a Catholic document, determined what Protestants were allowed to see in their local movie theaters. Some Protestant moralists could not bring themselves to welcome this achievement. *The Christian Century*, the flagship journal of liberal Protestantism in America, had started its own system of rating movies that had no effect whatsoever. Yet the editors were reluctant to acknowledge the contribution of the much more effective Legion of Decency simply because it was Catholic. They even suggested that the Legion of Decency determined its ratings according to how a movie depicted the Catholic Church. When the pope himself in 1936 suggested that American films were getting better, *The Christian Century* fell victim to an even more extreme expression of cultural sour grapes. It hinted that the Catholic Church was involved in a conspiracy to shore up the monopoly position of

Hollywood's "Big Eight" studios, all Jewish. Outsiders were ganging up to take revenge on the Protestant Establishment.

The Passing of the Protestant Nation

We come back to the question of how, given this situation, the United States could imagine itself as a Protestant nation. At the beginning of the twenty-first century, public rhetoric proclaims that notion less frequently. Cultural pluralism rooted in religious differences has become almost a boast of the American nation. That was not so earlier. The habit of writing about cultural pluralism in a positive way became common only after the decade of the 1960s. The earlier notion was that if the United States was to be truly one nation forged out of many, public and private social agencies had to ensure that newcomers acculturated themselves to something called the American Way. They did not have to change their religion, though few Protestants thought it a bad idea for Catholics to leave the church or for Jews to become Christians.

At the turn of the twentieth century, national leaders spoke a good bit about a melting pot. The metaphor was an ambiguous one. It might suggest that Americans were a new race. People from all over the world had come to the United States, merged their gene pool, and blended their cultures. More commonly it suggested that foreigners who did not look like Northern Europeans jumped in a big stew pot and emerged from the other side with blond hair and blue eyes, and clothed in neatly tailored suits and dresses. Social planners spent their days thinking up elaborate plans of Americanization. Oregon passed a law in the early 1920s requiring all children in the state to attend public schools. It was a not-so-subtle way to abolish Catholic religious schools. In 1925 the United States Supreme Court, in *Pierce v. Society of the Sisters of the Holy Name of Jesus and Mary*, struck down the law. What is sometimes forgotten is that the law was an initiative of social progressives, not social conservatives.

Yet if many Americans dreamed fondly of "monoculturalism," their actions guaranteed a much different result. The nation's white Protestant leaders had a strong desire for empire and economic growth—a desire that could be accomplished only by diversity (who, after all, was going to provide the labor if not cheaply hired immigrant workers?), and on a large scale. Besides, what Protestant leaders meant by the American Way was never entirely clear. It had to do with language, dress, standards of hygiene, respect for the Constitution, and patriotism, but the specifics were left vague. There was room for improvisation. Even a cursory history of American immigration reveals that immigrant groups did not simply conform to what an army of social workers told them they ought to be doing. They embraced the American Way on their own terms.

Every immigrant group that entered the United States made changes in the way it did things. The American Catholic Church was quite different from what it was anywhere in Europe, a fact lamented by more than one pope, including Pope John Paul II. American Judaism, whether Reform or Orthodox, was different from Jewish practice in Europe. Immigrants were determined to change themselves in order to become more American. One part of the story of American immigration is about the embarrassment felt by an older generation of immigrants in seeing the "un-American" behavior of later arrivals of their co-religionists. German Reform Jews agonized about how to handle the "uncouth" Yiddish-speaking Jews from the Russian Pale. Irish Catholics worried about being associated with the "superstitious" Italian Catholics or with "non-white" Hispanic Catholics. Every group made creative adjustments, ones that reflected their background as well as the influence of existing American institutions.

None of this means that Protestantism had no importance in America. After all, with one exception, every American president and vice president identified with Protestant culture. Outside of large cities in the Northeast, Protestant numerical dominance was overwhelming. Yet the analysis we have pursued in this chapter rests on other facts. Once you move away from national government and some other important American institutions—corporations and universities, for example—the portrait of the United States looks quite different from what is suggested by notions of unchallenged Protestant dominance. John Kennedy was the first and only Catholic president. But his success owed to Catholic mayors, governors, and a host of other Catholic politicians who ran local institutions in heavily populated regions of the country. Catholics did not run the universities now known as the Ivy League, but they built an impressive network of private schools that conservative Protestants now clamor, in a manner filled with delicious irony, to emulate. American Jews constructed a network of institutions parallel to the social and business institutions that excluded them. They had their own resorts, their own elegant clubs, and their own law firms.

The simple fact is that non-Protestant immigrants were responsible for shaping what the nineteenth century called entertainments and what we now call popular culture. The accomplishment, which joins religious culture to secular culture, was not a minor contribution, something at the margins of a grand American narrative that we give passing credit to in a history textbook. Oh yes, a Catholic signed the Declaration of Independence. Or, oh yes, a Jew helped finance the American Revolution. Catholics and Jews (along with African Americans who are the subject of a later chapter) made contributions to national life without which the present United States would be unrecognizable. It would not be recognizable to American Protestants. And it would not be recognizable to the rest of the world. Maybe the American Dream as delivered abroad was once a white Protestant concept. To the extent that the American Dream matters now throughout the world, it is a dream represented by African American Protestants, by Michael Jackson and by Michael Jordan. It is a dream created by Stephen Spielberg, an American Jew, or by Francis Ford Coppola, an American Catholic.

The myth of Protestant dominance did not so much fool people (how could it when Protestants were themselves so divided?) as provide a target for Americans who defined themselves against it. Protestant leaders recognized the challenge, and they made their own innovative responses. With respect to the institutions of commercial culture popular among immigrants, they had two choices. They could continue to "just say no" and to write more advice books that fewer and fewer people read. Or they could compete with a different product. How they did the latter is the subject of the next chapter.

Chapter Three

A Protestant (Counter) Culture

E very April at a star-studded event in Nashville, the Gospel Music
Association hands out the annual Dove Awards. The five thousand
members of the association promote not just gospel music but Christian
music broken down into some forty categories. These include rap, hip-
hop, and rock. In recent years Steven Curtis Chapman, Third Day,
Michael W. Smith, and Jaci Velasquez have carried home many of the top
honors. Kathie Lee Gifford hosted the awards show in 2000 and sang a
duet with Dolly Parton, one of the most popular figures associated with
Christian music. That year Glen Campbell won the Dove for "best county
album," and the St. Louis Rams quarterback Kurt Warner presented the
award for best song.

If the Dove Awards are not generally as well known across the United
States as the Oscars, they represent a very large and growing industry.
Companies involved with religious music make a great deal of money.
Christian music groups go on tour. They play to sold-out audiences in
large arenas. Americans anywhere in the country can find religious music
on their car radio dials.

The accommodation of Christian music to what young people like to
hear is a recent phenomenon. Not so long ago conservative Protestant
groups were dead set in their opposition to rock 'n' roll. Some of them
still wonder what happens to the Christian message when rock bands
named Barren Cross, Resurrection Band, and Bloodgood deliver it. It is
not just music that causes unease. Anyone who wanders through large and
well-stocked Christian bookstores, with prominent locations in suburban
shopping malls, will immediately see that Christian consumers want religious reading material that is in genre and appearance much like the fare

laid out on the tables of Barnes and Noble. The Christian Booksellers Association started organizing commercial outlets for religious reading material in 1949. Now their outlets stock Christian-style Harlequin romances, Bible-based diet books (*More of Jesus, Less of Me*), lovemaking guides, and exercise books. They also offer a choice of many different versions of the Bible in a bewildering range of formats.

Christian bookstores, in addition to books, carry other Christian "goods." They sell T-shirts (a picture of a basketball team in action with half of its members disappearing from the court in the Rapture—the label is "Fast Break"), bumper stickers ("Jesus is my rock and My Name is on the Roll"), greeting cards, coffee mugs, tablemats, and Frisbees. Videos and DVDs take up an increasing amount of floor space. Among the movie offerings is *Judgment*, starring Corbin Bernsen and Mr. T., which is advertised with the teaser "Can the Supreme Being Defeat the Supreme Court?"

A survey of the contemporary religious marketplace leaves one with the disquieting feeling that a very large part of it deals with the end of the world. Hal Lindsey's *The Late Great Planet Earth* first appeared in 1970 and found a huge reading public for the rest of the twentieth century. The volumes produced by Tim LaHaye and Jerry Jenkins have recently matched Lindsey's prophecies concerning the end of human history. One might have expected the events of September 11, 2001, to quell the seemingly insatiable appetite of the American public for graphic portrayals of catastrophes. Hollywood has destroyed New York City, Washington, and Los Angeles so many times that stunned witnesses of the televised images of the collapse of the Twin Towers had trouble separating them from the macabre creations of special-effects artists. Faced with the real thing, people might have drawn back and demanded a different product from mass culture. That did not happen. It is worth noting that the book of Revelation, the biblical primer for all disaster epics, has fascinated many different kinds of Americans, including President Ronald Reagan, especially when deadly events have threatened human history.

How to Compete with the Mass Market?
The Protestant Learning Curve

Where did all this begin? As we saw in chapter 2, democratic Americans in the early republic, including many newcomers who were not Protestant, became avid consumers of many new kinds of cheap entertainments. As the nineteenth century wore on, and cities grew in size, the number of these diversions increased at least as fast as the number of new churches.

Protestant ministers and other people concerned with the health of religion worried that they were crowding God out of public awareness. Americans read novels instead of devotional tracts. They went to a noisy theatrical production instead of a church meeting. They attended public lectures to learn about mesmerism rather than about sin. Some of their choices seemed to reflect not merely indifference to religion but hostility. In taverns, at horse races and prizefights, people escaped from moral regimens and enjoyed what every religious tract of the time told them they ought not to enjoy.

If it had only been the Catholic immigrants who paid attention to these activities, Protestants might have relaxed. That was not the case. Protestant warnings about the dangers of having fun convinced fewer and fewer Americans of any background. If Protestant moralists were going to defeat the kinds of popular culture they did not like, they had to invent a popular culture of their own. They did not entirely succeed. But the achievements were impressive.

The first important battle in what amounted to a long culture war was over reading material. Before the nineteenth century printed material was expensive. In colonial America most people, men and women, had at least rudimentary reading skills. Literacy rates in Protestant New England were probably as high as anywhere in the world at that time. Even so, very few families had the economic wherewithal to purchase books. An average Protestant family might own a Bible, a few devotional tracts, and perhaps an almanac. Given the scarcity of books, reading practices dictated that the same texts be read over and over, usually aloud to the entire family group. Since the books most commonly owned and circulated were religious in nature, Protestant ministers strongly encouraged the development of literacy. Able readers made good Christians, for they studied the Bible and read only books that contributed to spiritual and moral uplift.

Not all books and pamphlets in circulation were theological in nature, but a major part of the other items was seriously didactic in tone. Advertised titles, especially in history, suggest that people were not invited to read for pleasure, if pleasure connoted light entertainment and indulgence in escapist fantasies. Reading was an activity of self-improvement. At the time of the American Revolution it became a patriot's duty. Some types of ephemeral print material aroused uneasiness among colonial religious leaders. Chivalric tales, Indian captivity narratives, romances, plays, and ballads had no useful didactic purpose. They constituted the literary trash of the times. However, the vast majority of the fare that attracted colonial readers did not in any way threaten their virtue.

A strong sense of competition between religiously sanctioned fare and morally unhealthy reading material awaited the early nineteenth century, when cheaper ways of producing paper and new printing techniques lowered the price of reading material. The innovations also increased the number and the variety of books and periodicals. Protestant ministers began to express real alarm. A strong demand for nonprescribed types of reading, especially novels, posed a severe check on their enthusiasm for universal literacy. Ministers woke up to the fact that the book trade, in their judgment, encouraged wayward reading habits. Reading did not improve the mind. It debased it.

Mathew Carey's publishing firm catered successfully to popular taste and did not seem to care much whether people demanded works that upheld the Christian faith. Religious pessimists threw up their hands, doomed America to hell, and retreated into their churches to preach to the faithful. More supple Protestant strategists responded with a different tactic. If the book trade was capable of putting more material into the hands of readers, then Protestant authors needed to think up their own formulas to teach religion in ways that sold. These Protestant optimists believed that Americans would make morally responsible choices if Protestant authors adapted religious reading material to popular taste.

Using this strategy, the American Tract Society launched a highly successful campaign to encourage Protestant belief. Organized by wealthy Christian laypeople in 1825, the Tract Society merged forty small societies together and turned Christian publishing into a nonprofit business. Its philosophy was simple. If the book market of the young republic tempted American readers to consume morally questionable fare, the solution was to provide an alternative diet. It had to be equally attractive and even cheaper than what the competition offered. By 1827 the Tract Society had printed over three million items for distribution. That number climbed to over five million in 1828 and over six million a year later.

The American Bible Society, a close affiliate of the Tract Society and a precursor of The Gideons International, by the end of the 1820s produced annually over three hundred thousand editions of the New Testament. Though not a sufficient quantity to put it in the hands of every man, woman, and child in the United States, it marked a significant step in the direction of that announced aim. These two Christian societies pioneered in the use of new printing technologies. Together they outstripped in production the output of all the commercial publishers then doing business in the United States. Despite the fact that they distributed much of their material free, they took in a substantial amount of cash receipts.

Scale and cheapness were important parts of the strategy, but something else mattered just as much. Readers had to be enticed to read what was placed in their hands. The format and content of religious material had to be "pleasing." More and more Americans had the time and money to read but not necessarily more time for hard reflection. A high rate of literacy did not mean that American readers had long attention spans or much desire to tackle intellectually challenging books. Sponsors of the American Tract Society uttered the word "entertainment" cautiously, for "the prevailing thirst in the rising generation for the mere entertainment of high wrought fiction" was precisely what they wanted to scotch. They shared the prevailing Protestant view that fiction, that is, novels, degraded morals by encouraging readers to accept as part of their mental life stories that frankly departed from "truth." On the other hand, they were realists. Novels were here to stay.

The goal became to frame "entertainment" in ways that were "useful" and "instructive." Many tracts they published were not at all innovative. Didactic recitations of Christian beliefs continued as a staple in the Protestant book market. But the innovations were striking. Some of the tracts tried to convey moral lessons with "true tales," that were "short," "interesting," "striking," "clear," "plain," and "pungent." "Pungent" was an especially interesting adjective. It suggested almost a savory relation between the reader and a text, literally something to be eaten with relish. "True narratives" were not fiction, but they told an absorbing story. For most Protestant readers, they replaced dogmatic treatises, collections of sermons, and devotional books as the most popular form of religious publishing, except the Bible. They were one of the most popular forms of any sort of publishing in the first half of the nineteenth century.

Mason Locke Weems

Some Protestants moved forward more boldly than others. We encountered Mason Locke Weems in the last chapter because of his long association with the Catholic publisher Mathew Carey. He remains a familiar figure to many Americans because his famous biography of George Washington launched some of the most enduring anecdotes about America's first president. That biography is a good example of the "truthful tale." It eschews fiction but substitutes doubtful anecdotes that convey moral lessons. A case in point is the dubious story of Washington chopping down his father's cherry tree. Getting the facts exactly straight was less important to Weems than catching and holding the attention of his readers.

Reading should be morally uplifting, but if religion were to retain sway over American audiences the moral and the religious had to be as "dulcified as possible."

"Dulcified" is not exactly the word that springs to mind as the best characterization of the moral tales that Weems authored. What he wanted to soften was the preachy tone of religious tracts. Otherwise, he sought a graphic and frank description of the wages of sin, a description that did not omit a sensationalized and detailed telling of the sinful acts that demanded retribution. In *The Drunkard's Looking Glass*, one of his most popular books, Weems recounts the story of a man who, after falling for Satan's temptation to get drunk, violates his sister, kills his father, and hangs himself. Calamity follows upon calamity, all bloody, all violent. Drunkards die in their vomit. One inebriated young man falls from his horse, and the brutal impact leaves "no sign of a nose remaining on his face . . . completely scalping the right side of his face and head. . . . One of his eyes . . . was completely knocked out of its socket and, held only by a string of skin, there it lay naked on his bloody cheek."

Weems wrote moral tracts that were page-turners. As if his words were not graphic enough, he called on the skills of illustrators. If many nineteenth-century Protestants had doubts about the novel, they had another set of fears about pictures. Was it perhaps too Catholic to use illustrations to make religion vivid to believers? Weems thought not. His tracts usually carried engravings on their covers that were designed as "come-ons" to readers. They were almost without exception violent. In one, a man shoots another in the head, saying "There! G-d D-n you. Take that." To illustrate another, he asked his publisher to put it "instantly into the hands of some artist good at design who would give us at once the likeness of a very beautiful woman distorted or convulsed with Diabolical passion, in the act of murdering, with up-lifted axe, her husband in sleep." Weems was popular with American readers, but it took most of the Protestant clergy a long time to catch up with him.

By the 1830s the American Tract Society had stretched its definition of useful entertainment to permit the reprinting of selected portions of Weems's output, without the illustrations. Yet the religious narratives that became an important part of American publishing by the second half of the nineteenth century rarely repeated the boldness of Weems's moral sensationalism. The few ministers who wrote novels peopled their stories with virtuous heroes and mild sinners, none of them drunkards or adulterers. Fictional telling of Bible stories or of tales set in biblical times became a popular genre. An important cluster of American women writers filled their bestsellers with moral and religious homilies. By the end of the nineteenth century, even the sternest Protestant moralists were able to use these formulas to make their peace with fiction. The Protestant fear of the imagination had not been easy to conquer. It had taken a determined series of innovative Protestant writers to demonstrate that it was possible to please popular taste and improve it at the same time.

Moral Purpose as a Useful Fiction

Protestants had by no means driven off the market all the books they wanted to. Pessimists did not have to look far to find something to worry about. A number of American authors who wrote for the cheap book trade churned out long novels that appealed to popular interest in sexually salacious and violent events. They were serialized in newspapers and other periodicals. We saw in chapter 2 clerical reactions to James Gordon Bennett, whose *New York Herald* revolutionized newspaper production in the United States. Ministers faulted it for calling attention to violent crimes, including rape and murder. Their efforts to convince people not to buy the paper served only to increase circulation. Attempts to censor material rarely worked. *The Police Gazette*, one of the many new periodicals that appeared in the 1840s, printed illustrations suggestive of the seamiest sides of American urban life. Like novels, this sort of publication was here to stay.

Yet, in an odd way, the Protestant crusade to silence wickedness in the book trade did not entirely miscarry. Almost without exception the people who were the principal authors of the various sorts of sensationalized books and periodicals insisted on the moral usefulness of what they were doing. They were not afraid of the clergy, but they knew that most Americans held religion in high regard. Their task was to titillate as many readers as possible without offending them. Therefore, almost all of them claimed that morality was important to their purposes in writing.

For example, consider George Lippard. Before he became a bestselling author, he was a Methodist minister. To his way of thinking, he never changed careers. He simply found a better way to promote his faith in the work of the "Savior Jesus." In 1844 he published *The Quaker City*. It was a Gothic horror story, set in Philadelphia, that among other things described seduction, rape, enforced prostitution, torture, and infanticide. One passage held before the reader a very tangible and voluptuous female breast. All the same Lippard had a vision of a purified world when true religion would sweep away the hypocrisy that governed the Quaker City.

His work was graphic, because he wanted his readers to understand that evil was not an abstraction. The work of the devil had tangible forms.

Ned Buntline (E. Z. C. Judson) represents an even more interesting case of someone who was determined to square his literary output with a religious mission. Buntline was a moral scamp by almost anyone's definition. In his personal life he broke every one of the Ten Commandments many times and added to those violations a host of other criminal acts. His reputation did not hurt sales. Buntline was one of the most successful authors of America's famous dime novels as well as of the prurient urban exposé *The Mysteries and Miseries of New York*. The latter was much like Lippard's *Quaker City*. It led readers through the seamiest undersides of New York City's urban life. As an active and unrepentant participant in that world Buntline knew what he was talking about. Buntline's effort to cast himself as a moral crusader amounted to hypocrisy. But that is not the point. To carry his books to the widest possible readership, he had to declare his respect for "the true minister of God" and his intention "to do good" in everything he wrote. Buntline was doubtlessly playing a game. What is interesting is that he thought he had to.

Life Upon the Wicked Stage

In adjusting to a revolution in print production that reduced the visibility of traditional religious fare, American Protestants counted some successes and some failures. In either case, their task had only begun. Books were not the only area of commercial culture that detracted from America's mission as a moral beacon to the world. A second battlefield in the antebellum culture wars revolved around the theater. As we have seen, Protestants associated theatricality with Catholicism and characterized the celebration of the mass as stagecraft. Catholic priests seduced the senses of those who came to church and left the faculties of rational understanding to languish. Belief based on seduction was the religious equivalent of slavery. By this logic, Protestants concluded that devout Catholics took no responsibility for their moral actions.

In antebellum America commercial theaters posed some additional problems. They were disorderly places. Men from all social classes were the chief patrons. In many theaters the only women present were prostitutes who sat in the infamous "third tier" and sold their services between acts. The audiences were rowdy, in part because alcohol consumption was part of the fun. Patrons carried baskets of rotten vegetables to heave at performers who did not please them. The disorder inside the theater sometimes spilled out onto the streets. In one tragic incident in New York City, a crowd that gathered around the newly constructed Astor Place Opera House got out of control. On May 10, 1849, a largely working-class group came to protest the performance of an English actor, William Macready. Angry factions developed among the protestors, and in an ensuing melee, more than fifty people were killed or badly injured.

Urban disorder was a problem, and not just for the Protestant middle class. Protestant efforts to ban the theater had never worked very well. Theatrical managers in Boston struggled against Puritan prejudice. Everywhere they had to deal with largely successful clerical efforts to make sure that the playhouse and other forms of commercial entertainment could not do business on Sundays. But despite the obstacles, theater found a growing audience composed necessarily of many people who were at least nominally Protestants. What were the Protestant church leaders with strong moral scruples to do about that? What alternatives could they provide?

One alternative we have already seen. Revival ministers studied the stage techniques of actors. Charles Finney did not attend the theater, but he saw a connection between his profession and that of stage performers: "Now what is the design of the actor in a theatrical representation . . . but to throw himself into the spirit and meaning of the writer, as to adopt his sentiments, make them his own, feel them embody them, throw them out upon the audience as living reality." Finney's advice initially attracted a great deal of criticism. But he did not retreat. If ministers did not understand why the techniques of actors drew crowds, if they decried acting while pompously defending the "dignity of the pulpit," the churches would be emptied and the theaters filled every night.

Revival ministers and "respectable" stage managers had a common problem that they both learned to resolve. The problem was how to get a strong emotional response from an audience and at the same time keep order. The job of revival ministers was to awaken the transforming power of emotions and then to control them. Many theatrical managers, partly in response to Protestant criticism and partly to attract women and families to the performances, also sought ways to control the behavior of their audiences. They wanted their patrons to laugh and to cry, to feel anger and joy. But as managers of "legitimate" theater, they wanted them to leave rotten vegetables at home.

Better-behaved audiences raised the respectability of revivals and of the theater together. But even with polite audiences, and in theaters that banned alcohol and unaccompanied women, Protestants moralists felt uncomfortable. They advised Protestant church members to go to lyceum lectures instead. They told them to take long, quiet walks in New York's Central Park and meditate. They recommended attending an exhibition of a morally inspirational work of art. The reputation of visual art among Protestants had its own troubled past. The Catholic religious paintings and sculptures that decorated the great cathedrals of Europe carried the same dangers as the theater. They seduced the senses. Fortunately for American Protestants, a group of talented painters found a way to infuse their canvasses with religious significance without imitating Catholic representations of God or Christ or a pantheon of saints. They found in the natural landscape a subject that allowed them to depict God's presence in the world. Thomas Cole and Frederic Church, two of the best American landscape artists, became key figures in Protestant efforts to raise the tenor of popular culture.

It was less clear what to do with P. T. Barnum. Barnum was America's greatest showman in the nineteenth century. He was a native-born New Englander and not a Catholic. He did not drink and supported the temperance crusade. So far, so good. On the downside, Barnum was a Universalist, a church whose members did not believe in hell. For that reason many Protestants did not think that Universalists really qualified as Christians. Also troubling about Barnum was his love of deceiving people. That is how he made money. He gathered crowds to gawk at George Washington's nursemaid and the "Feejee Mermaid." Both were frauds. Barnum's New York Museum that opened in 1841 was part an educational display for naturalists, part a freak show, and part pure hokum. It contained a theater (called a "lecture room") that seated three thousand people and put on popular melodramas of the day.

Many Protestants moralists never liked Barnum and were especially incensed when he likened theatrical performances in the museum to church services. Barnum did that to justify keeping his museum open on Sundays. On the other hand, a lot of other Protestant leaders decided that Barnum was doing the public no harm. The crowds that thronged into his museum were exceptionally well behaved. Mothers felt comfortable bringing their children. Barnum's shows marked the birth of family entertainment in America. Barnum's greatest financial success was his nationally sponsored tour of the singer Jenny Lind. He presented the Swedish diva as a paragon of virtue. Along the tour route, Barnum made himself available to local churches to speak out against the demon rum, his most popular lecture topic after "The Art of Making Money." What Barnum offered to urban crowds was a lot better, most Protestants decided, than most of the competition.

Henry Ward Beecher:
The Flawed Hero of Protestant Culture

Henry Ward Beecher, more than any other Protestant cleric, illustrated the changes in Protestant attitudes during the middle part of the nineteenth century. Beecher was the brother of Harriet Beecher Stowe and a number of other talented children who had sprung from the loins of Lyman Beecher. Influenced by his father—one of the last great New England preachers who took Calvinism seriously—young Henry began his career as a minister with a dour view of the human condition. Like all Calvinists, he emphasized the web of sin that ensnared men and women, adults and children. In one of his early publications, *Lectures to Young Men* (1846), Beecher compiled a long list of pleasures to avoid. Damnation was the likely result of frequenting taverns, reading novels, drinking, gambling, smoking, theater going, card playing, and dancing. He would wish any son of his in the grave, he said, should he become a sexual libertine.

Beecher changed his mind. By the time he became an immensely popular preacher who presided over Brooklyn's large Plymouth Church, he had made his peace with many expressions of American democratic taste. Like Charles Finney, he learned from actors who knew how to unite the "man speaking" to the "man hearing." Ministers needed to know less about doctrine and more about voice, posture, and gesture. Beecher took no offense when people dubbed his church the "playhouse church." Although he acknowledged that there was plenty of wickedness on the New York stage, he became a regular patron of "legitimate" theater. Good theater, like good literature, improved people's moral behavior.

In time Beecher found very little in the popular culture of his day that threatened religion. He enthusiastically shopped in New York City's new department stores and loved the tempting display of wares in the store windows. It was another form of theater. He wrote for newspapers and himself edited a religious journal with over one hundred thousand subscribers. His collected sermons and lectures were bestsellers and turned him into a national figure. Beecher concluded that Protestant leaders could direct trends in popular culture and disarm whatever was harmful in it. To prove his point, he wrote a novel. *Norwood* appeared in 1867, and while perhaps not a classic of American fiction, it sold well. Beecher's career helped other ministers decide that serious religion was not the enemy of pleasure.

Then for a time Beecher's world fell apart. Early in the 1870s Victoria Woodhull broke the story that Beecher had had an affair with Elizabeth

Tilton, one of his parishioners and the wife of his best friend. Woodhull was a marvelous New York woman who threw herself into a number of radical causes, including Marxist socialism. In her mind the problem with Beecher was not that he sexually misbehaved (she had done that herself), but that he lied about it. Others were more concerned about the truth of the charge. If Henry had slept with Elizabeth, then all the advice he had given Protestants about how to have good, clean fun looked suspect.

Theodore Tilton sued Beecher for alienation of affection (he, not his wife, was the purported wronged party). A long trial proved little one way or the other except that Americans loved a scandal. The evidence showed that Beecher had had plenty of opportunity for seduction. Tilton trusted him and knew that Beecher often visited his home when he was not there. But no direct evidence put Beecher in bed with Elizabeth Tilton. His acquittal left the public judgment split. In the end the episode seems to have worked to the advantage of Beecher's career. His wife and his church stood behind him. To cover his legal fees, he undertook a lecture tour in 1876. Large crowds applauded him and made it possible for Beecher to ask $1,000 as a fee for each talk. That is a sum equivalent in real dollars to what celebrity speakers receive today. He played to sold-out houses across twenty-seven thousand miles in eighteen states. Beecher was more than a religious figure. He was a celebrity, an icon of popular culture who understood theater.

The Beecher scandal was a close call for male Protestant America. He had urged Protestants to back off in their confrontation with democratic popular culture. Just because Catholics liked theater did not make it evil. Unconvinced Protestants continued to try direct censorship. They backed state and local laws that made the sale and consumption of alcoholic beverages illegal. They applauded Anthony Comstock, the self-anointed knight of Protestant prudery, and his heavy-handed efforts to suppress abortionists, purveyors of information about contraception, smutty literature, naked statuary, gamblers, drinkers, and anyone who danced. But Protestant efforts to construct safe alternatives to immoral enticements continued to increase.

Moral Canopies

Somewhere around the middle of the nineteenth century Protestants discovered "muscular Christianity." It was a masculine reading of the Christian ethic that said less about turning the other cheek and more about physical strength. Rather than retreating in fear from the worldly temptations, manly Christians were urged to stride forth and conquer. One important expression of this impulse was the Young Men's Christian Association, the YMCA. The movement began in England and spread around the world. It had a powerful missionary component. But to attract recruits in the United States, Y leaders placed a large emphasis upon sports. They built gymnasiums in many cities. Young men who came to the Y were invited to pray. But simply participating in sports was almost as good. The main thing was to provide a wholesome environment for young men to spend time when they were not working.

Dwight Moody, who in the late nineteenth century replaced Finney as America's best-known revivalist, began his career in Chicago's YMCA. While aggressively pursuing worldly success as a salesperson, he enlisted in the Y as a civic enterprise. Quickly he became its president. In one letter that he wrote home about his attendance at religious meetings, he said, "Oh, how I do enjoy it." The phrase is significant. In his theological views, Moody moved from conservative to ultraconservative. He gave up business to become a revival minister and to found a Bible institute. He was a precursor of what would later be called Protestant fundamentalism. None of that prevented him from building a pleasurable social dimension into the religious institutions he founded. Among the responses Moody sought from his audiences was laughter. He enlisted the talents of Ira Sankey, a gospel singer who delighted Christians much like popular hit-parade performers of the twentieth century.

Attending a meeting run by Moody was a long way from the sort of religious experience that Elizabeth Cady Stanton, the great proponent of women's rights, had as a child. She recalled slogging her way through the snow as a little girl to sit in a cold church and listen for hours to joyless sermons. She thought that death might be preferable to the punishment of yet another discourse about the threat of eternal damnation. The pleasurable parts of Dwight Moody's Protestant work appealed easily to Protestant liberals. On theological issues, Washington Gladden and Moody stood a long way apart. Gladden made his career as a sponsor of the Social Gospel movement that proposed to use Christian ethics to reform American society. But Dwight and Gladden, both famous preachers, had moved into a new world that allowed Protestants to enjoy themselves, even when worshiping. Gladden's most telling recollection was that when he was twelve he learned to his great relief that he did not have to give up baseball to be saved.

Perhaps the most significant invention of Protestant religious recreation in late-nineteenth-century America was the Chautauqua Association. It provided in a beautiful setting by a lake in western New York what the YMCA movement provided for the city. Chautauqua was a logical progression from Methodist camp meetings whose history dated back to the early nineteenth century. Camp meetings brought people together for as long as two weeks to participate in intense spiritual exercises. But Methodist ministers learned to convene them in forest groves or along the Jersey shore. They became regularized events, with the dates announced long in advance. Regulars began to think of camp meetings as an annual family vacation. One of the most popular annual meetings was on Martha's Vineyard. Attendees worshiped, but they also played tennis and croquet and bathed in the ocean. Concession stands sold candy, ice cream, and even tobacco. Although young people did not find dancing approved as part of the social activities, Andrew Dickson White, the first president of Cornell University, observed them roller-skating with arms around each other to a waltz version of "Nearer, My God to Thee."

The founders of the Chautauqua Association, John Vincent and Lewis Miller, were both Methodists and familiar with the camp meetings sponsored by their church. In 1873, they created Chautauqua to provide a retreat for Sunday school teachers of all denominations. It quickly moved beyond that purpose. White American Protestants signed up for a season at Lake Chautauqua knowing they would pray, hear sermons, and attend devotional meetings. They also knew that Chautauqua boasted of a "Department of Entertainment" that organized concerts, fireworks, bonfires, and humorous lectures. The speakers were not all ministers. College presidents and popular authors eagerly accepted invitations to talk at Chautauqua. Six American presidents went there almost as a political necessity. To lead the American nation, a president had to do homage to this wholesome institution. Protestants had found a perfect recreation and a powerful symbol to reassure themselves that they still controlled the direction of America.

Programs at Chautauqua generated more programs. The Chautauqua Literary and Scientific Circle, which started in 1878, aimed to promote valuable reading not just for the people who actually attended Chautauqua but also for people who enrolled for a correspondence course through the mail. Every year men and women, who in their homes had stuck with the regimen of assigned readings and had sent in essays as proof of their disciplined study, journeyed to Lake Chautauqua for Recognition Day. The ceremony to honor them took place in the Hall of the Grove, an open-sided structure that permitted the participants to look beyond the busts of Plato, Socrates, Homer, Virgil, Goethe, and Shakespeare to the splendor of the wooded setting.

Chautauqua advertised the power of the Christian faith. It published testimonials from pleased Chautauqua students who came from all over the country. They said that Chautauqua had made them better Christians, a fact that they demonstrated by pointing to an improvement in their social and economic circumstances. A dry goods clerk boasted that the inspiration provided by Chautauqua gained for him a place of influence and usefulness in the world. A college student credited Chautauqua with allowing him to finish his program in three rather than four years. The words of mothers, mill workers, rail workers, seamen, and businessmen found their way into advertising copy. Chautauqua performed wonders, spiritual wonders and economic wonders. It cordoned off a safe Protestant world.

Advertising Takes Command

Foreign visitors to the United States express bemusement when they see on the urban landscape a neon sign flashing the slogan "Jesus Saves." This is proselytizing, American style. It seeks to have religion command the landscape. It tries to convince people to use churches as centers of their social life. Charles Stelzle, who in the early twentieth century ministered to working-class New Yorkers, published in 1908 *Principles of Church Advertising*. In 1910 he founded and managed to fill on most days of the week New York City's Labor Temple. It was a brownstone church on the corner of Fourteenth Street and Second Avenue. To compete with the lighted marquees of nearby movie houses, Stelzle emblazoned the name of the Labor Temple on an electric sign with letters two feet high. To provide information about church programs, he erected four large bulletin boards studded with electric lights. Inside, on Sundays, he ran a "continuous bill" of back-to-back attractions. Stelzle studied the competition. He went to vaudeville performances to get ideas about how to introduce "life and snappiness" into church programs. After World War I Stelzle left church work to become an advertising agent. The job was not very different.

The "science" of modern advertising encouraged Protestant churches to differentiate themselves by something other than church doctrine. For example, a Presbyterian church on Fifth Avenue did not try to attract members by saying that it was more Calvinist than all the other Presbyterian churches in New York City. Methodist churches did not sell themselves as a surer way to heaven than Baptist churches. Advertisers wanted churches to sound like happy places. "Know the handshake of St. Paul's," one church said in a newspaper ad that did not mention what kind of church it was. "The House of Happiness" might have sounded like a better place to go to other readers. Yet another advertised alternative was the church that took as its slogan, "Christianity Makes People Healthy, Happy, and Prosperous." In the twentieth century more and more American Christian churches held social hours for different age groups. Like Catholic churches, they sponsored bingo games and potluck suppers. They formed drama groups. They built their own auditoriums and gymnasiums. Some had swimming pools. The largest of them moved to the suburbs and offered free parking in lots that were big enough for a modestly sized sports arena.

Appropriately enough, Bruce Barton, a founding partner of one of America's largest advertising agencies, summed up the new spirit. *The Man Nobody Knows*, a book he published in 1925, stayed atop the bestseller list for two years. It was a slick updating of the historical Jesus that turned him into a prototype of the go-getting, canny American businessman. Jesus was "no pale young man with flabby forearms and sad expression" who roamed the Holy Land looking for enemies to forgive. He was a hard-nosed organization man. He picked up twelve men from the bottom ranks of society and turned them into a sales force that conquered the world. With a muscled body hardened by manual labor, the gregarious Jesus was the most sought-after bachelor dinner guest in Jerusalem.

Many Protestant church leaders were shocked by Barton's book. But Barton, who had been voted "most likely to succeed" by his class at Amherst College, had found a message with enormous appeal to Protestant America. The son of a minister, Barton intended religious leaders to take him seriously if they wanted Protestant Christianity to prosper. He had only gone a little bit further than Harry Emerson Fosdick, who ten years earlier had published *The Manhood of the Master*. No one could accuse Fosdick of simply writing promotional material for the American Chamber of Commerce. He was a well-known preacher in the Social Gospel tradition. In the 1920s he crusaded for a socially relevant Christianity against what he saw as the regressive positions taken by Christian fundamentalists. Yet his title said it all. Jesus was no sissy. He enjoyed nature, friendship, and an active social life. Physical exercise blessed him with good health and the energy to pursue a clear plan of action.

Fosdick and most other Protestants in America were not opposed to the image of a businesslike Christ. Business was what Protestants did best. The true opponents of this image of Christ were Catholic. Fosdick wanted social reform, but he expected the leadership for the reform of unregulated capitalist enterprise to come from businesspeople who pledged to follow Christian rules of behavior. Fosdick thought he had found one in John D. Rockefeller Jr. Rockefeller gave most of the money to build Riverside Church on the upper West Side of Manhattan. When this interdenominational church opened in 1931, Fosdick was its first pastor.

To many intellectuals who have no particular use for organized religion, Barton and Fosdick and the audiences they reached are symptoms of the shallowness of American religious commitments. That judgment underestimates the depth of religious feeling of those who attend America's large houses of worship. What arguably is shallow is popular or mass culture. But even that evaluation is too sweeping. A better assessment is that many Protestant religious figures were enormously inventive in adapting religion to American democratic culture. Trying to make religion enjoyable was a lot better than trying to impose religious conformity by law. The label *Protestant* covers many attitudes and beliefs that affect secular behavior as well as worship practices. If Protestant leaders were going to help shape American behavior, they had to catch a lot of people outside of church.

The Challenge of Contemporary Mass Culture

In the twentieth century Protestants made one heavy-handed attempt at censorship, and it failed. That was national Prohibition, which tried to dry up the United States from the end of World War I until the first term of Franklin Roosevelt's presidency. Other things were censored, like books and movies. But as we saw in the case of Hollywood's Production Code, Protestants played a secondary role. Some of the best Protestant innovations, the YMCA movement and Chautauqua, continued operation in the twentieth century. The explicitly religious part of their mission disappeared, but that did not make them less effective in upholding ideals of wholesome entertainment.

One thing did change. At the end of the nineteenth century, many of the Protestant leaders who worked hard to purify the commercial offerings of American culture were liberals. Closing down saloons, making the theater a safe environment for families, building museums and parks as places for redemptive recreation—these were Progressive reform measures designed to improve the lives of all Americans. Paternalistic or not, the initiatives had the goal of helping working classes and immigrants. By the middle of the twentieth century Protestant liberals were less certain about their missionary drive to determine the moral behavior of everyone. At the end of the century, it almost seemed as if the field of cultural cleansing had been abdicated to Protestant conservatives, or fundamentalists. In the pursuit of family values, the conservatives were ready to do what they never would have done in the nineteenth century—make common cause with Catholics and conservative Jews.

Some of the shift was apparent in the 1950s when Hollywood's Production Code began to run out of steam. It had been an interesting experiment. Almost everyone agrees that the code did not harm the quality of American films. The years 1933 to 1950, in fact, mark a golden age in American filmmaking. The rationale behind the Production Code was spelled out in a thoughtful document that listed good reasons why film executives—who had a great deal of power to shape the way people, especially children, thought—ought to be careful about the moral content of their product. But attitudes changed. By the 1950s people were asking whether it was really morally useful for mass entertainment to pretend that sex did not exist. Would that make young people more sexually responsible? Or did sexual naïveté almost guarantee unwanted pregnancies?

The death of the Production Code did not immediately threaten what many Protestants celebrated as America's clean-cut image. Religious books sold well. Pop singers hit the charts with songs about "The Man Upstairs." Hollywood invested lots of money in producing biblical films that drew on both Old and New Testament stories. *Father Knows Best* and *Leave It to Beaver* were the standard sitcom fare of early television. But a lot also was changing. *Playboy* magazine went through the mails. Elvis Presley's once-censured gyrating hips became the style of American dance. By the early 1960s Americans no longer needed to travel to Europe to buy *Lady Chatterley's Lover*. Movies not only talked about sex, they also showed people having sex. Liberal Protestants moved with the times and stopped trying to control the content of popular culture.

Nonetheless, commercial mass culture is a vast and varied market. American Protestant religion still claims for itself a sizable market share. The Dove Awards represent a national phenomenon. Protestant filmmakers produce videos that reach a large audience. And the oldest form of Protestant cultural excitement, the revival, is alive and flourishing. American evangelism remains a highly visible part of American popular culture. Its practitioners are skillful entertainers who have become savvy exploiters of print media, radio, and television. Billy Sunday, Aimee Semple McPherson, Billy Graham, and Oral Roberts all understood that the United States provided a market for religious messages that extended well beyond the people who attended weekly religious services. They invented strategies of Christian show business. The televangelists of the late twentieth century built on the success of Charles E. Fuller's great radio hit *The Old-Fashioned Revival Hour* and Herbert W. Armstrong's *Radio Church of God*. They even learned from a Catholic. Bishop Fulton J. Sheen, in his *Life Is Worth Living*, demonstrated in the 1950s what television could do for religion.

Pat Robertson will never be elected president of the United States, but he has secured an important place in the history of American popular culture. Robertson founded the Christian Broadcasting Network (CBN) in 1960. That was the year in which the Federal Communications Commission (FCC) ruled that radio and television stations no longer were required to donate time to religious groups as part of their public-service responsibilities. Before the FCC changed the rules, liberal religious groups like the National Council of Churches had been the principal beneficiaries of free airtime. Radio and television executives preferred dealing with groups that stressed ecumenical peace. They made the more contentious conservatives buy airtime. When competition hit the religious airwaves, the conservatives were prepared.

Robertson proved himself to be something of a media genius. He converted to Pentecostalism, an unusually expressive form of Protestantism wrongly associated with people of low economic standing. Robertson certainly had never known social deprivation. His family was well off. His father served for thirty-four years in the House of Representatives and then in the Senate. Nor was Robertson's decision to become a Pentecostal a result of poor education. He earned a bachelor of arts degree at Washington and Lee with Phi Beta Kappa honors. He then went on for a law degree at Yale and a master of divinity degree at New York Theological Seminary.

Robertson built CBN into one of America's largest cable channels though it devoted over 50 percent of its programming to religion. Its centerpiece was the *700 Club Program*, which made television stars out of Jim and Tammy Bakker. Robertson easily survived the scandal that brought down the Bakkers. They had left CBN to found their own cable network, PTL (Praise the Lord). An equally spectacular sexual scandal involving Jimmy Swaggart threatened the reputation of televangelists. But the ever-respectable Robertson continued to do well. He used the profits he made from his media empire to found the Christian Coalition, a powerful political lobby, and also Regent University. Robertson takes his religion very seriously. Television is for him a way to usher in the triumphant return of Jesus Christ. To him the disaster of September 11, 2001, might just possibly have been a divine judgment foretold by his television ministry. In that case, Americans had no effective political or even military way to respond. To Robertson the smart ones would fall back on God. He was ready to serve them with television programming that promised morally safe entertainment until the very last day of the world.

In considering Protestant strategies for policing the standards of American secular culture, we have not yet considered one of their strongest institutions—the organizations of American women. That is the subject of the next chapter.

Chapter Four

American Religion and the Second Sex

In 1896 Susan B. Anthony stood before delegates to the annual convention of the National American Woman Suffrage Association. She had done this many times before, and at the age of seventy-six she could look back on many personal victories. This time she was less sure of her ability to persuade the delegates. Her intent was to convince them to vote against a resolution that, according to Anthony, "will be a vote of censure upon a woman . . . who has stood for half a century the acknowledged leader of progressive thought and demand in regard to all matters pertaining to the absolute freedom of women." The woman in question was Elizabeth Cady Stanton, Anthony's close friend and long associate in the struggle for women's rights.

The disputed resolution aimed to disassociate the association from a project that Stanton had undertaken with a zealous energy unusual even for her—the composition and publication of the *Woman's Bible*. Its first volume appeared in 1895, the second in 1898. Stanton wrote in the introduction: "From the inauguration of the movement for woman's emancipation the Bible has been used to hold her in the 'divinely ordained sphere,' prescribed in the Old and New Testament." That sphere, according to Stanton, was an inferior one. A scripture that made women bear the blame for Eve's role as Adam's temptress in the Garden of Eden, a Bible that presented women as the cause of sin and death in the world and thereby sentenced them to silent subjection to men, was unsatisfactory.

Anthony's plea failed. The resolution disassociating the suffrage cause from the *Woman's Bible* passed by a vote of 53 to 41. The delegates feared that the *Woman's Bible* was too controversial. Suffragists were fighting for a sufficiently unpopular cause to make gratuitous association with another seem a bad idea. Stanton was a giant of their movement, and therefore a magnet for publicity. Most of the delegates thought that her fame made it all the more necessary to repudiate her attack on the authority of divine scriptures. They were, after all, holding their meeting in the Church of Our Father in Washington, D.C.

Stanton had some excellent reasons to pick a fight with the Christianity of her day. Opponents of suffrage, of education for women, and of all other efforts to accord women legal equality with men loved to quote Scripture. Their favorite verses included the creation of Eve from Adam's rib (Gen. 2:21–23), Eve's suggestion to Adam that they eat the forbidden fruit (Gen. 3:5–6), and Paul's command that women keep silent in religious assemblies (1 Cor. 14:34–35). Stanton and the committees that worked with her on the *Woman's Bible* found many other offensive passages. Their aim was to collect all the verses in the Old and New Testaments relating to women and to provide a corrective commentary on passages that seemed to justify women's subordination to men.

Stanton had long been a free thinker. "I do not believe," she wrote in the *Woman's Bible*, "that any man ever saw or talked with God" or that "God inspired the Mosaic code." Even so, Stanton had been reared in a strict religious environment and recognized the power of religion. In fact, the sacred aura of the Bible still affected her deeply. Protestant Christianity was part of her cultural heritage, so much so that she recalled "the shudder that passed over me on seeing a mother take our family Bible to make a high seat for her child at the table." Stanton's goal was to revise religion, not renounce it. Yet that proved to be too radical a project.

Stanton naturally wondered why. She wrestled with the puzzle of why the majority of women, including suffragists, acquiesced in doctrines that dictated their subordination. "So perverted," she said in pondering reasons to explain the piety of women, "is the religious element in her nature, that with faith and works she is the chief support of the church and clergy; the very powers that make her emancipation impossible." What she especially could not understand was that many women in the United States and Europe believed, despite all evidence she had collected to the contrary, that Christianity gave women nobility and a full equality with men.

To sustain that belief, Protestant women compared their faith with other world religions, past and present. They noted that paganism sacrificed female virgins to appease angry gods. Islam made the status of women totally subject to the whims of their husbands. Muslim men were free to take multiple wives and to divorce one who had ceased to please them with the wave of their hand. Hindus burned widows alive. Even

Judaism, the only other religion that in their minds was free of barbarism, was thoroughly patriarchal. In contrast, according to the women who opposed Stanton, the New Testament revolutionized the status of women. Christ instituted new laws of love and forgiveness that were especially suited to the temperament and intuitive powers of women. Because of this change women arguably had more important roles to play than men in constructing a Christlike world.

Stanton agreed with her critics that some religions made matters worse for women than Christianity, at least Protestant Christianity. But better in this case was not good enough. Women, although they comprised the majority of church members in the United States, enjoyed in some perverse way being ruled by male elders and preachers. In this assumption at least Stanton was wrong. Nineteenth-century American women found in their churches important ways to express themselves and to join with their sisters in seeking ways to improve American society. In this chapter we will examine the reasons for Stanton's frustrations but also consider why women at least as intelligent as Stanton clung to their faith.

Churches and the Sponsorship of Public Domesticity

The main reason that people, whether men or women, attend religious services is to worship God. In churches and in synagogues and in mosques, they reaffirm their faith in doctrines that give meaning to their lives. Remember, however, that religion is about something else. Unless we imagine that religious fervor is sexually determined, that women because of some peculiar gene formation are more naturally given to prayer than men, we must look for reasons other than faith to explain women's devotion. For the moment our focus is on Protestant women.

Middle-class women in nineteenth-century America learned a set of cultural norms that strongly linked their expected roles as wives and mothers with the traits of nurturing, moral sensitivity, and self-sacrifice. Rather than learning how to support themselves, they were taught to aspire to economic dependence in a home provided by their husband. Their most important social role was to teach their children the difference between right and wrong. Yet women were not that dumb. The private world of domesticity, they learned, had public extensions. Churches, for example, served as an important extension of domestic space. The easy movement of women between their home and their place of worship unchained them from the hearth and stretched the social roles they played as wives and mothers.

For Stanton and for other women who fought to improve the status of women, the most obvious symbol of what was wrong with women's lot was their exclusion from participating in the most important rite of American democracy. Yet even without the vote American women found ways to address and influence politics. Politics is, after all, any activity that aims to affect the decisions made by people who hold elected or appointed positions. Women's political work began in their churches. By the 1830s Protestant women were organizing church-based clubs. These clubs were sexually exclusive. Only women could belong. Only women served as the club officers. Only women could without invitation deliver speeches. In their church clubs women talked about things other than their children or how to cook savory meals for their husbands. They talked about public issues, often the same issues that men talked about. They acted in ways we now call political lobbying.

Women's church organizations worked with the poor and with prostitutes in urban neighborhoods. The information they collected taught America's first social workers how poverty rather than innate sinfulness destroyed lives. They were in the forefront of the antebellum temperance movement. Who better than women understood the strong correlation of drunkenness with wife-beating and child abuse? Many of the women trained in church organizations joined the abolitionist movement and participated in street demonstrations to support candidates who took a stand against slavery.

A sticking point developed when some women suggested that they ought to express their views in forums that men attended. In challenging what was then a strong social prohibition against women addressing mixed assemblies, Sarah (1792–1873) and Angelina (1806–79) Grimké tried with mixed success to challenge the rules of middle-class respectability. Born in Charleston, South Carolina, to a wealthy slave owner who saw no place for women in public life, the two sisters grew up with plenty to rebel against. They had extraordinary courage. Moving to Philadelphia and joining a Quaker assembly, they became abolitionists. In the 1830s, working with William Lloyd Garrison and Theodore Dwight Weld (who Angelina later married), the two sisters began to speak in public assemblies attended by both sexes. Their efforts drew a sharp rebuke from their Quaker brethren. That was perhaps surprising because Quaker women spoke in their religious meeting. More predictable was the public denunciation from New England Congregational ministers. The latter group, citing the Bible to prove women's weakness and dependence, said that when a woman "assumes the place and tone of man as a public reformer . . . her character becomes unnatural."

For the time being, not many American women tried to cross the line that the Grimké sisters had stepped over. They recoiled at the mere idea. We should not be surprised that many women who became social activists respected the gender distinctions drawn between men's roles and women's roles. What the Grimké sisters did compromised the special moral quality of women's work. What was the point, women asked, in becoming coarse platform performers like men? Most male orators cared only for their egos. The Grimké sisters were right about the symbolic importance of women being able to speak wherever they wanted. But their failure to convince others still left women with many ways to blur gender distinctions.

Making Domesticity a Science

The famous Seneca Falls Convention held in 1848 was the first women's rights assembly held anywhere in the world. Although it met in the Seneca Falls's Wesleyan Church, it had no religious sponsorship. Lucretia Mott, Elizabeth Cady Stanton, and the other women who came together in western New York set goals for women's legal and political equality endorsed at the time by no Christian denomination. Yet most of the women delegates belonged to churches. They had worked in church organizations and had taught Sunday school. Their redrafting of the Declaration of Independence to include women in the phrase "all men are created equal" was radical even though they still accorded women a special role as moral leaders. The cultural stereotype that most of the women at Seneca Falls wanted to overcome was the association of women with self-sacrifice. They were not content to think of middle-class women as a permanent volunteer army who asked for no benefits for themselves. They demanded the right to work and to control their own property. But for the most part, they presented their demands as things necessary to preserve the sanctity of marriage and to provide for the protection and safety of women.

Middle-class women in America aimed to be pillars of respectable society and used their religious affiliations as a badge of respectability. Arguably, respectability held back their demands for greater social and political equality. That is only to say that most people, whether men or women, are not by nature revolutionaries. They work to better their circumstances while at the same time seeking happiness in their daily lives.

Religion encouraged women to say a lot of conventional things about goodness that might in our day seem saccharine and dull. In Susan Warner's hugely successful novel *The Wide, Wide World*, published in 1850, admirable Christian women spend a lot of time in the kitchen talking about quilting and other domestic arts. The only liberating aspect of the story is that men have scarcely any role to play. The hardest decision faced by the heroine was what color Bible to buy. The wide world that Warner held up to women in some five hundred pages of text revolved around small achievements, small jealousies, and very small talk.

We may suppose that nineteenth-century women read Warner's novel and others like it for solace. That is only one side of the coin, however. A search for consolation is not a sufficient reason to explain why women went to church or why they read books. If reading taste is our guide to women's lives in nineteenth-century America, we need to remember that women were the primary readers of fiction. That was a small but significant defiance of conventions. Moreover, nineteenth-century fiction came in many forms. Women purchased Warner's book, but they also read the popular stories of Walter Scott, stories where daily life and the place of women in that life was anything but dull. Whatever we imagine to be the boring features of domestic routines blessed by religion, we must not mistake our standards for the standards that nineteenth-century women used to evaluate their lives.

The career of Catherine Beecher is instructive. She was the oldest daughter of the famous New England Congregational minister Lyman Beecher. Lyman Beecher had two wives (the first one died) and thirteen children, many of whom went on to careers associated with religious vocations. Among Catherine Beecher's famous siblings was her brother Henry, whose career we considered in the last chapter. He was not the only man who disappointed Catherine. She was also the sister of Harriet Beecher Stowe, the novelist who wrote *Uncle Tom's Cabin*. Perhaps the most famous woman in nineteenth-century America, Stowe presented her influential novel to readers as something that came to her in a religious vision. If anyone took the claim seriously, then Stowe was a passive conduit rather than a skilled artist. Her book milked sentimental images of the power of feminine self-sacrifice to alter the moral conduct of others. Uncle Tom, the everlastingly loyal slave who died at the hands of Simon Legree rather than resist, was in that sense nothing but a woman.

Despite the fact that Stowe supported suffrage, many later feminists wrote her off as someone whose heart was in the home. She coauthored with her sister Catherine *The New Housekeeper's Manual*, a book that tied her to the dull enterprises of cooking and cleaning that enslaved house-wives. Domestic economy, later named home economics, has quite properly received more respectful evaluations in recent years. Catherine Beecher's best-selling book *A Treatise on Domestic Economy*, published in 1842, was without question aimed at homemakers. Though the chapter titles, including "On the Care of Parlors," "On Washing," and "On Sewing, Cutting, and Mending," are not exactly a list of dream subjects for feminists, Catherine Beecher's intention was not to encourage women to stay at home. She never did.

Lyman Beecher with reason regarded Catherine as a strong-willed child. She believed in Christianity and considered the Bible the bedrock of moral instruction. She read it to the children she taught at the Hartford Female Seminary, an institution she founded. But she doubted the truth of the Calvinist tenets of original sin and predestination. Despite her father's urging, she never experienced conversion nor particularly worried about that failure. Christianity to her meant performing good works. She was once engaged but never married. Domestic economy was not for her the credo of a simple wife who wanted to learn how to cook and sew. It was a strategy for elevating the value of women's work, whatever that work was, and for justifying an education for women equal to that given to men.

Beecher wanted to raise domestic economy to a science. In her long manual she provided information for women about architecture, hygiene, the chemistry of cooking, the efficient arrangement of domestic space, and budgets. Beecher crusaded to show that homemaking and mothering were not intuitive activities, picked up through idle gossip with other women or from an oral tradition handed down by mothers from generation to generation. They were subjects that required training, including a basic education in mathematics and science. Beecher did not forget religion. In a poorly managed home, Christianity, like every other important aspect of life, foundered. Nonetheless, Christian management merited monetary compensation.

There were limits to her program for liberating women, but those limits were often tested. In one significant episode of her life, one involving the defense of her friend Delia Bacon, her resentment at the way men stacked the deck in their favor turned to bitterness. Delia came from a large and talented Hartford family and had studied for a year at Catherine's female academy. Her brother Leonard became a leading minister in New Haven. Delia herself was something of a prodigy who wrote historical fiction. Her most famous literary enterprise was her engagement in the controversial effort to prove that her distant ancestor Francis Bacon had written Shakespeare's plays.

It was another controversy that drew Catherine Beecher into a public battle to protect her former student. Alexander MacWhorter, a young minister with promise, began a courtship with Delia in 1847. Delia was older than MacWhorter and according to his later insinuations a good bit wiser. The courtship ended in mutual public recriminations. He accused her of indecorous behavior, and she accused him of breaking a promise of marriage. Leonard Bacon rose to his sister's defense and demanded that the Congregational Church formally censure MacWhorter. Beecher took her friend's side and unwisely urged Delia to pursue the matter in a trial she had no chance of winning. MacWhorter had too many friends among New England's most prominent clergymen, including Catherine's father. In the end he received only a mild reproof. Delia suffered public humiliation. Beecher was furious. She had seen firsthand the injustice that resulted from women's unequal power within the church and within society. Yet Beecher would not have backed Bacon if she believed that she was sexually permissive. About some matters Beecher was altogether proper. Domestic science had no answers for the problems of her friend.

From Domestic Science to Home Protection

In the late nineteenth century the phrase "home protection" appeared in the women's movement. More than domestic economy, it provided a slogan for women to claim more of a voice in legislative matters. "Home protection" was the motto of the Woman's Christian Temperance Union. The WCTU was the largest women's organization created in nineteenth-century America, in fact the largest organization of any kind if you exclude political parties. The hatchet-wielding Carry Nation, who belonged to the WCTU, epitomized for many Americans an unsmiling type of female religious zealot who sought revenge for the lack of joy in her life by attacking the pleasures of everybody else. Nation was a much more interesting character than that. Born in Kansas and married briefly to an abusive alcoholic, she used her six-foot frame to break up drinking establishments all over Kansas. "A bulldog running at the feet of Jesus, barking at what he doesn't like," she was arrested many times. Her boldness made her a popular speaker at America's most famous male colleges.

The story of the WCTU is more accurately the story of Frances Willard, who served as the organization's president from 1879 until her death in 1898. The WCTU was founded in 1874 during one of the early meetings of the Chautauqua Association. In its early years, it limited its activities to struggles against the demon rum. But when Willard took over, she insisted that if women wanted to redeem America society, they had to concern themselves with a whole chain of related issues. Willard's causes, all justified as home-protection measures, included rights for trade unionists and women's suffrage. Temperance controlled a husband's brutality. Trade unions made possible better wages for those responsible for the economic support of families. Women's right to vote provided a political voice for mothers.

Willard did not consider herself a radical but as someone who wanted to make American society live up to its ideals. She never married, but most of the women who joined the WCTU did. Nothing in its platform challenged traditional Victorian ideas about sex and marriage. When Willard staged the large annual meetings that brought thousands of WCTU delegates together, she arranged the speakers' platform to look like a home parlor, decked out with plants, easy chairs, warm-colored rugs, and a Bible placed conspicuously in view. She believed that a "woman's touch" was a powerful force for social change.

In Willard's opinion, women's problem was not religion but their own laziness in the struggle to secure a religious nation. A Methodist by upbringing, she blamed the world's problems on the inclination of women and men to spend their leisure hours in frivolous pursuits. Middle-class women had too much time on their hands and not enough ambition to do much more with their leisure than read novels. Women, in her mind, could raise families and still have enough hours in the day left over to work for social betterment. She especially recommended journalism as a useful activity, and the WCTU had its own large press run by women. Among the daunting titles of the books she wrote for women was *How to Win and Do Everything*.

A Few Women Preachers, Very Few

Willard, along with most of the other women we have considered, assigned a sacred purpose to women's social work. Her White Ribbon women (white ribbons were the badge of WCTU membership) were to "spread the pure light over nations far and wide." Most of them attended to their sacred mission without confronting the exclusionary practices of religious institutions. No school of theology accepted women as students. No Christian denomination admitted women as regular candidates for the ministry. Few church assemblies, as the Grimké sisters had learned, permitted women to speak. Women's religious clubs had done nothing to eliminate a fundamental problem that kept women in a humiliating position of subordination. So long as Paul's injunction kept women silent in religious assemblies, whatever women did carried a stigma of unimportance.

The few women who wanted pulpit roles quoted Joel 2:28. It read "your sons and your daughters shall prophesy." It was too insignificant a passage to challenge Paul and to tumble the barricades that stood in the way of making women church leaders. Only a few American women got through those barricades in the nineteenth century. But at least the few who became ordained preachers of established Protestant denominations received some publicity. What mattered was the mere demonstration that women could be effective pulpit orators.

Perhaps the most famous was Phoebe Palmer. From the late 1830s through the 1860s, she and her husband pursued a career as itinerant pastors that took them on tours through the United States and the British Isles. They were swept up in the enthusiasm that was dubbed the Holiness Revival in Anglo-American Methodism. Phoebe Palmer tried to push Methodists into a more enthusiastic recognition of the visible evidence of sanctifying grace. God's grace was an ecstatic experience, not a staid recitation of words. Yet despite her important role in promoting a religious impulse that eventually spread beyond Methodism into the Pentecostal movement, the Methodist Church never ordained Palmer. One reason, in fact, that the main branch of Methodism kept a guarded attitude toward the Holiness Movement was precisely the encouragement that its emotional services gave to women's active participation.

In 1853, the Congregational Church, in many ways still the repository of New England Puritan stiffness, took what might have signaled a radical change in policy. It ordained Antoinette Brown Blackwell as its first female minister. Antoinette Brown, who was born in Henrietta, New York, in 1825, spent much of her life organizing one kind of reform movement or another. She graduated from Oberlin, one of the country's few coeducational institutions. She then was permitted to study, but not stand for a degree, at Oberlin's theological school. Before her historic ordination she preached for four years in a church in South Butler, New York. The breach that Blackwell made in the dyke of male privilege turned out to be small because her term as an ordained pastor lasted only one year. It did not tempt the Congregational Church to alter its usual procedures that kept women out of leadership positions. Later, after her marriage to Samuel Blackwell, she joined the Unitarian Church and continued to give sermons. The number of women who spoke in church increased. But the list of women who pursued a career in the ministry of a large Protestant denomination was very short.

The situation becomes more interesting if you turn to some of the alternate religions that spread in nineteenth-century American democratic culture. For example, throughout the nineteenth century a number of independent-minded women became leading participants in the popular investigative craze known as spiritualism. Billed as a scientific endeavor to prove the existence of life after death, spiritualism beginning in the 1840s drew prominent people into the parlors of mediums who advertised themselves as channels of communication to the other world. Kate and Margaret Fox, two teenaged sisters who became spiritualism's first celebrated act, satisfied their audiences by producing spirits who rapped out answers to questions posed to them by their living auditors. Within a few years other mediums boasted of spirit controls who played musical instruments, spoke through the medium who fell into a trance, and appeared as gossamer apparitions.

The vast majority of the mediums were women who were heavily criticized for unconventional and unfeminine behavior. Because many of them led itinerant lives, much like revivalist preachers, they rarely settled into domestic life with a brood of children. Some of them never married. Some of them married more than once. Mediumship was a career, and the women who pursued it meant to make an income that freed them of financial dependence on men. They were well represented in the women's rights movement in the latter part of the nineteenth century and counted as their clients leaders of the movement, including Susan B. Anthony and Elizabeth Cady Stanton. Spirit messages were more encouraging to female equality than the Bible.

Despite their novelty, female mediums made many concessions to conventional gender stereotyping. The work they had chosen, they claimed, had been forced on them by their spirit controls. They would have preferred to stay at home. But the insistent voice of the spirits, most of them male, left them finally with no choice but to go on the road. Mediums also denied active agency in their performances. Before they could receive spirit messages, they had to fall into a semiconscious trance. Male spirits took over their bodies and used them. Despite the sexual innuendos and the passivity they ascribed to themselves, female mediums filled their autobiographies with happy memories of how they subdued audiences of skeptical, unruly males and turned them into devoted fans. Their mission was triumphant.

New Churches and Women

Spiritualist churches continue to exist today. But most spiritualists, whether men or women, showed little sustained interest in organizing a religion alternate to the already established denominations. There were plenty of other religious seekers in nineteenth-century America who did. Interestingly, many of them played a distinctive part in rethinking gender roles and family organization. The Church of Jesus Christ of Latter-day Saints, or the Mormons, which Joseph Smith launched in the early 1830s, shocked notions of middle-class respectability by endorsing the practice of a man taking more than one wife. The Oneida Community of Perfectionists, organized by John Humphrey Noyes in 1848, instituted a system of rotating sexual partnerships that his critics insisted amounted to "free love." Smith and Noyes were savagely attacked on the grounds that their religious innovations degraded American women. In fact, it is not at all clear that women suffered under these arrangements. The main problem was that as experiments in family arrangements, their terms were cut short. Oneida became a community of silversmiths. And the Mormons were forced by the American Congress to renounce plural marriage.

Something else kept the American Shakers from gaining a permanent foothold. Led initially by Mother Ann Lee, the Shakers shared all work, including church work, equally between men and women. The Shaker divinity had male and female characteristics, and Ann Lee herself was heralded as the second coming of Christ. All of this was heady stuff for religious women in America. Yet by the middle of the nineteenth century it was clear that the Shakers had saddled themselves with a principle that prevented their growth. They were pledged to celibacy. Believing that they lived near the second coming of Christ and the end of human history, they saw no need to defile themselves in sexual activity. Shaker communities survived by bringing in new members, but they competed poorly in the marketplace of American religious pluralism. Today American Shakers count only a handful of aging members.

Millennial expectations in America found expression in other religions that proved to be more enduring. A woman founded one of the most important. Belief in the imminent second coming of Christ had been part of Christian teaching since the early days of the church. The book of Revelation, which had been penned sometime in the first century of the common era by a mysterious figure named John, gave the Christian world a rich set of allegories and symbols by which it might discern when human history was approaching its end. From time to time someone arose to proclaim the imminence of the triumphant descent of the warrior Christ to fight the battle of Armageddon and begin the Last Judgment.

In the 1840s that role fell to William Miller, a New England Baptist who had spent his adult life in a quest for religious certainty. Using his own method to crack the prophetic codes contained in Revelation and also in the book of Daniel, he believed he could count the actual number of days in history that separated the destruction of the temple in ancient Jerusalem from the second coming. His calculations made him certain that Christ would return to earth sometime between March 1843 and March 1844. Miller was an indifferent preacher with none of the rhetorical skills associated with famous evangelicals of his time. Nonetheless, publications generated by Joshua V. Himes, a man who met Miller in 1839, spread Miller's message widely through the Northern states. His publicity campaign created for Millerism a wide network of expectant followers. They faced a severe disappointment when the world passed through 1843 and 1844 without a trace of a descending Christ.

Miller's career was over, but the prophecy game he started was not quite up. Some of his followers decided that Miller had correctly calculated the date but had misinterpreted the event that had happened. A farmer named Hiram Edson declared that although Christ had not appeared on earth, he had in heaven entered the holiest part of the Jewish temple in preparation for the Last Judgment. At this point, Ellen Harmon White, who was born in 1827, and her husband James White entered the story. Along with Joseph Bates, they joined Edson's reinterpretation of Miller's prophecy to another religious movement that enjoined Christians to keep a Seventh-Day, or Saturday Sabbath. Because of spiritual visions that she began to receive in 1844, Ellen White became the leader of this new religious initiative. She was the founder and first head of the Seventh-Day Adventist Church.

White's visions were clearly within the tradition of divine revelation, even if most of her revelations had to do with practical matters of church organization and the conduct of daily life. She made the Adventist Church a center of dietary reform. Her followers gave up alcohol, tobacco, tea, coffee, and all meat. She gathered them in Battle Creek, Michigan, much like the Mormons gathered their members in Kirkland, Ohio; Nauvoo, Illinois; and finally the Salt Lake basin in Utah. In Battle Creek, White worked with John Harvey Kellogg to build one of the best hospitals in the United States. Kellogg went on to invent granola and a flaked wheat cereal that his brother, W. K. Kellogg, commercially exploited. Battle Creek became the center of America's breakfast food industry. After White's death, Seventh-Day Adventism maintained its character as part church and part medical establishment. A disproportionately large number of its members work in some area of medical practice. In Loma Linda, California, it maintains a large medical school and hospital. The church never marketed Kellogg's Corn Flakes, but it did have its own line of health-food products.

Mary Baker Eddy

White's success suggested that health was a natural subject for religious women. Nineteenth-century women, more often than men, seemed to fall victim to debilitating illnesses that put them in bed for months on end. In founding a church, Ellen White made no intentional assault on patriarchy. She did not join the woman's suffrage movement. What she did do was arguably more important. She gave women encouragement to control their own bodies. As we will see in a later chapter, nineteenth-century women had many good reasons to avoid the practices of so-called regular medicine. Spiritual practices might not heal them. They did not at least make physical pain part of a useless treatment.

The nineteenth-century American woman who most boldly seized the mantle of religious leadership, drawing upon associations between religion and health, was Mary Baker Eddy. One can almost write the history of her life, which lasted from 1821 until 1910, as a series of encounters with men who failed her. Eddy's first husband died, leaving her with a son with whom she was never close. A second husband was unfaithful, perhaps the least of his cruelties to her. In 1862, suffering from numerous physical ailments, she consulted Phineas P. Quimby, a well-known "mental healer" who lived in Maine. Quimby helped her and is the one male person, aside from her third husband, whom Eddy should have remembered more generously than she did. She regarded his death in 1866 as another betrayal.

Shortly after Quimby disappeared from her life, Eddy fell hard on a sheet of ice and suffered a serious and painful injury, possibly a dislocated spine. This time she healed herself, rising dramatically from her bed on the "third day" after her accident. From that day forward Eddy imagined herself as a religious leader on a par with Jesus. Other men who worked with her in the days when she was setting down the doctrines for Christian Science disappointed her in one way or another. When she published the first edition of *Science and Health* in 1875, she saw no reason to thank anyone.

Eddy had many critics. People had to pay to learn the healing powers of Christian Science, an original sort of church financing that struck many other religious leaders as extortion. When the state of Massachusetts tightened up its rules governing the licensing of physicians, it tried to put Christian Science healers out of business. Eddy backed away from none of the challenges. The Church of Christ, Scientist, with its imposing "Mother Church" in Boston, was the creation of a determined woman who combined a passion for writing religious treatises with skills for organizing and financing a large, centralized institution. Eddy paid some attention to the prevailing assumptions about gender. She liked to be called "mother." After her church was safely launched, she delegated more authority to the minority of men in the church than to women. She never liked to speak in public. She did not support the woman's suffrage movement or in other ways protest women's inequality. Yet it is hard to think of any other woman who more defiantly used a religious vocation to break through the constraints that Victorian culture placed on women's conduct.

Missionary Women in the World

Religious sponsorship allowed women to move into the world of public affairs. However, although their work enlarged the boundaries of the separate sphere that defined women's work, it did not shatter it. Nor did women necessarily want that. They shared deeply engrained assumptions about the essence of female nature that amounted to biological determinism. They honored them even in situations where they found themselves taking on duties normally reserved for men. The example we can use to illustrate this point has to do with women missionaries in foreign fields.

American Protestants began thinking about their duty to spread the good news of Christ to "heathen" lands early in the nineteenth century. Congregationalists formed the American Board of Foreign Missions in 1810 and sent its first group of missionaries to India two years later. Numbered in that intrepid band were Adoniram Judson and his wife, Ann Hasseltine Judson. The pair proved a disappointment to the Congregationalists, for during their long ocean voyage they became convinced that Protestants who maintained the rite of infant baptism were insufficiently "reformed" from the Catholic faith. In Calcutta, they submitted to rebaptism as adults and became members of the Baptist denomination. Much cheered by this well-publicized conversion, American Baptists formed their own mission board and joined the highly competitive business of converting the world to Christianity.

Ann Hasseltine Judson was the first American woman to be assigned missionary responsibilities outside the United States, though that role fell to her only because of her husband. When the Judsons left India and moved to Burma, their work split along predictable gender lines. Adoniram compiled the first English-Burmese dictionary, one that remained in use for many years, and he preached the gospel while trying to persuade local leaders of the good intentions of the missionaries. Ann stayed at home with women and their children, performing duties consistent with those of a nurturing mother. Matters abruptly changed, however, when Adoniram was arrested and thrown into prison. Ann now had to do everything. She negotiated with local leaders to secure her husband's release and wrote letters to the United States. She eventually traveled back to America and addressed public assemblies. When she died at the end of that trip, the many tributes to her life made nothing of her ability to step into a man's role. In posthumous myth, she became the apotheosis of the self-sacrificing woman.

Adoniram was at least not afraid of strong women. His second wife, Sarah Hall Boardman, was equally resourceful. She worked helping to translate English works into Burmese and published her poetry in religious publications. Adoniram's third wife, Emily Chubbuck, managed to outlive him. She also was a literary person who before her marriage was a well-known author of fiction who published under the pseudonym Fanny Forester. As the wife of a famous Protestant missionary, she gave up writing fiction and penned biographies instead. Her work continued to reach a large audience.

A large number of other American missionary women went abroad in the course of the nineteenth century. Some went in the company of their husbands. Others went as single women and served as teachers and nurses. The physical hardships they encountered, the debilitating illnesses they suffered, and the new social roles they were called upon to play gave abundant testimony to the fact that women were capable of dealing with challenging obstacles. The opportunity to escape from the barriers imposed on them by their culture may explain why missionary work appealed to them. It may also explain why many American women in the twentieth century became anthropologists. But as in the case of Ann Judson, the hagiographic literature devoted to the memory of women missionaries stressed their femininity. Even in the heathen lands of Asia or Africa, they were able to preserve it. The women in question did not necessarily question that judgment. Living in other countries often reinforced their belief in the superior position of women who lived under Christianity. We are back to the problem that bothered Elizabeth Cady Stanton. American women used their knowledge of comparative religion to defend the faith they had.

No Strangers to Racism and Ethnocentrism

White Protestant women did not have to go abroad to activate their sense of privilege. Like their husbands or their fathers or their brothers, they believed that Protestantism defined American norms. People who arrived in the United States from other countries could become Americans but not without changing many of their habits. If they came from non-Protestant countries, the task was harder. American Protestant women shared with American Protestant men the conviction that Catholics would never amount to much in America until they left the church. The prejudices of their Protestant upbringing kept them from learning some useful lessons.

The experience of American Catholic women, despite significant differences of class and national background, mirrored in some important ways the experience of American Protestant women. On any given Sunday they and their children comprised the majority of those attending mass. By the end of the nineteenth century Catholic women were organizing clubs within their parishes that performed charity work primarily within their own communities. Catholics had their own prejudices that led them to avoid contact with Protestants. Catholic women often had broader experience than Protestant women. More of them had jobs since many immigrant women had to work to help their families stay economically afloat. Economic necessity is hardly a privilege, but in this case experience with work gave women power in Catholics neighborhoods. No one doubted that women were needed.

Catholicism was patriarchal and allowed only men to become priests. Even so, it gave different accents to gender stereotypes. Catholic women had the Virgin Mary, a powerful icon of female power that could be found in every Catholic Church and every Catholic home. Worship in a Catholic Church was evenly split between the attention focused on Christ and the attention focused on Mary. At a secondary level of worship, devout Catholic women had a pantheon of saints to pray to. They too were almost evenly divided between male and female figures. Close to a majority of Catholic churches carried the name of a woman. Not one Protestant church did.

Finally, the communities of nuns gave Catholic women a model of self-sacrificing, chaste women who were also determined and strong. Nuns did not have the sacramental powers reserved for the priesthood. But they formed all over the United States activist groups that staffed the schools and hospitals that American Catholics constructed. They did not marry or bear children. Freed of family responsibilities, including sexual duties owed to husbands, they could follow vocations not generally open to other women. Nuns were resourceful managers. With meager resources at their disposal, they could figure out ways to perform organizational miracles. At the very least nuns demonstrated that women, placed in independent circumstances, could manage without men.

Protestant women living in the United States were right about one thing. All religious faiths, in adjusting to the circumstances of democratic America, wound up giving more importance to women than was the case with those same faiths located elsewhere in the world. Jewish temples in America during the first part of the nineteenth century followed Reform practice and ended the custom of letting men perform religious rituals while women sat in the balcony. The experience of orthodox Jews from Russia and Eastern Europe who came to the United States in the latter part of the nineteenth century also softened the rigor of Jewish patriarchy. Jewish communities in the United States were almost always in a process of reinventing themselves. In the process Jewish women sought education. They became labor leaders and social workers. They were mothers and also professionals. When American feminism entered a new period of activism in the 1960s, a Jewish mother and graduate of Smith College provided it with a manifesto. Betty Friedan published *The Feminine Mystique* in 1963 and opened a discussion of why happily married women with delightful children were desperately bored with their lives.

Women Gain Equality

The question that Elizabeth Cady Stanton asked at the end of the nineteenth century was why women acquiesced in religious doctrines that committed them to second-class status. At the beginning of the twenty-first century the question is worth asking again. That is especially true since the Southern Baptist Convention, by far the largest American Protestant denomination, began the century by passing a resolution to remind women within the Southern Baptist fold that they owed a duty of obedience to their husbands. The enthusiasm with which conservative wings in all religious faiths have endorsed family values has been a reaction to the notion that women have an equal right with men to enter the workplace and pursue careers. Most Protestant religious denominations in the United States, even the Southern Baptists, have expanded women's roles of leadership in the church. But as a percentage of the total occupational population, more women are doctors and lawyers today than they are preachers.

One may, of course, make a list of twentieth-century women who have been important figures in the religious life of the nation. Aimee Semple McPherson's career as a Pentecostal revivalist preacher took her from China to Detroit to Los Angeles. She was among the first evangelists to understand the importance of radio, and her Church of the Foursquare Gospel set a standard for media savvyness that only a very few later religious entrepreneurs surpassed. Evangeline Booth built the American branch of the Salvation Army into one of the largest private charity organizations in the entire world. Dorothy Day, the wealthy, sophisticated convert to Catholicism, led the Catholic Worker's movement that fed the hungry, sheltered the homeless, and made labor activism a feature of twentieth-century American Catholicism.

Less famous women, however, were responsible for changes that opened the doors of leadership in the largest denominations. We end this chapter with the story of Georgia Harkness. When in 1972 she rose to address the General Conference of the United Methodist Church she was greeted with sustained applause before she opened her mouth. She was then eighty-one and found a much different reception than when in the early 1940s she argued, "the church is the last stronghold of male dominance."

Harkness was born in Harkness, New York, in 1891 into a "definitely Christian home" and was graduated from Cornell University with Phi Beta Kappa honors in 1912. She had little to do with her degree except to teach high school, but later, with a Ph.D. in the philosophy of religion from Boston University she landed a job as an assistant professor of religion and religious education at tiny Elmira College. She spent the rest of her life in an academic career, writing over thirty-seven books. A position at the Garrett Biblical Institute made her the first woman in the United States to hold a professorship in theology. In 1926, she was also ordained as a "local elder" of the Methodist Church that under certain restrictions allowed her to administer sacraments and to preach but not to be a full member of the Methodist conference. Her longest struggle, then, became one to win full equality for women within her church's ministry. That finally happened in 1956, though on that occasion Harkness allowed "able and discerning men" to do the speaking. "I have long since learned," she said, "that this is often the surest way to get something passed."

Harkness helped to get something radical accomplished, although she used conservative means and realized that respectability was something that women within the church could not afford to lose. She never married, but in the latter part of her life, living in California and teaching at the Pacific School of Religion in Berkeley, she shared her home with Verna Miller. She enjoyed gardening and entertaining her students with home-baked cookies and pies. From all the evidence she was a very content person when she died in 1974.

Harkness's life suggests one way of responding to Elizabeth Cady Stanton's question. Organized religion was a space of activity that American women succeeded in making their own. If at the beginning of the twenty-first century they had not established their claim to full equality, they had managed some important victories. Those who stood in their way were on the defensive. Why at that point should women abandon what had been one of their most visible and important contributions to American culture? If women did abandon their churches, the exit would cast an ominous shadow on the future of organized religion in the United States. Some people think that many of the countries of Europe—France, England, and Germany among them—have entered a post-Christian era. The majority of people in those countries have long since stopped going to church. What signified the final nail in the coffin of European Christianity was a religious indifference among women that equaled the level of religious indifference among men.

On the bright side, the barriers that Georgia Harkness and other women broke down in their churches came at a time when other barriers fell as well. White Christian denominations put aside their sense of superiority to other world faiths, and also their racism. Elizabeth Cady Stanton wondered why white women tolerated social and political discrimination. She never wondered why she and many other women in the suffrage movement saw nothing wrong with discriminating against African American citizens.

Chapter Five

The African Future of Christianity

I n 1995, Louis Farrakhan, the leader of one important group of Black Muslims in the United States, organized what he publicized as the "Million Man March" in Washington, D.C. The purpose of the assembly was to demonstrate pride among African American men, a group of the American population that was overrepresented in the nation's prisons, among drug users, and among fathers who could not support their children. Opinion polls suggested that Farrakhan was not a popular man in the United States. His speeches, directed at black audiences, were laced with hostility toward white Americans, and especially toward Jews. Even to the majority of African Americans, Farrakhan espoused an unacceptable strategy of racial militancy. He represented a threat to the ideal of achieving racial comity, an ideal that had been etched in American consciousness by Martin Luther King Jr. when in 1963, also at a mass rally in Washington, he spoke about his dream of black and white children together. King, unlike Farrakhan, had an integrated audience.

The Nation of Islam, or Black Muslims, burst into general visibility in the mid-1960s. They were part of a sharp turn toward confrontational radicalism that marked protest movements after the United States escalated its military activities in Vietnam. The American press treated the Black Muslims much like they treated the Black Panthers. They were an angry group that, having given up on the American promise of equal justice for black citizens, had turned toward a politics of disloyalty. Newspapers gave a lot of publicity to Malcolm X's remark following the assassination of John Kennedy that "the chickens had come home to roost." Cassius Clay, America's most famous convert to the Black Muslims, changed his name to Muhammad Ali and in 1967 refused induction into the United States Army. "I have no quarrel with the Vietcong," he said to young black males who were proportionately by far the largest group of Americans drafted to fight in Southeast Asia. The Selective Service Agency rejected Ali's claim of religious pacifism and tried to put him in jail. The boxer, who was stripped of his heavyweight championship title, vindicated his claim of religious exemption only after the American Supreme Court in 1971 reversed the decision of lower courts.

The passing years softened the reputation of the Black Muslims. Malcolm X's best-selling autobiography, widely adopted as required reading in American high schools and colleges, included an account of his travels to Arab nations. Islam, he discovered, did not countenance a philosophy of racial division. The message of conciliation that he began to preach at the end of his life led him to break with Elijah Muhammad, the leader of the Black Muslims. That move, many people thought, set the stage for his assassination in 1965. As for Ali, he became an American hero, a man thunderously applauded when in 1996 he carried the torch that lit the Olympic flame at the Atlanta summer games. When radical adherents of Islam, linked to the Al Qaeda network of Osama bin Laden, steered passenger airplanes into the twin towers of the World Trade Center in New York City and into the Pentagon in Washington, Ali quickly and with no qualifications denounced the atrocities. In this instance it was Jerry Falwell, a white Baptist minister, who made remarks that recalled what Malcolm X had said about chickens coming home to roost.

Farrakhan, in fact, represents only one part of the Black Muslim movement that splintered in the 1970s. Wallace D. Muhammad, the son of Elijah Muhammad, was educated in Egypt and speaks Arabic. Like Malcolm X, he concluded that Islam, properly interpreted, was not compatible with militant black separatism and the cultivation of hostility toward "blue-eyed" devils. He sought to convince those who followed him that being Islamic in no way conflicted with loyalty to America. His former organization, named the World Community of al-Islam in the West, pointed the Nation of Islam toward orthodoxy.

Farrakhan nonetheless is an important figure in contemporary America. The Million Man March signaled that he too wanted a Black Muslim movement that was 100 percent American. In a very long speech he made on the occasion, Farrakhan made his own tribute to American "exceptionalism," to the promises embodied in American values that made the United States unlike any other nation in the world. Like others before him who had felt excluded from those promises, he told the demonstrators that they "were gathered here to collect ourselves for a responsibility God is placing on our shoulders to move this nation toward a more perfect union." The United States was redeemable because the preamble to its Constitution pledged an eternal mission of self-improvement. Other groups had struggled against discrimination and had finally shared in the benefits of America's promise of equality. It was now the turn of African Americans.

George W. Bush, elected president in 2000, pledged as a major initiative of his administration to place the federal government into partnership with faith-based charities. Religious faith, he confidently predicted, could change the lives of social delinquents by giving them a motive to find jobs and to work hard for economic success. He was embarrassed when someone mentioned Farrakhan as a possible partner. Could radical Black Muslims provide the faith resources that Bush was looking for? Someone should have reminded him that America's religious landscape is more complicated than groups represented by the Federal Council of Churches. The Million Man March aimed to do precisely what Bush's initiative had in mind. It proposed to use spiritual resources to help African American men avoid drug addiction and delinquency. Every man who took part in the march pledged "to strive to improve myself spiritually, morally, mentally, socially, politically, and economically for the benefit of myself, my family, and my people." With the goal of reducing recidivism, Black Muslims have made American prisons their principle place of recruitment.

There is something else that must be said about Farrakhan, not to excuse his anti-Semitism, but to explain his appeal to some African Americans. The most important thing about African American religion, over its long history, is not its distinct theology, nor its music, nor its links to Africa, nor its participatory style of worship. Important as those things are, they were made a lasting part of African American worship by something else. What kept African American churches different was their deliberate separatism. In a multicultural, multiracial society, some sort of separatism is built into the order of things. It may be bad, but not necessarily. Much depends on who controls the terms of separation and for what purposes. In the religious lives of black Americans, deliberate separatism was an essential strategy for keeping hope alive. In so many other aspects of daily life, African Americans had segregation imposed on them as a racial curse. In establishing their own churches, they exercised choice. Black churches, almost all of them Protestant, had many purposes beyond that of worship.

America and the Story of Exodus

The biblical story of Exodus, of the Jews fleeing from Egypt into the desert and then to the promised land of Canaan, has been incorporated into the mythic stories of more than one group of American immigrants. The Puritans who arrived in Massachusetts Bay in 1629 linked their passage to the New World to the trials of ancient Israel. They left England on board the *Arbella* to find a place to practice religion as they thought God intended it to be practiced. Like the Israelites, they wanted a place to be themselves, where they could keep out those who heard a different voice from God. What they imagined from the Old Testament's second book was that they were a new "covenanted" nation.

Parts of the Exodus story did not fit the experience of New England Puritans. For one thing, while they "dissented" from many of the practices of the Church of England, they were determined not to separate from that church. That is, they wanted to be a model for the purification of the English Church (hence the name Puritan), a role they could play only if they stayed within the church. In Boston and in the other settlements of Massachusetts and Connecticut, they professed loyalty to the king, who was also the head of England's church. Many of their fellow Puritans did not even leave England. The ones who stayed participated in the English civil war, instigated the beheading of Charles I (1649), and supported the protectorate government established by Oliver Cromwell (1653–58). None of these events quite turned England into Egypt or the Stuart monarchs into Pharaoh. When Cromwell's death brought the Stuarts back to the throne, the colonial Puritans recognized that they were still a long way from Canaan. As they tamed their "howling wilderness," they had to share their territory with many people who disagreed with them.

The 1776 Revolution gave newly minted Americans reasons to reinvent the Exodus story as a national myth. They were real separatists now, no longer part of corrupt England. Freed of the burden of monarchy, the former colonists, both in the North and in the South, began thinking of their national destiny as one blessed by God. So long as Americans remained virtuous, so long as they organized churches, they could be a modern chosen people. Not just England but the "Old World" in general became Egypt. Its oppressed peoples sought refuge in the United States.

For most immigrants the reality of the American promised land was flawed. They did not immediately experience America as a land flowing with milk and honey. For African slaves, who were forcibly carried to the English colonies, the Exodus story took on a different meaning altogether.

They got nothing from the American Revolution or from the Constitution. Egypt, the land of bondage, was republican America. Even free Africans in the United States found that their freedom was severely circumscribed. Pharaoh was every slave master and every white politician who acquiesced in the institution of slavery. Abraham Lincoln served as a Moses of sorts, but he was unable to take the emancipated American slave into a promised land. Like Moses, he died before anyone reached Canaan.

For African Americans, the inversion of the Exodus story began before and continued long after emancipation. Carried to Egypt, they were turned into property and made totally subject to the will of their masters. They carried with them African religions, African languages, and African customs. However, the conditions forced upon them in their new place of residence made it difficult for Africans to build communities and institutions that preserved the traditions of Africa. No one taught them to read or write. Many Africans in the Northern states lived in different circumstances than Africans in the South. Although slavery still existed north of the Mason–Dixon line, other forms of labor, most significantly contract or free labor, proved more profitable to Northern business than slavery. Yankee freedom, however, operated according to very different rules depending on a person's color.

The hypocrisy of Northern whites was not lost on Southern slaveholders. In responding to abolitionists, they pointed out that all freedom meant for blacks in the North was the freedom to be abused. Slave masters at least had to provide their slaves with room, board, and medical care. Emancipation in the North proved to be an ominous foreboding of racial divisions that were to poison American experience even after a bloody war that freed slaves everywhere in North America. The North invented Jim Crow, the pattern of segregation that characterized life in the Southern states through much of the twentieth century. Most free blacks living in the North in the first half of the nineteenth century could not vote. They were not allowed to attend schools with whites. And with respect to almost all forms of public accommodation and transport, they faced exclusion or a humiliating relegation to inferior rooms or compartments.

Yet anyone who suggests that freedom is no better than slavery does not know much about either condition. Freedom makes options possible, however difficult they might be to pursue. With freedom, Africans in the Northern states began a determined effort to define themselves as very much in the American grain. Acculturation is a process of loss as well as of gain. In the case of free blacks living in the North, the most significant loss was the practice of African religion. What replaced it was by and large

Protestant Christianity. However, the loss of an African heritage was not complete. When African Americans joined Protestant churches, they joined the ones whose rituals most recalled African practice. They responded to the revivals led by Methodists and Baptists, adapting the emotional style of those denominations to their own needs.

How to Use Freedom

Option One: Back to Africa

If the United States was Egypt, then Canaan had to be somewhere else. For free blacks in the North, that was one conclusion derivable from the Exodus story. It dictated a reverse immigration of free blacks from the United States back to the ancestral land of Africa. This idea made an early appearance among African Christians in the English colonies. In the 1770s, John Quamino and Bristol Yamma, two Africans who had been brought to Rhode Island as slaves but then freed, developed the idea of sending former slaves who had become Christians to settle in Africa as missionaries. The plan, which gained the backing of some prominent white Congregational ministers in New England, never went anywhere because the American Revolution intervened. Nothing more happened with the idea until in 1816 thirty-eight former American slaves landed in Sierra Leone. This effort at establishing a colony was the first concrete result of what became known as Back-to-Africa movements.

Reverse immigration became an important notion because it represented a choice. But there were some questions that complicated the mythology of a return voyage. Why Africa? Many of the Africans who had been transported to the English colonies by the slave trade had begun their bondage in Africa. Other Africans had enslaved them and then sold them to white slave traders. True, slavery in Africa was sometimes a less degraded form of servitude than it became in North America. But it hardly pointed to an Edenic past. To African Americans who had gained freedom in the United States, had learned to speak and write English, and had adopted a religion largely unknown in Africa, Africa did not represent a promised land. They were being asked to undertake a missionary voyage to bring Christian enlightenment to a benighted continent.

There was another problem. White Americans became too enthusiastic about the idea. Africans, who were encouraged to return to a "homeland" as Christian missionaries, were arguably doing work for whites. Could they undertake a mission of enlightenment to Africa without being implicated in racist ideologies that regarded all black people as inferior? Cooperation with a Back-to-Africa movement became especially suspect after the formation of the American Colonization Society (ACS) in 1817. It was founded and funded by white Protestants. Arguing that the United States could not endure as a democratic republic with slavery, the ACS began the political movement for emancipation. Yet freeing slaves was only one part of its program. The other part was to preserve America as a white nation. Leaders of the ACS did not believe that emancipated slaves were fit to live in the United States. White Americans had a moral duty to help them resettle in Africa even though most of them had not been born there. Many of them traced their American roots back for several generations. Never mind. Though white colonizers deplored the place that southern states had given Africans, their own notion of free America had no place for black Africans at all.

For their own reasons a few African American leaders agreed with the conclusion that Africans had no future in the United States. As we will see, Back-to-Africa movements, cut loose from white sponsors, resurfaced after the Civil War. But most free blacks in the North before 1865 chose not to accept a white plan that denied them an American homeland. In 1817 James Forten called a meeting in Philadelphia that was attended by three thousand blacks. Denouncing schemes of the American Colonization Society to exile free blacks to the "savage wilds of Africa," he got the meeting to pass a resolution declaring, "Whereas our ancestors (not of choice) were the first successful cultivators of the wilds of America, we their descendants feel ourselves entitled to participate in the blessing of her luxuriant soil, which their blood and sweat manured." Forten knew that most of the black Americans who had returned to Africa had died. The regions where they were settled were extremely inhospitable to good health. One settlement begun in an area just north of Sierra Leone in the early 1820s did manage to survive. Financed originally by the ACS, it became in 1847 the independent nation of Liberia.

Option Two: Separatism American Style

Forten's protest meeting was held in Philadelphia's black Bethel Church, which had been founded by Richard Allen. Allen and Absalom Jones, another important African American church leader, thought that Forten was absolutely right. Several decades before, Allen and Jones had made a different application of the Exodus story. Their strategy rested on premises totally opposed to those of the ACS. It was a strategy based on religious separatism. It allowed free blacks to claim an African heritage yet at the same time to insist on their right to live on American soil as full American citizens. Going back to Africa was to accept another form of mistreatment. What African Americans needed to do instead was to exit religious institutions that treated blacks as inferiors.

In the 1780s, just a few years after the first proposal to return Africans to Africa had surfaced, Allen, a former slave, was living in Philadelphia. He was a Methodist and worshiped in St. George's Methodist Episcopal Church. Absalom Jones was also a member of the congregation. The majority of the members of St. George were white, but it drew from Philadelphia's large, and in relative terms, prosperous black community. Allen and Jones were used to the segregated seating policy of the church. However, on one Sunday in November 1787, the growing number of black worshipers caused confusion about where they were supposed to sit. According to Allen, he and the other "colored people" were told to go to the "gallery," the balcony. They did and took "seats over the ones we formerly occupied below, not knowing any better." Apparently the white elders had other seats in mind, for while Allen was kneeling in prayer at the beginning of the service, he "heard considerable scuffling and low talking." He raised his head and saw a white trustee pulling Absalom Jones off his knees and saying to him, "You must get up—you must not kneel here." He denied Jones's request to finish his prayers, and other white trustees moved into the area to force the black worshipers from their places. According to Allen, "By this time prayer was over, and we all went out of the church in one body, and they were no more plagued with us in the church."

The exodus was spontaneous, but the decision to stay away was deliberate. Subsequent events turned the moment into what John Mifflin Brown one hundred years later memorialized as the "most decisive act of our religious colored people in the United States." Allen and Jones rented a storeroom and worshiped "by ourselves." In 1793 Allen founded the Bethel African Methodist Episcopal Church and a year later Jones organized the St. Thomas Episcopal Church. Originally, Allen's "Mother Bethel," though a separate black congregation, stayed within the jurisdiction of the white Methodist Episcopal Church. In 1816, despite vigorous white opposition, Allen won a court battle that turned the African Methodist Episcopal Church into an independent denomination. He became the church's first bishop.

Religious separatism soon became the norm for African American Christians in the Northern states. In 1800 in New York City Peter Williams and others who had left their white Methodist church founded the Zion Church. It too became a national denomination and took the name African Methodist Episcopal Zion Church. Black Baptists formed separate black congregations as well, the African Baptist Church in Boston in 1805 and the Abyssinian Baptist Church in New York City in 1809. In these places of worship, free blacks avoided the humiliations that were part of their usual encounters with whites.

The motivation for forming independent black churches initially had nothing to do with creating a different theology or a different style of worship for black Christianity. The motive was to announce that discrimination was intolerable. Black religious leaders discovered that independent churches could be used to address many of the economic needs of the African American community. Allen and Jones helped found, in addition to their churches, the Free African Society. It was the first nonchurch organization in the United States that blacks created for themselves and then continued to operate without white patronage. Many subsequent African American fraternal organizations used it as a model. Usually church based, they served a variety of community needs, economic, social, and political. Allen, the year before he died in 1831, became president of the National Negro Convention, a political organization founded to protest racial discrimination. The history of the separatism that came to characterize African American religion always blended secular concerns of the black community with spiritual concerns.

African American Religion Under Slavery

Many of the important transformations that differentiated black Christianity from white Christianity took shape in the slave South. Both before and after the Civil War the vast majority of African Americans lived below the Mason–Dixon line. Even as late as 1940, long after the lure of jobs in industry had prompted many Southern blacks to relocate in large Northern cities, 77 percent of African Americans still lived in states that had once formed the Confederacy. From direct evidence we know very little about the religious practices of the first slaves in America. They left no written records. We do, however, know a lot about the religious beliefs of West Africa. The conditions of slave life made it difficult to sustain African traditions carried to North America. Nonetheless, aspects of African culture managed to survive. They affected the way slaves interpreted the Christian message.

For a long time in the South little or no effort was made to convert slaves to Christianity. Slaveholders balked at the notion of bringing their slaves into the same religious fold as members of their own families. Doing so implied a common humanity. In these circumstances illiterate slave populations passed elements of African culture down from generation to generation with storytelling and ritual performance. As long as the slave trade continued, new people who arrived from Africa revitalized oral traditions. Even after it ended, twenty years after the adoption of the American Constitution, slaves smuggled into the coastal islands of the Carolinas and Georgia renewed African practices. African traditions became weaker the farther you moved away from the coast. Slaves who lived on small farms isolated from the black communities on large plantations had no ready ways to remember much about an ancestral past. Still, when in the latter part of the eighteenth century white evangelicals finally decided to open a missionary drive among the black population, they found that the minds of black slaves were not blank slates.

Missionary activities created tangled layers of crossed communication. Those who spread the message and those who heard it assigned a different meaning to the words. White Baptists and Methodists were not even sure what message they wanted to preach. In the beginning some of them were antislavery, but emancipation was not a message they could preach in the South. Missionaries had to convince the slaveholders that they were not trying to stir up trouble. Slaveholders went along with plans to convert the slave population only when they became convinced that the message of Christianity could be tailored to make slaves more efficient workers. They wanted white missionaries to talk about obedience and to remind slaves that revered Old Testament figures kept slaves.

But there was trouble in store. Black ministers were absolutely crucial to the success of the Protestant crusade. In the South, slaves preferred worshiping apart from their masters. Like free blacks in the North, they established their own churches. In 1821 the Gillfield Baptist Church in Petersburg, Virginia, had a black membership of 441 people. The tightening of slave codes in the South eventually made such open expressions of religious separatism illegal. That was especially true after several black leaders used religion to spark insurrection. In 1822, Denmark Vesey, a leader in the African Methodist Church in Charlestown, South Carolina, planned a large slave uprising. He told slaves in his congregation that God would deliver them from bondage as God had delivered the children of Israel. Vesey's plot was discovered and put down before it happened.

Nine years later slaveholders were less lucky in the case of Nat Turner. Turner, acting as a black religious prophet, led a bloody uprising in August 1831. Turner apparently had developed very early in his life a notion that

God had chosen him to free black people. Over two days and two nights he and seven other slaves killed their master, his family, and about sixty other whites. The rebellion was savagely suppressed and Turner executed in November 1831. It left slave masters scared, however. Even though they had the weapons, they were the minority race on many plantations. They moved swiftly to put black lay preachers out of business. For the rest of the slave period, black religious separatism went underground.

Slaveholders could suppress rebellion, but they could not control the way their slaves used Christianity. Black slaves who responded to Christianity, no matter what a white preacher might be saying, changed the message to suit their purposes. African American Christianity emerged in the slave quarters as an eclectic blend of Protestant Christianity, African ritual practice, and cultural innovation original to the American slave population. It was a powerful invention. Slaves understood Christianity as a message that made clear the injustice done to them. It did not usually encourage insurrection for the simple reason that insurrection in the slave South was suicidal. The opposite of insurrection was not supine passivity. Black Christianity made virtues out of meekness and humbleness only because Christianity promised the earth to people who practiced those virtues.

To most Americans, and for that matter to most non-Americans, music is the most distinctive feature of the African American Christianity created under slavery. The spirituals, or what W. E. B. Du Bois called the "sorrow songs," were scored for concert performance in the late nineteenth century. The Fisk Jubilee Singers, a talented group formed at one of the first black colleges created after the Civil War, arranged the music of the black slaves for enthusiastic audiences in the United States and Europe. Spirituals influenced the blues, jazz, and even rock 'n' roll. Jerry Lee Lewis and Elvis Presley were the white children of the slave past.

The "Negro" spiritual was only one element in distinct worship practices. In their secret meetings slaves valued emotional participation. Rhythmic responses to spoken words joined them in a spiritual bond. The ritual of the ring shout, described by many observers of slave religious meetings, involved chanting, dancing, and clapping. Individuals stepped forth from a circle of worshipers and performed with the participatory support of those who remained grouped in the ring. As was true in African culture, slaves did not draw sharp boundaries between the sacred and the secular or between the natural and the supernatural. They were European categories. No wonder white observers of slave religion often misunderstood what they saw.

Slaveholders thought they heard in black religious music and story-telling an obsession with the afterlife. The spirituals promised deliverance "over Jordan," which to whites meant that slaves accepted their peculiar status in this life. Black spirituals in fact treated eternal time and temporal time as equivalent. Singing the "sorrow songs" did not suggest to the black slave that they were passively waiting for deliverance in another life. Deliverance might not come during their lifetime. Moses did not reach Canaan. But it might come tomorrow. The deliverance was not certain for any individual but it was certain for God's oppressed people. While waiting, the community made religion a way to deal with the trials of daily existence, a way that made survival possible while recognizing the injustices done to them.

Post-War Religious Separatism
and the Reemergence of Back-to-Africa Movements

Slaves dared the wrath of their masters and stole away under the cover of darkness to hold their own religious meetings. They were determined whenever they could to avoid white supervision. More slaves became Baptists rather than Methodists because Baptist missionaries allowed them more autonomy than the hierarchy-conscious Methodists. White Methodists arguably gave more pastoral attention to the slaves they converted and worried more about the doctrinal soundness of how slaves interpreted Christianity. The slaves after a time saw these concerns of white missionaries as an intrusion, and they were right.

After emancipation the independent black denominations that had been formed in the North spread to the South. The African Methodist Episcopal Church and the African Methodist Episcopal Zion Church worked aggressively to recruit from the vast field of potential new members created by the Union victory. By the 1880s the former counted some four hundred thousand members, mostly now in the South, and the latter about three hundred thousand members. A third denomination, the Colored Methodist Episcopal Church, organized in 1870, also built a substantial membership. Black Baptists were harder to count because they were much more loosely organized than the Methodists. The National Baptist Convention, which is today the largest umbrella organization of African American Baptist churches, was not formed until 1895. Before that, independent black Baptist congregations sometimes came together at a regional or state level, but not regularly. Nonetheless, a census taken in the 1880s produced a count of over one million African American Baptists. Some African Americans in the North chose to worship in mostly white churches, but they were a distinct minority of the African American Christian population.

The story of Exodus remained important to the black religious imagination. The United States had abolished slavery, but black Americans were still living in Egypt. During the period known as Reconstruction, when freedmen in the South voted and held elected office, black churches became the centers of political activity. They also became schools. Learning how to use freedom was a religious mission. Black ministers gave political advice. They ran for office. No one in the black community suggested that they had crossed some fine line separating church and state. When Reconstruction ended in 1877 and blacks in the South were systematically stripped of their political rights, black churches were just about the only places where community leaders might organize resistance. Ministers became "race men," people who took pride in their skin color. Black ministers rarely challenged the white power structure. But the potential for churches to organize protests was one reason why black churches were so often the targets of arson.

Some black leaders, bitterly disappointed with the failure of Reconstruction to deliver basic political and economic rights to freedmen, revived the movement for a return to Africa. They argued that black people had no other options if they wanted to turn the promise of freedom into a reality. After the Civil War, Back-to-Africa movements focused on Liberia, a country that although established by the white-dominated ACS was now an independent nation. The black leaders of the cause avoided white sponsorship. In 1877 the Charleston-based Liberian Exodus Joint-Stock Steamship Company purchased a boat, the *Azor*, and started an advertising campaign. It claimed that over one hundred thousand black Americans "had signified their desire to go to Liberia." The boast proved to be a vast exaggeration. The *Azor* made only one trip to Africa, successfully transporting fewer than two hundred people to Liberia. In numerical terms, colonization never attracted more than a small number of African Americans. Yet numbers do not tell the whole story.

Bishop Henry McNeal Turner, a nationally prominent leader of the AME Church, was the most charismatic proponent of the Back-to-Africa movement. In the late nineteenth century Turner had good reason to be disillusioned with American democracy. Working in Georgia during Reconstruction, he had believed it possible to open government to all citizens. When the American Congress and the Supreme Court allowed states to nullify protections extended to blacks by the Thirteenth, Fourteenth, and Fifteenth Amendments, he changed his mind. The Back-to-Africa movement became his religion. The movement built black pride even if most American blacks chose to remain in the United States. In 1896 Turner declared, "God is a Negro." Blacks needed to overcome a debased image of themselves that the white majority had created. To do that, Turner thought they needed a Christian God who looked like they looked. White Protestants had already done something like that for themselves. They had created portraits of a white Jesus that erased from his features any suggestion that Christ was a Jew.

Turner died in Canada, not in Liberia, frustrated that all of his religious and political initiatives had yielded so little. Yet the legacy left by the Back-to-Africa campaign was not trivial. In the black community, the myth of return, or escape, to Africa had a power comparable to what the frontier myth had for white Americans. Images of an untamed frontier abounded in nineteenth-century American culture—in novels, in newspapers, in paintings. Yet only a small percentage of white Americans ever got in covered wagons and moved west. California's population boom came in the twentieth century long after the epoch of a Wild West depicted in Hollywood movies. But again, numbers do not tell the whole story. The West symbolized possibility. It symbolized a means of escape if things in the East got so bad that individuals lost hope of social advancement. To African Americans the phrase "Back-to-Africa" carried a similar hope of redemption. It expressed a judgment on America for the promises it had not delivered. It represented a possible option should disappointments in the United States continue to mount.

The Exodus story had some concrete consequences beyond the few people who returned to Liberia. It motivated a number of freedmen to leave the South and migrate to Kansas. In that relatively unpopulated state, once a famous battleground in the free soil movement, black migrants, dubbed the "Exodusters," founded independent black communities. They expanded the search for geographical independence by going to Texas and then to Oklahoma. Benjamin Singleton, an ex-slave from Tennessee who figured prominently in the Kansas settlements, received encouragement from black ministers. The Exoduster movement faced many discouragements. White Southerners used strong-armed methods to discourage anything that might reduce the region's supply of cheap black labor. The large number of settlers imagined in the initial heady promotions of Exoduster fever did not materialize. In that sense it was another disappointment, another blocked opportunity for the majority of African Americans to achieve legal equality. Yet the accumulation of symbolic initiatives mattered. Memory of what had been dared in the past was terribly important when the civil rights movement finally began in earnest. In the 1950s and 1960s African Americans cashed in on their belief in the power of the spirit to accomplish the work of temporal redemption.

The Long Wait for Inclusion

Through the first half of the twentieth century, the African American quest for equality yielded a long string of disappointments. Some African American leaders began to wonder whether the strategy of religious separatism had outlived its usefulness. White Americans were in almost all cases happy enough to be separate from black Americans. Southerners could justify Jim Crow laws by telling themselves that blacks preferred to stick with other blacks. So what if the public accommodations afforded to them were inferior? What did it matter whether segregation was self-imposed or imposed by others? In 1880, H. C. C. Astwood, a missionary of the AME Church, proposed deleting the word *African* from the name of the denomination and calling it the Allen Methodist Episcopal Church. Blacks, he argued, would get further if they interpreted the universality of Christ's kingdom as one that recognized no distinctions based on race.

Daniel Alexander Payne, the church's senior bishop from 1873 until his death in 1893, took a similar line. He sharply criticized Turner's Back-to-Africa enthusiasms. Unavoidable circumstances had made the AME Church, like all American churches, "a race church." That did not make it an eternally good idea. "The ultimate development and perfection of the Church of the Living God," Payne said, "will not be on the plane of race; but on the plane of humanity." Since Payne saw no quick entrance of America into Christ's kingdom, he did not think that the AME Church should disband and send its members off to join white churches. What he resisted was turning race separatism into an ideal. He feared that the religious divisions that proliferated in the United States, perhaps especially in black communities, would harden into useless bureaucratic structures. How could American Christians, black and white, establish racial comity if they could not create a unified Christian church?

Payne had a point. Protestant denominationalism was an encrusted structure that encouraged schism rather than merger. Never mind whether black Baptists would ever get together with white Baptists. A more immediate issue was whether black religious groups could establish a united front among African Americans. Leaders in the black community recognized that the lack of religious unity weakened the struggle for equality. Yet various attempts to merge the three major black Methodist denominations—the AME Church, the AME Zion Church, and the Colored Methodist Church—got nowhere. Both in small Southern towns and in large Northern cities, many African Americans worshiped in small churches that had no organizational ties to any other church.

Observers have passed conflicting judgments about the record of black churches in the period of Jim Crow. Some people continued to suggest that the separatism of the black churches had backfired. Rather than preparing blacks to combat discrimination, it doomed them to perpetual second-class status. Three or four major African American denominations competed with an unaccountable number of storefront churches and missions. Ego-driven personalities ran too many black religious bodies and exacerbated rather than healed jealousies in the black communities. In Northern cities too many churches, too much flamboyance, too much wasting of precious capital in fatuous projects thwarted the development of a strong African American political voice. Politically, the leadership in the largest black denominations drifted into an acceptance of the status quo.

Writing in the 1950s, the black sociologist E. Franklin Frazier expressed a mixed opinion of what "Negro" churches had accomplished. Whatever bonding they had managed, they had tied African Americans to folkways that had retarded their common intellectual life. Black ministers lacked education. Insofar as they served as models to black communities they poorly equipped their parishioners to deal with the modern world. Other critics complained about a lack of militancy. Many black ministers were simply frauds who skimmed off money from collection plates to raise their own standard of living. Critics had little praise for Daddy Grace or Father Divine and their large urban missions.

Nor did they have much use for the larger-than-life figure of Marcus Garvey. Garvey, who was born in Jamaica, was easily the best-known leader in New York City's Harlem community during the 1920s. He founded the Black Star Steamship Company with the intention of encouraging black Americans to leave the United States. Garvey wanted to build black pride in any way that he could. His associate, George Alexander McGuire, wrote a Negro religious catechism suggesting that God was black. Religious movements based on black power returned to the Exodus story. Blacks were not merely an oppressed people seeking release from Egypt. They were a chosen people, superior in every way to whites.

The problem with black churches was not that they were otherworldly. They were plenty worldly. What bothered critics was that black churches too often focused on the wrong causes of the worldly problems that held back African Americans. The churches ministered to social despair but did not address possible solutions. The joyous participation that rocked church meetings built solidarity. It was useful up to a point. But religion also needed to create values focused on discipline and on intellectual labor. To the critics, black churches had failed to do that.

Yet what, after all was possible? If the African American community had been middle-class and well educated, or if the passage of American blacks into positions of economic security had been no more difficult than it had been for Irish Catholics, black churches would have been different institutions. Every black congregation, every black minister had to give a lot of thought to what it meant to live without power. What did African Americans who joined churches want? What resources were they seeking to make their lives bearable and sometimes joyous? If black ministers failed, they failed in the same way that white ministers of poor congregations failed. They did not attack capitalism and the wage system. Preachers in white Pentecostal churches that often served those at the bottom of the economic heap more regularly assaulted trade unions, and Jews, and Communists. If you are poor and without power, it is not always safe to name the real enemy.

Lynchings and the endless church burnings had made that clear to African Americans since the end of Reconstruction. Sometimes rather than naming the enemies, it was better to outdo them. If some black ministers were flamboyant, it was because flamboyance was a visible sign of economic success. That explains why blacks responded favorably to Marcus Garvey, despite his prosecution for fraud and mismanagement of other people's money. It explains their fascination with the largess of Father Divine. It clarifies their loyalty to Adam Clayton Powell Jr., the Harlem congressman and leader of the Abyssinian Baptist Church. Powell may have been corrupt and immoral. But anyone who so thoroughly rankled white racists had to be doing something right.

Besides, most black ministers were not flamboyant. They spoke their minds with a boldness underestimated by their critics. They comprised a group of black leaders who most vehemently attacked Booker Washington's notorious capitulation to Jim Crow in his speech at the Atlanta Exposition in 1895. The miracle is that independent black churches effectively organized large portions of the black community and taught leadership roles to men and women. There was no end of grievance present at a Sunday religious service in a black church, even if an outsider to the congregation might miss altogether the disguised ways in which the communicants had learned to voice their protests. The criticism that black churches failed to unify the African American community is totally misplaced. People do not live their daily lives in communities of thirty-million inhabitants. They build networks among people they know and trust. In economically unstable urban neighborhoods where many black migrants from the South settled, churches struggled to create familiar, supportive environments.

The African American writer Richard Wright was for much of his life a Marxist. No more than any other Marxist did he believe that the oppressed of the earth would find their ultimate social redemption through religion. All the same, he wrote appreciatively about the work of black churches. He knew why African Americans "keep thousands of Little Bethels and Pilgrims and Calvarys and White Rocks and Good Hopes and Mount Olives going with their nickels and dimes." He never expected them to unify black Americans into a revolutionary force. What they did was, in fact, more important. "Our churches are centers of social and community life. . . . [T]hey cook and serve meals, organize baseball and basketball teams, operate stores and businesses and conduct social agencies. Our first newspapers and magazines are launched from our churches." It also turned out that this blending of sacred and secular activities was capable of releasing political energy.

Churches and Civil Rights

When Rosa Parks decided that she was too tired to obey an order that she move to a seat farther back on a city bus in Montgomery, Alabama, she set off a protest movement that won swift backing from the black churches of the South. The civil rights movement, as it unfolded in the late 1950s and spread across the nation in the 1960s, ranks among the most spectacular examples in American history of the use of spiritual language to change the nation's political agenda. Martin Luther King Jr. seized the moment to exchange his ordinary pastoral duties for a public career that won him the Nobel Prize for Peace and respect around the world. No one in American life had so powerfully mixed the sacred and the secular since Abraham Lincoln delivered his second inaugural address.

Lincoln was not a minister. He belonged to no church and only occasionally attended religious services. He did not, like so many politicians, tell Americans that God blessed their land. He told them instead that God judged all nations. Martin Luther King came to public life from the other side of the church state line. He was the preacher who became a skilled politician, though without holding an elective or appointive office. He fought for civil rights, for the rights of workers, for the better treatment of the poor. His protests based on passive resistance tried to shame the moral consciences of Americans. To call King a political lobbyist because he worked to change the nation's laws is rather like calling Gandhi an opponent of empire. The statements are correct but they leave out so much. They do not mention how essential to their work was the religious inspiration of the two men.

King was nurtured in the separatist tradition of black Christianity. He was minister to Atlanta's Ebenezer Baptist Church, just as his father and grandfather had been. Yet he quickly ran afoul of the National Baptist Convention that his grandfather had helped found. The Reverend Joseph H. Jackson, its conservative leader from 1953 until 1983, was not interested in activist politics. He used his power to silence King and his allies. King then went on to found the Progressive National Baptist Convention. His reading and education took him beyond the separatism of the black churches to the integrated world of Boston University. King was aware that integration often meant one or two blacks in a sea of white faces. Nonetheless, his frame of reference became national. It was time to conclude the story of Exodus by turning the United States into a promised land for all of God's children.

Yet separatism still had a role to play. In his moving last sermon that he delivered on April 3, 1968, at Mason Temple in Memphis, King evoked the Exodus story in intimating his own death. Like Moses, King had climbed the mountain and looked over into Canaan. He intimated to his congregation that he might not live long enough to make the descent into the promised land. Never mind. The important thing was that for African Americans, as a people, the end of the time in the wilderness was almost over. King understood that religious separatism was both metaphorical and practical. The promised land that he spoke of was the United States. Africa was a heritage but it was not a place to go. At the same time every group had to find its own way into the American promised land. Mere arrival was not enough. Many American immigrant groups, and certainly black Americans, experienced the United States for a long time as Egypt. What kept alive the hope that the United States might transform itself into Canaan was the Declaration of Independence. Americans had written down a pledge to guarantee the equal rights of all people. The best part of American history was the story of how succeeding groups who found themselves excluded from that pledge fought back. Like most immigrants to the United States, the subject of our next chapter, African Americans discovered that American freedom, when it worked, allowed both separatism and integration. It meant the freedom to be more than one thing, to have more than one identification, to have more than one allegiance.

In the end that was perhaps the most remarkable thing about African American Christianity. Despite its chosen separatism, despite its association with Back-to-Africa movements, despite its sense of grievance and deep anger with America's failure to deliver on its promises, African American Christianity kept alive a strong faith in what America was supposed to be. African Americans, in their religious lives and in their communities held together by churches, practiced better than anyone else what the country's founders had prescribed. They suffered defeats because of a poverty forced upon them. Their own lives fell far behind the moral standards set by their religion because of racial discrimination they had not chosen. And yet in their religion they celebrated American ideals they continued to revere despite everything.

Some people think that if Christianity has a future in the United States, in fact if Christianity has a future in the world, it lies with Africans and with people of African descent. If trends continue, black Christians in the world will soon outnumber white Christians. The white sponsors of the American Colonization Society had started something quite remarkable, even if the end of the story would have astonished them.

Chapter Six

Immigrant Religion and the Right to Be Different

T he events of September 11, 2001, changed many things about the way people think in America and around the world. The United States abruptly lost the confidence that it had once had in its domestic security. Only in the worst years of the Cold War had Americans imagined the possible destruction of their cities. Now the fears are not so much about rogue nations. Enemy nations can at least be dealt with using military strength as a deterrent. Americans after 9/11 fear rogue individuals who might be living anywhere and who can without the assistance of any foreign government engineer events of mass destruction. Every stranger becomes a suspect, especially if he or she is Muslim.

The United States is accustomed to congratulating itself on its success as a nation of immigrants. In successive layers for more than two hundred years, various groups have entered the country from the north, south, east, and west. Because most of these groups managed to make a place for themselves, inciting in the process relatively low levels of social violence, we easily forget that the process of acculturation was difficult. Many disappointed immigrants found themselves treated as pariahs. They worked hard and died in poverty. Most, of course, had children who did better in material terms than they had. They became patriotic citizens and joined a chorus of voices proclaiming the United States a promised land.

The Immigration Act of 1965 seemed to renew America's confidence in its ability to absorb newcomers. Laying to rest nativist fears of cultural difference, it repealed the previous system of immigration quotas that since the 1920s had both severely restricted the number of immigrants and had also favored peoples from Western Europe as a source of new citizens. The purpose of the old law was to freeze the cultural mosaic of

America as it existed in the late nineteenth century. The new law not only allowed a far greater number of immigrants into the United States but also encouraged diversity. People came from all over the world, from Asia, from Africa, and especially from Latin America. Their presence reheated the controversy about what constituted an American identity.

Arguably, this new immigration was different in some important ways from the so-called "new immigration" of the late nineteenth century. The United States offers more social services than it once did. More children go regularly to school and for longer periods of time. The fact that immigrants into the United States put strains on these services makes the question of who is or is not legally in the country more contentious than it was before. Many earlier immigrants went back to their homelands after several years of residence in the United States. That caused no anxiety. Now, however, many immigrants travel to and fro across borders with an ease unknown in the past. Many of them carry two passports. Who then among the millions of people who arrive in the United States really want to settle in the country and become loyal citizens?

The shrinking world makes that last question especially important. The intense divisions that tear parts of the world apart do not disappear when people move across the Atlantic or the Pacific. Globalization with all its attendant ways of modern communication means that a missile dropped by Israel on a Palestinian neighborhood, or a bomb placed by a Palestinian in a club filled with Jewish teenagers in Tel Aviv, has an instant impact on ethnic communities in New York City. September 11th forced Americans to recognize that people living legally in the United States had ways to protest American actions in the world with means of mass destruction. One day of terrorism engineered by a small number of people could taint the reputation of an entire community trying to adjust to life in the United States. American leaders bent over backwards after 9/11 to assure Muslims that they were not a special focus of fear. But they were.

No one knows for sure how many people of Islamic faith live in the United States. Estimates range from three million to nine million. Black Muslims constitute a significant portion of that number, but everyone agrees that immigration from many parts of the world has in recent years been the primary source of Islamic growth. Twelve hundred mosques existed in the United States in 2002, an increase of 25 percent from the total in 1994. Many of the men who come to pray in these sometimes large, imposing structures are Arabs. Most Arab Americans are Christians, the descendants of Syrian and Lebanese immigrants who arrived in the United States in the late nineteenth century and settled in California,

New York, and Michigan. However, the percentage of those who are Muslim is growing.

Even before 9/11, Muslims in the United States were having trouble imagining themselves as part of a collective American identity. Few political figures thought it necessary in their speeches about American inclusiveness to expand the Judaic-Christian tradition to include Muslims, even though Christianity, Judaism, and Islam are closely related in their origins. For much of the nineteenth century American Christians had depicted Islam as a primitive religion. Opponents of Mormon polygamy likened it to the "barbaric" practices of Islam. Today, Muslims from Arab countries as well as from Asia and Africa are often viewed suspiciously as the "new Catholics," a group whose religious traditions do not align easily with the American separation of church and state. Critics noted that many Arab leaders had no taste for democracy. During the Iranian hostage crisis that marred the last year of Jimmy Carter's presidency, American television carried images of crowds of Muslim self-flagellants that to Western eyes set Shiite religious practices somewhere in the Middle Ages. A decade later, the Gulf War further distanced many Americans from any sympathetic understanding of the Islamic world. Recent Palestinian suicide bombers only confirmed their view that Muslims set no value on human life.

Most children of Muslim families in America attend public schools. Muslim parents naturally spend time worrying about how to protect their children, how to rear them in the United States without their developing low opinions of themselves and of their religious heritage. How should Muslim children act? Should Muslim girls cover their hair, or should they dress in ways that call the least attention to their religious distinctiveness? What should Arab children say when a history lesson turns to the creation of modern Israel? Should they remember that Palestinian schoolchildren use maps where the state of Israel does not exist, or should they learn the American lesson of religious tolerance that promotes coexistence between Palestinians and Jews? How far should respect for the American Constitution lead them into critical stances toward many Islamic governments in the world? Even without opening their mouths Muslim schoolchildren have in today's world plenty of reason to fear harassment from their peers in a public school environment.

In their worries Muslim parents resemble the parents of many earlier immigrants groups. How long did it take ethnic Catholics to feel comfortable in social situations with American Protestants, let alone Jews? Without insisting that nothing has changed in today's world, we should remember that Americans have questioned the loyalty of almost every group arriving in the United States. Anarchist immigrants from Europe were blamed for a bomb that exploded in Chicago's Haymarket Square in 1886. The bomb killed very few people compared to the nearly three thousand who died in New York City's Twin Towers. Yet the press raised alarms that frightened Americans for the rest of the century. Progressive reformers started campaigns for cultural assimilation. Even the most optimistic among them doubted whether all "foreigners" could be turned into useful Americans. The Danish-born journalist Jacob Riis, in his famous book *How the Other Half Lives*, caught the sympathetic attention of turn-of-the-century Americans with photographs depicting the terrible damage inflicted on immigrant children by dilapidated tenement housing. Humanitarian though he was, however, he saw the raw immigrants as menaces to American society. They had to be changed. His fears, along with those of many other Americans, led to the restrictive immigration laws of the 1920s.

The Lessons of the Past

European Catholics

To generalize about the experience of any large group of immigrants is risky. No group is homogeneous. Individuals have very different reasons for coming to the United States, although those who choose to stay in America clearly want to escape parts of their past. The longer groups stay in the United States, the more they change particular things about how they remember their national origin. They reinvent their culture in a new environment. In American experience religion has often been an important component of that invention. Because religion is protected by the Constitution, it is a useful way to proclaim and protect difference. For that reason alone, immigrants whose religious traditions in their homelands opposed the separation of church and state became ardent defenders of the First Amendment to the American Constitution.

The Irish were the first large group of European Catholics to arrive in the United States. Humiliated by their social position at the bottom of the economic heap, they suffered further discrimination because of the alleged bad fit between their religion and American democracy. Middle-class Protestant Americans dismissed them as ne'er-do-wells who belonged in prison. Native-born wage earners feared them as a group of unskilled laborers who would drag down everyone's standard of living. Many

German Catholics arrived at almost the same moment but fared somewhat better. As mostly skilled laborers, they had more in common with German-speaking Protestant immigrants than with the Irish. They lived in their own neighborhoods, frequented their own beer gardens, and wherever possible worshiped with other German Catholics.

Although most Irish Americans remained part of the working class throughout the nineteenth century, they nonetheless made political headway. It is easy to list the ways that their Catholicism hurt them. But it also helped. The Irish dominated the American Catholic hierarchy. Identifying with the church made the Irish a powerful voting bloc in many American cities. Irish politicians and Irish bishops often had close ties. St. Patrick may well have helped the Irish more in the United States than he had in Ireland. His name graced the largest Catholic Church in America, which opened in 1879. The annual St. Patrick's Day parade in New York City still loosely marks Irish Catholics as a distinct American group.

The Polish and Italian Catholics who began to pour through Ellis Island in the last quarter of the nineteenth century did not immediately regard the Irish-dominated church as a welcoming institution. The differences between them and Irish Catholics were not economic. Poles and Italians too were working class. These differences lay in culture that affected their practice of Catholicism. The most famous place of Italian American worship was Our Lady of Mount Carmel church located on 115th Street in New York City. It was one of the three most important shrines dedicated to the Virgin Mary in the Western hemisphere, the other two being Our Lady of Guadaloupe in Mexico City and Our Lady of Perpetual Help in New Orleans. The pope had "coronated" a statue of the Madonna of Mt. Carmel and sent it to New York City to the Italian parish. It was specifically intended to help keep the notoriously anticlerical southern Italians loyal to the church. The pope knew that the Italian immigrants needed something to call their own, something that Irish American Catholics were not likely to provide.

The strategy worked, even if southern Italians in Manhattan retained some anticlerical feeling. They identified with the church and presented their children for baptism. Women went to mass. Priests presided at marriages and were called to give last rites. But for the most part Italians celebrated their Catholicism in street festivals and in their homes. Wandering through Italian neighborhoods during the Easter season made clear to anyone the differences not only between Italian Catholics and Protestants but also between them and other ethnic Catholics. The smells from the bakeries, the pictures of saints displayed in windows, the noise from religious spectacles performed in the streets made Italian American Catholicism a form of street theater.

Catholicism in the United States at the beginning of the twentieth century was anything but a universal church. During the nineteenth century the Vatican engineered a remarkably successful campaign to regularize Catholic worship in all countries. The Latin Mass followed the same form everywhere. But American Catholicism remained a system of ethnic parishes with distinct customs. Economic success among other things eroded the barriers that separated European Catholics in America. But only after World War II did German and Irish and Italian Catholics begin to think of themselves simply as American Catholics. They worshiped in the same big church and their children were free to marry one another. However, if some important national divisions within the church disappeared, others emerged.

Catholics from the South

Today the most significant split in America's Catholic population is between Catholics of European heritage and Catholics of Hispanic heritage. The story of the latter began in what are now the states of New Mexico, Arizona, and California. These were areas whose first European settlers were Spaniards. After conquering the Mayan and Aztec peoples of Mexico, some of them then moved north across the Rio Grande. In 1821 those areas north of the Rio Grande became part of Mexico when it gained its independence from Spain. Most of the people there were either American Indians or mestizos, a blend of the original peoples of Mexico and the Spaniards. Some of the Indians and all of the mestizos were Spanish speakers and Catholic.

As a result of America's war with Mexico that began in 1846, the areas that became the states of California, Arizona, and New Mexico fell to the United States. Texas had won independence from Mexico in 1836, but joined the Union in 1845. The former citizens of Mexico who lived in these areas became a peculiar kind of immigrant. They became Americans by *being* somewhere, not by *moving* somewhere. They remained far closer to their country of origin than European immigrants. To them the new border separating the United States and Mexico was artificial, and they traveled back and forth across it often. They were poor, but for a time they constituted the majority culture. Many Anglos had gone to California in search of gold in the 1840s but they concentrated in the northern part of the state. In 1870 San Francisco was a sizable city. Los Angeles was not.

Outside of California the only significant number of Protestant Americans living in the regions taken from Mexico before the Civil War were in Texas.

In the last two decades of the nineteenth century, American Protestants discovered the perfect weather of Southern California. Los Angeles suddenly grew rapidly, as did San Diego and Santa Barbara. Pasadena became a garden city of American Methodists who moved from the Midwest. By the first decade of the twentieth century, the Spanish-speaking Catholic residents of Southern California could no longer call themselves the majority. In addition to their poverty, they now had to deal with the attitude of the newcomers, who seemed to despise their way of life. Protestants were predictably disposed to treat them badly. However, European-American Catholics who also were newcomers to the area did not necessarily have a much higher opinion of their religious compatriots.

Many American Catholic priests who moved into the Southwest and Southern California did not speak Spanish. They disapproved of the sort of Catholicism they found there because they did not recognize its particular forms of eclecticism. Catholicism in Mexico had replaced the religions of the native people but not without an accommodation to pre-existing beliefs. American Catholics of European background tried for several decades to reform the practices of Hispanic Catholics. The first American Catholic bishop sent to regularize Catholic practices in New Mexico bore the distinctly non-Hispanic name of Jean Baptiste Lamy. He took strong exception to the work of Jose Martinez, a priest who prior to the American period had enjoyed great popularity among the poor. He was, however, married, one of the nonstandard Catholic practices the Vatican was determined to extirpate.

Lamy had the power to oust Martinez, and he did. The poor went to Martinez to confess anyway. In the years of initial cultural contact, Catholics in the region had no reason to trust priests who spoke no Spanish. The Catholicism of Mexico was older than the forms of Catholicism Europeans created in America in the nineteenth century. Hispanics in the Old Southwest demanded their own clergy, and in time they got them. The Catholic Church in California finally managed a sort of peace between the Catholics of European descent and the immigrants from Mexico. But the latter put their religion to a different use. Caesar Chavez, the leader of California's low-paid immigrant workers in the 1960s, found that Catholicism enhanced solidarity among his followers.

The cultural mosaic of American Catholicism became even more complicated when Spanish-speaking Catholics entered the United States in large numbers from regions other than Mexico. At the end of the Spanish–American War, Puerto Rico became an American territory. Large numbers of Puerto Ricans made permanent homes in New York City and other cities along the East Coast. Although the United States did not retain Cuba as a colony, it maintained a semi-guardianship of the island in order to protect America's substantial economic interests there. When during the 1950s its policies backfired and the United States had to accept Fidel Castro's revolutionary victory over the repressive dictatorship of Fulgencio Batista, large numbers of Cuban exiles swelled what was already a substantial Cuban population in Florida. Then, as a result of the Immigration Act of 1965, immigrants entered the United States from other parts of Central and South America. They settled in cities across the country, replicating with considerable ingenuity familiar parts of their home culture. In Plainfield, New Jersey, one can find communities of Ecuadorians who distinguish themselves not just by their country of origin but also by what city in Ecuador they come from.

Hispanics now constitute some 25 percent of the American Catholic population. The National Conference of Catholic Bishops set up an office for Hispanics in 1969. That was only one year before Patricio Flores, a former migrant worker, became the first Hispanic to be named a bishop in the United States. The church's belated recognition of the importance of its Spanish-speaking members has not yet unified various Hispanic groups. Puerto Ricans sharply distinguish themselves from Chicanos, and the Cuban community in Miami is notoriously conservative. Visibly, the Catholicism of various Hispanic groups differs because of what it has incorporated for their own particular environments, pentecostal ecstasy in some cases, Rastafarian and voodoo practices in others.

If history suggests anything, a common Hispanic Catholic identity will in time override national particularities. The particularities will not disappear, as they have not disappeared among European Catholics. The Irish in America wear the green on St. Patrick's Day. French Catholics look upon Mardi Gras in New Orleans as their special contribution to American culture. Polish Catholics differentiate themselves from other American Catholics by their devotion to the Black Madonna of Czestochowa. Nonetheless, the differences cease to be culturally isolating. People maintain them because they can cross them.

In the end, most Catholic immigrants, wherever they came from, managed to establish a strong American identity. Catholic ethnics are fervent patriots. A pride in being Catholic American got some unwitting help from Rome. In 1895 Pope Leo XIII addressed American Catholics, and also European Catholics who might be susceptible to American influence, in an encyclical *Longinqua Oceani*. In it he acknowledged the achievements of the American Catholic Church but warned against the effort to think of American church/state relations as the norm for the Catholic faith. Four years later he issued another encyclical *Testem Benevolentiae* that many people interpreted as a further attack on the heresy of "Americanism."

For the next half-century, anti-Catholic Protestants in the United States cited Leo's encyclicals as proof positive that Catholics would never accept the American Constitution. American Catholics understood the documents differently. Whatever the pope said, the American Catholic Church was the envy of European Catholics, even in Italy. The Italian popes, in fact, had far greater problems with the Italian state than the American hierarchy had with any level of American government. The American church was culturally plural and often divided. But American Catholics took pride in thinking of themselves as a breed apart, a breed apart not only from American Protestants but from European Catholics as well. Pope John Paul II still is not very happy with the independent-mindedness of American Catholics. But at least they go to church, often in greater numbers than their counterparts in Europe. Immigrant experience, and the problems attendant to becoming more than strangers in a strange land, gave them reasons to stay religious.

Our New Zion

The history of Jewish immigration into the United States tells a similar story about the transformation of ethnic particularities into a shared religious identity that is distinctly American. The first Jews in America settled in Rhode Island and in a few Southern cities during the colonial period. They were Sephardim and were part of the large diaspora of Jews out of Iberia following decrees by Ferdinand and Isabella that outlawed the practice of Judaism and Islam in their realm. Jews left Spain at the same moment Columbus set out to find a westward trade route to India. In the first part of the nineteenth century a larger group of Ashkenazi Jews arrived in the United States from the German-speaking areas of Central Europe, regions that had benefited from Napoleon's decree of Jewish emancipation. Much influenced by the European enlightenment, they settled all over the United States and established the first Jewish theological school in Cincinnati. By the second half of the nineteenth century many of them had achieved economic success and were reasonably well established among social elites in large American cities. They practiced Reform Judaism.

Matters changed dramatically when in the 1880s an even larger wave of Jewish immigration flowed out of Russia and Eastern Europe. These new arrivals were fleeing pogroms. They had lived in areas that had not been touched by Jewish emancipation. Russian Jews still lived in shtetls. Their intellectual and cultural life was centered on traditional Jewish practice. They spoke Yiddish. When they came to the United States, what they ate, how they spoke, how they dressed marked them as different. The difference was evident not only to American Christians but also to American Jews who already lived in the United States.

For a long time German-speaking American Jews and Yiddish-speaking American Jews did not get along. The former thought the new arrivals were crude and superstitious. Why, they thought, would anyone look to the Torah for rules about how to behave in the modern world? The latter, even if they were not observant, were horrified by Reform. The religious Jews in the new immigration were Orthodox. They could not see in the customs of German Jews anything that they recognized as distinctly Jewish. The arrival of the Yiddish-speaking Jews did, however, have one unifying result. It prompted a wave of anti-Semitism in America that gave American Jews a common enemy.

In 1877, the wealthy Jewish financier Joseph Seligman arrived in Saratoga Springs with his family for a vacation. In a snub that made national news, the Grand Union Hotel refused him a room. Doors suddenly closed that had once been open. American Jews who had helped found city and country clubs were told that their children could not become members. American law firms would not hire Jews. The boards of America's leading corporations adopted similarly restrictive policies. Restrictive covenants in wealthy residential communities excluded Jewish homebuyers. The patterns of discrimination multiplied and eventually infected America's elite universities. Whatever their professed devotion to principles of academic excellence, they adopted quota systems that gave advantages to Christian applicants over Jewish applicants. Harvard led the way.

The victims of American anti-Semitism were not in the first instance the immigrants from Eastern Europe and Russia. They clustered together in crowded urban neighborhoods by choice and by necessity. Discrimination was an insult. But owning property in Connecticut was not as important to them as maintaining communities where their customary ways of life looked normal. Anti-Semitism first affected the American Jews who had already risen up the economic scale. Even so, within a generation many

Yiddish-speaking Jews had learned English, had received a university degree, and had made some money. They were prepared to fight prejudice against all Jews. The two large communities of American Jews tended to stay socially and religiously apart until after World War II. Then the Holocaust created an urgent sense to drop all social barriers that divided Jews.

Anti-Semitism had a second important effect. Because it kept Jews out of socially elite clubs and resorts and because it discouraged Jewish entry into certain professions, American Jews began to build their own economic and social institutions. Jews created their own clubs, their own law firms, their own resorts in the Catskills, and their own wealthy residential neighborhoods. They also took advantage of new economic opportunities and dominated businesses that new urban technologies made possible. As we saw in chapter 2, Jews along with American Catholics saw business opportunities in American popular culture. They also contributed to high culture. Discrimination never discouraged Jews from seeking education. In numbers far greater than their percentage of the total population, they distinguished themselves in every humanistic and scientific discipline. German and Eastern European Jews became American Jews, distinct in some ways from other Americans and also distinct, perhaps in more ways, from Jews elsewhere in the world.

A Special Case

Some stories of immigration and assimilation have happy endings. Others do not, at least not yet. One of the stories without a conclusively happy ending involves American Indians. Like the Mexicans who were absorbed in the United States after the Mexican War, American Indians were not immigrants to America. Mexicans at least by the terms of the Treaty of Guadalupe Hidalgo became American citizens. Indians did not have that option after they lost their wars against the United States. The wars made them foreigners in their own land. The terms of peace dictated conditions of acculturation. What Indians retained within their control were their ancestral forms of religion. How they struggled to use those forms of religion to gain control over their lives is a story that has only begun to receive a full telling.

The history of cultural contact between European Americans and American Indians is not an unrelieved saga of brutality on the one hand and capitulation to overwhelming force on the other. Misunderstandings were mutual. But Americans had the weapons. Apologists for what happened insist that Americans never made it a general policy to kill the people who stood in the way of their settlements. But they did kill them when other means of displacement failed. Europeans called the Indians savages to excuse the butchery. If it took something close to genocide to civilize them, then so be it. A long series of wars had by the end of the nineteenth century brought all Indian populations under the jurisdiction of the United States.

European Americans expressed their "benevolence" toward the people they had conquered by seeking to Christianize them. Much the same impulse prompted American evangelical groups to bring Christianity to slaves in the American South. Indian tribes, according to Christians, believed in many gods and were unable to make simple distinctions between men and other animals, or between nature and the spirit world. Their unscientific attribution of events in the natural world to spirit interventions rendered all of their "primitive" social customs unsuitable for life in the industrial age. Thus, in 1872 when Indian tribes had been subdued and organized on reservations, the federal government commissioned Christian missionaries to educate them. In the nineteenth century the only parochial schools financed by the federal government were situated on Indian reservations.

The results of the self-styled benevolent effort to separate Indians from their past was mixed. Indians regarded mission schools with the same suspicions that many immigrant groups regarded public schools. Education was within certain conditions welcome enough. But the price Indian tribes paid by putting aside their language, traditional dress, and religious practice was possibly too high. Many American Indians became Christian and abandoned tribal ways. Others became nominal Christians and practiced Christian rituals without abandoning their participation in deer dances, sweat lodges, and kachina rituals. Some managed to ignore Christianity altogether and reinvent teachings about the creation of the world and about human destiny held sacred by their ancestors. Clearly the recent growth of a movement for Indian rights has resulted in a strong resurgence of traditional tribal religious practices. It has also made possible a pan-Indian identity. "American Indian" is in some cases a more useful way to define tradition than to insist always on distinctions that separate Apache and Navaho and Ute.

American Indians have learned from the experience of other American groups that a religious identification can serve political ends. In 1978 Congress passed the American Indian Religious Freedom Act, which declared "it shall be the policy of the United States to protect and preserve for Americans their inherent rights of freedom to believe, express, and exercise their traditional religions." The language is not quite as permissive as it might sound. In *Reynolds v. United States*, the Supreme Court in 1878 upheld the federal law against Mormon polygamy. The decision established the principle that whatever the sanctity of religious belief, laws can restrict religious action when it violates criminal laws. With this in mind, the Supreme Court refused to grant to the Native American Church the right to smoke peyote as part of its religious ritual. What Indians gained from Congress was more a recognition of past wrongs than a granting of new rights. The law in effect said that the former American policy of devaluing Indian culture had been a mistake. Congress would never again outlaw the Sioux Sun Dance as it did in 1883.

Without question, a growing number of Americans understand and appreciate traditional Indian beliefs. But their admiration has a dangerous double edge. While it may change discrimination into respect, it can also promote unintended parodies of Indian practice. Promoters of New Age religious movements seize upon shamanistic practices and vision quests as models for non-Indian people trying to restore a sense of wonder in a world deadened by dreary technique and bureaucracy. Admiration of this sort can freeze options. Black artists in America learned this during the so-called Harlem Renaissance of the 1920s. Their white admirers praised their work for its "primitive" qualities. Pulsating black rhythms released inhibitions that had stunted the emotional life of white Americans. Jazz, to some white enthusiasts, was not so much art as therapy. Although white patronage produced some economic benefits for black artists, it did not change the balance of power between white and black Americans. Environmentalists may respect "primitive" Indian religions because they do not give humans dominion over nature. But their respect will not do much to restore land to Indians.

Why the Working Class Stayed Religious

The importance of religion to various immigrant groups in part explains why religion remained in relative terms important to the working class. Compared to European trade unionists, American wage earners stayed involved in religious institutions. The most negative way to explain this phenomenon is to say that American wage earners stayed in churches because they had nothing else to turn to. Frederick Engels explained the failure of American workers to build strong trade unions and a labor-based political party on their ethnic and religious divisions. A unified class consciousness was impossible. Immigrant European workers could not break through their parochial national backgrounds to do something that directly answered to their economic and political needs. They only had their churches.

Were Marxists right in saying that churches dulled the consciousness of oppressed workers and hid from them the cause of their oppression? Put so bluntly, the answer to the question must be no. Yet religious institutions in the United States were often unresponsive to the collective economic interests of workers. They frequently let themselves be used to oppose trade unions. As soon as America's industrial revolution began to divide urban populations into those who owned factories and businesses and those who worked for these companies, owners called upon religious institutions to improve the work habits of wage earners. Protestant church leaders complied since it was axiomatic to them that good work habits offered evidence of moral virtue. These habits included punctuality and diligence. They also included temperance, or the willingness to forego the pleasures of drinking during work hours.

Middle-class entrepreneurs did not leave things to chance. When the pillars of nineteenth-century American communities invited evangelical ministers to town to lead revivals, they hoped to improve the local business climate along with moral standards. One way to judge the success of a revival led by Charles Grandison Finney during the 1830s was by the number of laborers who joined churches. Instead of frequenting taverns and drifting from town to town, they settled down in Rochester or Utica and raised families. Wealthy church laypeople gave generously to support the Young Men's Christian Association because their employees who went to Y centers for recreation were reliable workers. The argument is not that moral behavior hurt workers. It did not. Labor newspapers in the second quarter of the nineteenth century preached the rewards of temperance and discipline as strongly as any newspaper that opposed trade unions. The contentious issue is who financed the message and whether those who did kept other messages from coming through.

What do we say about John Wanamaker, a good Christian who made a fortune by founding a large department store in Philadelphia? During the labor troubles that roiled America in the late nineteenth century, he invited Dwight Moody to preach in Philadelphia with the intention of quelling labor discontent. Wanamaker did not like trade unions. Financing a revival by a minister with proper economic views was cheaper than bribing legislators. Reinhold Niebuhr, the most important theologian in the United States during the twentieth century, took a job with a church in Detroit after finishing his training at the Yale Divinity School. He spent most of the decade of the 1920s as a pastor before the joined the faculty of Union Theological Seminary. In Detroit Niebuhr witnessed firsthand the power of conservative Christian money. When a few church leaders invited labor organizers to speak in their pulpits, the car makers who contributed significant amounts of money to those churches demanded a retraction of the invitations. They got what they wanted.

Economic class in America divided large church denominations. Episcopal churches house the rich. Pentecostal churches do not. Wealthy Protestant church leaders boasted that Christianity made the American economic system successful. It benefited everyone, workers and factory owners. Businesspeople boasted that their money supported charity work among the poor. It financed the Social Gospel movement of the late nineteenth century, a movement that tried to remind all churches that Christ ministered to the poor. They themselves warned that unless churches met their social obligations to the least privileged in American society, wealthy Americans appropriately would become the target of social anger. Yet, on balance it is hard to argue that American Protestant workers went to church because churches dependably championed their economic interests.

Catholic Workers

The issue is even more complicated among Catholic workers, who by the latter part of the nineteenth century constituted the largest part of the working-class population in American cities. On the one hand, papal encyclicals in the nineteenth century attacked the abuses of unrestrained capitalism. The Catholic Church was hostile to liberalism in all of its forms, and the free market was one form of liberalism. The papal social message was paternal. The rich owed obligations of charity to the poor, an obligation most of them were not taking seriously. Since popes did not depend on American businesspeople to butter their bread, their pastoral concern for the poor was genuinely moving.

On the other hand, the Catholic Church reserved an equal contempt for many of the social solutions proposed by the left. Terence Powderly, an American Catholic, became the leader of the Knights of Labor, the most idealistic of all trade unions in late-nineteenth-century America. Powderly had the radical idea of uniting all American workers across lines of religion, race, and national background. His proposed union made no distinction between skilled and unskilled labor. For a moment in the late 1870s and 1880s, the Knights of Labor surged in membership. Then for a number of reasons its membership roles collapsed. The idea of "one big union" was replaced in the 1890s by the much more conservative confederation of skilled labor dubbed the American Federation of Labor (AFL).

One of the biggest obstacles that Powderly faced was the opposition of his own church. Since Powderly's one big union proposed a social mixture of Catholics with Protestants, the Catholic hierarchy opposed the idea. Church leaders feared that the Catholic minority would disappear into the Protestant majority. They stopped just short of condemning the Knights of Labor and of excommunicating any Catholic who joined. Its opposition was plain, however, and put Powderly in an impossible position. For someone like himself who saw unity as the only way to advance the interests of American workers, the church's position was reactionary.

It seemed equally reactionary when it silenced Father Edward McGlynn. McGlynn worked in New York City and identified strongly with Catholic workers. In 1886 he ignored the warning of Michael Corrigan, New York City's powerful archbishop, and campaigned openly for Henry George, who was running on an independent ticket for mayor of the city. George had the backing of labor because of his famous proposal of a "single tax" on profits made from ownership of land. George was not a socialist in any classic sense of that word, but he believed that most of the wealth in the United States was unearned and ought to be confiscated. Archbishop Corrigan cared nothing about the single tax. But he did care about the connection of New York's Catholic Church to Tammany Hall, which would suffer if George won. McGlynn was briefly excommunicated for his defiance and then sent as a pastor to Newburgh, New York, where he kept his mouth shut.

So why did American workers stay loyal to their churches? Many, of course, did not. The religious activism of American workers is striking only when compared to European workers. Still there is something to explain. The answer does not lie in false consciousness. Many wage earners approved of the values that religion taught. Moral behavior enriched their personal lives and moved them up to positions of responsibility in the workplace. In other cases, wage earners were able to control the social message of their churches. The Bible, both the Old and New Testament, contained many passages promising greater justice for oppressed people. Eugene Debs, the American labor leader who became the country's most famous socialist politician, knew all of them and laced his speeches with Scripture. Not all churches opposed trade unions. Moreover, not all religious workers were Christians. Jewish immigrants plunged into radical labor politics and found support for their work in the traditions of their faith.

American churches, in ways that were both political and apolitical, gave immigrant workers in the United States an important form of social identification. Churches were means of binding immigrants into communities of people with shared values. In a foreign land, religious communities provided a more instant sense of familiarity than anything offered by labor organizations or political parties. If the American working class had been less culturally divided, those workers would have gone to church as infrequently as French and English workers. As it was, religion served local ethnic communities that in time learned to create a broader form of social identification. The only answer to the question of why wage earners stayed in churches is that they wanted to.

The Case of Asian Americans

With this mind we conclude this chapter on immigration by looking at one of the great success stories. It is the story of Asian immigrants, who collectively overcame the worst forms of discrimination that the United States was able to construct. In this case the new arrivals flowed not through Ellis Island in the New York City harbor but through ports of entry on the West Coast. As early as the 1840s, the same decade that brought so many Irish to the United States, young Chinese men appeared in California and worked in a variety of occupations in San Francisco. The United States gained its first Chinese restaurants and laundries. Some Chinese laborers took up farming. They also formed part of the work force that completed the transcontinental railroad.

Most Chinese men probably intended to return to China after a few years of work. The Chinese Exclusion Act, passed by Congress in 1882, by cutting off further Chinese immigration, certainly was intended to encourage their return. The law prevented Chinese men who were already in the United States from sending for their families in China to join them. Nevertheless, by the end of the nineteenth century the number of Chinese immigrants had grown. They had distinct neighborhoods not only on the West Coast but in New York City as well.

By that time a sizable number of Japanese had also arrived in the United States. Many of them had originally settled as contract laborers in Hawaii, and then moved to the United States when it annexed Hawaii in 1898. Although the Japanese encountered the same racial hostility met by the Chinese, they were able in greater numbers to arrive in family groups or to arrange marriages with mail-order brides. The United States moved to limit Japanese immigration through a "Gentleman's Agreement," which President Theodore Roosevelt negotiated with the Japanese government in 1907. That was better than the blunt insult used in the case of the Chinese exclusion. Nonetheless, Japanese residents in the United States suffered equally with the Chinese under a law that applied to no other group of immigrants. They were not allowed to become naturalized citizens.

This barrier was an unintended effect of a naturalization law passed by the first American Congress in 1790. It said that only free whites were eligible for naturalized citizenship. The phrase, which lingered in subsequent renewals of the law, was aimed at Africans who might be brought to the United States in the slave trade and then freed. In 1870, however, people of African "nativity and descent" were added as a category of people who could become naturalized citizens. Who, then, was left out by the phrase "free white"? American Indians. Who else? Not southern Europeans, who were sometimes darker than northern Europeans. Not Hispanics, either, who were accorded legal status equivalent to "Caucasians" following America's war with Mexico. The Chinese and Japanese, the yellow and brown peoples of Asia, became victims of the law that Congress did not repeal until 1952.

The law mattered for reasons that went beyond the fact that this class of immigrants could never vote. When the first generation of Chinese and Japanese immigrants proved themselves to be extremely successful farmers in the rich California valley, white Californians used their status as noncitizens to take away their right to own land. Japanese farmers tried to get around the law by putting their land title in the names of their children. They were citizens by virtue of having been born in the United States. Although whites sought to make that practice illegal as well, Asians were able to attain a high level of economic success. The gains were far from secure. When Pearl Harbor was attacked in December 1941, Japanese-Americans on the West Coast, many of them citizens, were rounded up and confined in camps for the duration of the war. They were forced to sell their property at far below its market values or simply to abandon it.

Racism is constructed in many ways. In the case of Chinese and Japanese immigrants, stereotypes used to justify discrimination almost always depicted them as pagans who had no regard for the ethical standards taught by Christianity. Asians were depicted as sly purveyors of every sin known in the West. The Chinese lured young white women into their josh houses, broke their moral inhibitions with opium, and sold them into prostitution. Although Protestant missionary societies were active on the West Coast, the reports of conversion did not ease racial tensions. The advice given to Chinese and Japanese Christians was that they return to their homelands and set up missions there.

In explaining cultural misunderstandings, we must remember that the Chinese and Japanese had their own prejudices. They wanted to set a distance between themselves and "white" Americans. To maintain the integrity and purity of their own people, something especially important to the Japanese, they practiced their own forms of exclusion. Japanese children went to public schools in California and Oregon and Washington. But the Japanese parents warned their children not to make friends with other children and forbade them from accepting invitations to enter non-Japanese homes. These social prohibitions had the desired effect. Prior to World War II the rate of intermarriage between Japanese Americans and non-Asians in California was close to zero.

To maintain community identity and to enforce social boundaries, Asian immigrants used religion. Chinese men brought with them not only Buddhism but also Taoism and Confucianism. Most first-generation Japanese immigrants, the Issei, were Buddhists upon their arrival. They stayed Buddhist and were not seriously intimidated by the charge that Buddhism was an inferior religion compared to Christianity. But they also adapted Buddhism to the American environment. Since Buddhist "churches" did not exist in Japan and since the Japanese worshiped at Buddhist shrines only on special occasions, the Japanese people in the United States had to learn and imitate the notion of "organized religion," American style.

The Japanese government sent Buddhist missionaries to the United States to look after the welfare of immigrants. They rethought Buddhist practices to resemble in some outward ways the practices of other religious groups. American Buddhist Churches held regular Sunday services and ran Sunday schools. They became community centers that sponsored Boy Scout troops as well as courses in traditional Japanese arts. The history of the American Buddhist Church has to be strictly separated from the interest that non-Asian Americans took in Buddhism over the course of the twentieth century. Zen meditation centers with a largely Anglo clientele have their own history. The American Buddhist Church existed for the Japanese.

Within the second generation of Japanese Americans, the Nissei, were a substantial number of converts to Christianity. Most of them were Protestant, usually Baptist or Methodist. They also formed churches. The services, usually in English, did not depart in any striking way from the services found in any "white" Methodist or Baptist church. Japanese and Baptist Methodist churches did not by any church rule exclude from membership non-Japanese people. But social practice had that effect. Their membership was almost entirely Japanese.

Since 1965 Asian immigration into the United States has been large and visible in almost every part of the country. Virtually every Asian country is now represented in the American population. Their immigrants have built religious institutions. Collectively, Asian immigrants have been economically successful and have pursued educational opportunities with an intensity seen previously in the United States only among Jewish immigrants. The Chinese and Japanese whose families have been in the United States for several generations are heavily represented among professional and academic elites.

The Chinese and Japanese are an elite group in another way. Having used an ethnic identity, forged in part through religious institutions, to promote community goals, they are now in a position to relax community boundaries. Japanese Americans can be fiercely protective of their cultural traditions but they now operate in an environment where some of those traditions have become as American as apple pie. Sushi bars are part of American fast-food operations. Buddhism no longer seems an exotic religious faith. Japanese Americans who in the first part of the twentieth century married strictly within their own communities now have one of the highest rates of out-marriage among any identifiable ethnic or racial group. They marry other Asians. And they marry non-Asians.

In these circumstances where people have identities in more than one community, Asian churches still serve as important reminders of one primary allegiance. However, they are no longer the only resource, or even the most important resource. Japanese Americans can feel an affinity for Buddhist culture but also think of themselves as many other things. They may be a Republican or a Democrat, as a graduate of the University of California, as a member of a law firm representing American corporations, as a person who does not like raw fish. That is, they now give the politics of identity a plural spin. They may say "I am a Japanese American Buddhist." But that is only the beginning of who they are.

To be sure, some groups in America maintain very tight boundaries. The Amish of Pennsylvania and Hassidic Jews in New York City use their religion for the sole purpose of remaining a distinct community loyal to God. They cross as few boundaries as possible. Fundamentalist Protestants move more aggressively in the world around them but worry a lot about contamination to their faith. They are uncomfortable with pluralism and want for themselves and their children a single identity. This observation is preliminary to understanding why public schools and the teaching of science raise such controversy. That is the subject of the next chapter.

Chapter Seven

Science and the Battle for the Souls of Children

T he most ticklish questions that arise from efforts to protect free religious practice concern requests from this or that religious group to be exempted from laws that apply to all other American citizens. An American Indian wants to use peyote as part of a religious ritual even though peyote is on a list of prohibited drugs. A man cites religious pacifism as a reason to refuse an otherwise compulsory induction into the armed services during wartime. A woman cites church teaching as a reason not to accept a homosexual as a tenant although state law forbids discrimination against renters based on their sexual preference. Parents want their child excused from biology classes because the state education curriculum requires all children to study Darwinian evolution, a theory that the parents regard as satanic.

All of these cases are difficult. The last one, however, and all others involving the education of children raise perhaps the most intractable problems. They place in conflict two cherished American principles—the right of parents to instill in their children moral values rooted in a strong religious faith and the responsibility of the state to provide the best possible education for all children in all subjects. In *Wisconsin v. Yoder*, an extraordinary case that reached the Supreme Court in 1972, the justices allowed the Amish to take their children out of school before the mandated age required for other children. The Court accepted the argument that public education threatened the values of this small, tightly parochial religious group. But the *Yoder* case was ringed with so many provisions that the exception it allowed has not been accorded to other religious petitioners.

In fact, under present interpretation of the Constitution religious claimants for exemptions from general laws have little chance of success so long as the intention of the law is not to harm religion. This is so even if judges recognize that abiding by the law places substantial burdens on someone's religious practice. Yet how do we define intentional harm? In the many cases that have come before the courts involving the teaching of evolution by natural selection, the religious plaintiffs have clearly believed that teaching Darwin is meant to destroy faith. It undermines the credibility of any religion that regards the story of creation as told in Genesis as literal fact. The claim of scientific neutrality does not impress them. Science is not neutral if it teaches as fact something that somebody's religion says cannot possibly be true.

In extreme cases no one cares whether science tramples on an outmoded belief. Imagine, for example, a religion that teaches the doctrine that the world is flat. Adherents of this religion contend that their children cannot attend a public school without encountering teachings that ridicule their belief. A round globe representing the world sits on the teacher's desk. Everything that children learn in science classes assumes that the earth is spherical. In history they hear about great advances in human technology that permitted people to sail around the world. A state superintendent of education will claim that the roundness of the earth is a general principle of knowledge and that teaching the principle is not intended to discriminate against any particular religion. It does in this case, but no one cares.

John Scopes versus Charles Darwin

With respect to Darwinian biology, a lot of people seem to care. The so-called Scopes-Darwin trial, which took place in Dayton, Tennessee, in 1925, was supposed to have settled the issue. It did not. What is remarkable about that case is how a local dispute that never reached the American Supreme Court became a national cause célèbre. The echoes of the battle still reverberate in school board meetings around the country.

The facts of the 1925 trial were simple enough. Tennessee was one of several states that had passed a law making it a crime to teach any theory that denied the story of the divine creation of human kind as taught in the Bible. The framers of the law had in mind Darwinian evolution. At the time quarrels were raging within some major Protestant denominations between liberal theologians who sought to "modernize" the major doctrines of Christianity in accord with reason and science and conservative church leaders who insisted on keeping the fundamentals of the Christian faith intact against any scientific theory that threatened them. Darwinian theory was one such theory and the Tennessee law banned it.

Evidence suggests that the Tennessee statute made little practical difference. The biology taught in the state's public schools rarely advanced far enough to make students aware of what issues concerning divine providence *On the Origin of Species* had placed in jeopardy. But the American Civil Liberties Union (ACLU), an organization founded after World War I to protect the legal rights of people who espoused unpopular causes, saw another issue. It decided to challenge Tennessee's law as a violation of constitutionally protected free speech. The ACLU said nothing about religion. It argued simply that the law muzzled teachers from saying what they believed to be true, in this case a set of scientific ideas that had won general acceptance among biologists.

The ACLU advertised for someone who would openly break Tennessee's law with the aim of standing trial for the crime. For the legal team of the ACLU, a guilty verdict in the trial court was essential. Only an appellate court had the authority to declare the Tennessee statute unconstitutional. Without a guilty defendant, they could not take the case on appeal. What happened proved to be a lot more sensational than the ACLU had anticipated but sadly for its cause of little legal significance.

In the small town of Dayton, John Scopes, who taught science and coached the school's baseball team, became the ACLU volunteer. He taught evolution to his class and was arrested. His trial attracted over one hundred out-of-state reporters, who descended on a little town of eighteen hundred people in the hills of Tennessee. The caustic H. L. Mencken, representing the *Baltimore Sun*, seized the opportunity presented by the prosecution's case to satirize the absurdity of American democracy in action. Mencken called the opponents of John Scopes yokels, morons, and gaping primates. The trial also brought to town two other famous Americans, the controversial lawyer Clarence Darrow, who worked with the ACLU, and the great populist William Jennings Bryan, who leaned left in politics but was a rock-solid fundamentalist in religious matters.

The twelve-day trial produced no fireworks, except for Darrow's famous cross-examination of Bryan. That was meant to demonstrate that Darwin or no Darwin, Scripture was filled with contradictions that defied common sense. Otherwise, trial matters were mostly bogged down in questions of procedure that excluded scientific testimony as irrelevant. The only salient question was whether John Scopes had knowingly broken a state law of Tennessee, and everyone agreed that he had. The jury found Scopes guilty, and the ACLU appealed the decision. The appeal did not go well. The Supreme Court of Tennessee found a procedural irregularity in the lower court proceedings and remanded the case for retrial.

The second trial never happened. Scopes had paid his fine and left town to study geology at the University of Chicago. With his degree he left teaching and went to work for American oil and gas companies. Meanwhile, the Tennessee law stayed on the books with the question of its constitutionality unresolved.

Today, state laws and judicial decisions make the teaching of Darwinian evolutionary theory legal everywhere. Several other related questions have not been put entirely to rest. The most contentious one is whether biology classes might or should include the teaching of alternative theories of evolution. One fashionable alternative is creation science, which has tried to establish academic respectability by creating an Institute for Creation Research in California. The courts have struck down several state laws requiring the teaching of creation science, but opponents of Darwin have not given up. The school district in Cobb County, Georgia, requires all science textbooks to state that evolution "is a theory, not a fact." Teachers in discussing the origins of life are supposed to give equal weight to evolutionary and biblical teachings. Christian parents who support the policy insist that they, not their opponents, are promoting an open discussion of different points of view.

William Jennings Bryan died five days after the trial of John Scopes. Some suggested that Darrow's humiliating cross-examination broke his spirit. Perhaps. Even leading fundamentalists felt they had lost the cultural war in Dayton and for the next fifty years turned inward and stopped fighting political battles. Bryan, nonetheless, left a troubling set of questions for those who believed that repeating mantras about the neutrality of science settled every moral issue. Bryan wondered why American biologists were more likely to have abandoned their religious faith than other Americans, including other kinds of scientists. He wondered why college seniors were less likely to believe in God than college freshmen. Did those results suggest neutrality?

Bryan was not much of a philosopher, but he understood correctly that what people believed about religion determined a great deal about what else they believed, and vice versa. To Bryan, a world without a belief in divine providence was not just a world where most people no longer believed in the virgin birth. It meant a world overtaken by nihilism. What's more, science did not always put people on the high ground of moral insight. One of Bryan's main opponents was Henry Fairchild Osborn, a distinguished biologist associated with the Museum of Natural History in New York City. He wrote several books aimed at Bryan's "foolish" efforts to deny the truth of Darwinian science. Darwinism was not

Osborn's only scientific crusade. He was an ardent eugenicist who believed that science had proved the superiority of white Nordic races to all others. The truth will make us free only if those who speak for truth are still searching for it. In that respect, neither Bryan nor Osborn served as models.

The Truth about the Warfare Between Science and Religion

At the beginning of the twenty-first century, virtually no one in the West doubts the importance of science to economic and technical advance. Religious conservatives in the United States oppose Darwin but not science. They do not think that Galileo and Copernicus were wrong to challenge clerics with the notion that the earth revolved around the sun. They do not protest weapons research or efforts to map the human genome or attempts to find a cure for cancer. Darwin remains anathema to them because the principle of natural selection seems to banish any role for divine providence in the scheme of creation. That fear is real, as we will see later. Yet so does the big bang theory of cosmic creation that to date has provoked little protest from fundamentalists. This exceptional negative evaluation reserved for Darwin suggests that the so-called war between science and religion has had a peculiar and unpredictable history.

Andrew Dickson White, an eminent nineteenth-century historian and the first president of Cornell University, published a two-volume book in 1896 that he titled *The History of the Warfare Between Science and Theology*. White recognized that the clash between science and religion was really a series of battles over some but not most scientific claims. The objections came from some but not all religious believers. Europeans through most of Western history did not separate religion and science as distinct fields. Science simply meant knowledge, and theology in that sense was science or a systematic way of knowing God. Theologians often made significant advances in understanding the natural world. What created conflict was any discovery that upset the harmony that everyone believed joined together all forms of knowledge, or science. Christian philosophers taught that human beings had to take some things on faith. That teaching did not usually contradict the notion that human beings learned many things by observation.

At the time Andrew Dickson White wrote his book, religion and science in the United States were not in a state of protracted battle, despite the recent publication of Charles Darwin's famous book. Nor did White wish to start one. White wanted to improve the prestige of scientific knowledge. He supported the policy of Ezra Cornell, the university's benefactor, who did not wish to include religion as part of university instruction. Cornell had no divinity school, no department of religion, and no compulsory chapel. Nonetheless, White did not consider himself an opponent of religion. He may not have believed that Joshua stopped the sun in its tracks or that Noah had managed to cram two of every kind of animal onto his small ark. But he believed in God and often went to church. A typical Protestant in many ways, he thought that Protestantism's superiority to Catholicism lay in its ability to harmonize religious teaching with new information about how the world worked. Science and religion progressed together so long as neither got stuck in untenable dogma. White, in short, represented a class of nineteenth-century intellectuals who believed that science, by revealing the wonder of God's firmament, prepared the way for an end of religious bickering. An era of universal social harmony based on Christian ethical teachings was at hand.

White really stood at the end of an era. Up to that time, there had never been a party of religious faith that stood against a party of reason. There were rather people who disagreed about what these terms meant. They disagreed about how human beings should proceed if they wanted to discover how the world worked and why it was here in the first place. The American Puritans who settled Massachusetts Bay in the seventeenth century were not open-minded. They were intolerant people who banished Roger Williams and Anne Hutchison for persisting in religious error. They hanged Quakers and witches. Even so, the leaders of the Puritans were intellectuals who established Harvard College within a decade of their arrival. Puritan ministers in New England had studied at Cambridge in England, the same intellectual universe that produced the very religious Isaac Newton in the generation that followed them. What made them intolerant was their conviction that people, using their powers of reason and logic, albeit aided by Scripture, could discover truth. In their view God had not created a world with many different appropriate ways to carry out God's wishes. Puritans might have appreciated words later attributed to Einstein that God does not play dice. The laws that governed the world were discoverable, or at least sufficiently discoverable so that people could with confidence lay down firm rules to govern the conduct of churches, of governments, and of individuals.

Puritans did not stop with Harvard. They also founded Yale and Princeton to ensure that the colonies had a steady supply of well-educated ministers. To his later critics, the Massachusetts clerical leader Cotton Mather was a crabbed narrow thinker who led witch-hunts in Salem. He took as his solemn responsibility the protection of Puritan orthodoxy from new ideas. Yet Mather spent his long life writing learned books that exhibited encyclopedic knowledge and impressive language skills. Mather's intellectual weakness, from a later perspective, was less his unwillingness to consider new ideas than his conviction that ideas, once settled, remained settled. For Mather, what was True needed an aggressive defense and learned explication. It did not need revision.

By the end of the seventeenth century and throughout the eighteenth century, a class of learned Americans with secular interests took their place as intellectual leaders alongside ministers. Wealthy men involved in trade and Southern landed gentry collected large libraries. Graduates of colonial colleges became lawyers and politicians. They thought about government and the problems of maintaining civil order. They did not, however, in these activities intend to usurp the position of ministers. Knowledge of all kinds was complementary to religion.

It is true that during the revivals of the 1740s, a group of itinerant clergy had appeared in New England who challenged the intellectual pretensions of the educated clergy. They claimed that book learning had nothing to do with whether the spirit of God moved in a man or woman. Ministers who knew too much allowed their passion for reading to crush the direct presence of God. James Davenport and other itinerant pastors among the New Lights, as the revivalists were called, came very close to setting an irreconcilable conflict between faith and reason. Davenport publicly denounced his fellow ministers as blind guides and burned the religious books they used in a huge bonfire in New London, Connecticut, in 1743.

But we need to be careful before attributing anti-intellectualism to all revivals. Protestant evangelical styles came in many sizes and shapes. The most famous ministers associated with the Great Awakening of the mid-eighteenth century were Jonathan Edwards and George Whitefield. The first was a man of vast learning. Arguably the best philosopher that the American colonies produced, he maintained a lifelong interest in investigating the natural world. Long before Edwards wrote about sinners in the hands of an angry God, he wrote about the natural life of spiders. Whitefield, although not in the same league as Edwards, was a solid member of England's educated class. He studied at Cambridge and kept himself current with eighteenth-century currents of thought, whether theological, political, literary, or scientific. The most celebrated revival preachers of the nineteenth century were not people who wanted to set learning and science in opposition. Charles Finney ended his career as president of Oberlin College.

The appearance of individuals who went to college without intending to devote their lives to religion did make it increasingly common for people to imagine distinctions between one sort of knowledge called religious and another sort of knowledge called science. But through the colonial period and into the early nineteenth century everyone who went to an American college studied the same classical curriculum. A college education was supposed to develop mental faculties that served a person no matter what calling that person followed in life. Future ministers studied classical languages and thinkers just as James Madison did.

The Enlightenment

The Age of the Enlightenment, the label given to European history in the last half of the eighteenth century, got its name because leading philosophers of the age stressed the importance of human reason. It was the foundation of their attacks on tradition and authority. One target of reason was the divine right of kingship. Another was the dogmatism of Christian church officials. During the French Revolution, Louis XVI and many French nobles went to the guillotine. Many priests did as well. French radicals elevated natural revelation over scriptural revelation and blamed Catholicism for many of the nation's ills that had led up to the revolution. To replace the religion that had blindly worshiped God, they set up a state religion to worship the republican French nation.

In the American colonies the ideas of the Enlightenment never came close to driving such a deep schism between state politics and organized religion. The era of the American Revolution, which began in earnest with the passage of the Stamp Act in 1765, perhaps had the effect of diverting people's attention away from their churches. By the late 1780s, when the American Constitution was written, the majority of the now former English colonists did not count themselves members of any church. American church life underwent a disruptive transition from a time when churches relied on state support to an era when they had to finance themselves. Virginia led the way to disestablishment when it adopted its famous Statute for Religious Freedom in 1786. Drafted by Thomas Jefferson, it became a model for the religious clauses contained in the American Constitution's First Amendment.

Some American religious leaders viewed these shifts as calamitous. But as we have seen, the men who wrote the Constitution never sought to base their republic on religious skepticism. Deism, the religion associated with many of the American founders, privileged reason and observation over scriptural revelation. The most radical Deists replaced the idea of Christian providence with the idea of a mechanistic universe. A creator had started the mechanism going but then had left the universe to run itself. American Deists did not hold many ministers in high esteem. However, they believed in a creator God who cared enough about God's creation to establish the right to life, liberty, and the pursuit of happiness. God also rewarded good and punished evil. In the minds of Deists, reason and science opposed dogmatic thinking, not a well-founded religion.

Organized religion made a strong comeback in the American nation after 1800. During the very same period American science and technology came of age. American churches grew at the fastest rate during the early years of the Industrial Revolution. For educated Americans, religion and science pointed to the same thing: an orderly universe. William Paley, an Anglican priest and tutor at Cambridge University, gave Western thinkers a powerful image that helped hold the universe of reason and the universe of religious faith together. In *Natural Theology*, a book he published in 1802, he asked people to think of the world as a watch, that is, as an intricately crafted machine whose parts moved in perfect unison to effect a clearly intended purpose. Suppose someone happened upon such a remarkable piece of craftsmanship and had no idea where it came from. What could that person conclude? For one thing, something or someone had designed the watch. Moreover, since the mechanics of the watch were understandable and served a human purpose, the watchmaker wanted to benefit humans. The watchmaker God, Paley said, was the God that people everywhere had always believed in. They just had not fully realized that the best proof of God's existence lay in God's reasonableness.

Paley's image pleased many Deists because it downplayed if not outright eliminated the need for Scripture. If God were reasonable, God surely would not have done many of the things that the Bible said God did. God would not have put Adam and Eve in the way of temptation they could not resist. God would not have sent a flood to wipe out people God had created. Or, if God had, God would have made sure that the generations of humans who came after the flood were a whole lot better than they were. In short, a reasonable God would not have created a world so badly flawed that God had to send God's own son to earth as a sacrificial redeemer. God would have created human beings with the moral sense to recognize good and evil and a will free to choose the paths of righteousness. God would have left it at that.

Yet if the idea of a watchmaker God did not require scriptural proofs of God's existence, many American Christians in the first half of the nineteenth century cited Paley as scientific confirmation of their faith. The world might be like a watch, but even the best watches broke down and needed repair. Paley's proof of God left room for providence even if the age of miracles was over. Protestant denominations taught that while the miracles recorded in the Bible were real occurrences, God now moved with a regularity that scientists could trust. A Christian could believe in the virgin birth of Christ but dismiss as a charlatan anyone in the nineteenth century who claimed to have witnessed a miracle. As it turned out, such charlatans abounded in nineteenth-century America. But even people who insisted that God still acted in wondrous ways believed that human beings understood the world much better in the present than they had in biblical times. Moses saw a burning bush. Nineteenth-century Americans built something that was equally awesome: a steam engine.

During the first half of the nineteenth century, Americans who pursued careers as natural scientists were conventional Protestant Christians who went to church. Benjamin Silliman provides a good example. He graduated from Yale in 1796 when the only science offering at the college was a course in natural philosophy and astronomy. He took the course in the junior year. President Timothy Dwight, a staunch Calvinist who led a revival of religion at Yale in 1802, chose Silliman as a bright young man who could be trusted with the important task of expanding Yale's scientific curriculum. He offered Silliman a new professorship in chemistry and natural history and then sent him off to Philadelphia to learn something about the subjects. Silliman also spent a year in England and Scotland, where he studied geology, zoology, and medicine. Then he returned to his alma mater. At Yale Silliman collected the country's largest mineral collection and founded the *American Journal of Science*. He taught his classes and also lectured outside New Haven in order to build popular interest in scientific endeavors. In his mind, science and religion were almost the same thing: "I can truly declare, that in the study and exhibition of science . . . , I have never forgotten to give all the honor and glory to the infinite creator, happy if I might be the honored interpreter of a portion of his works."

American geologists, many of whom had learned their science from Silliman, participated in controversies generated by new discoveries in the fossil record. Almost all of them agreed that the earth was older than many biblical scholars had thought. Most geologists took the new calculations in stride and concluded that the seven days of biblical creation were not literally twenty-four-hour periods. On other matters recorded in the Bible, they remained steadfast in regarding them as real events. Geologists in England and the United States, for example, continued to believe that they found evidence of the flood in rock deposits.

To ordinary Americans, science meant simply that they could judge the truth of any claim, however extraordinary, by using their powers of observation. Demonstrations of religious claims became a form of popular entertainment. Mesmerists put on public exhibitions. Joseph Smith got witnesses to certify that they had seen the Golden Tablets that he translated into the Book of Mormon. Spiritualist mediums invited anyone who wanted to see evidence of life after death to come to a séance. Science did not promise them that the natural world held no amazing surprises for them. It only meant that they could strip the veil of mystery from the surprises. With this assurance they greeted technological advances—steamships, railroads, telegraphs—as the unfolding of a providential plan. Religion and science were both ways to master the world.

What Now Is Miracle?

This is not to say that everyone agreed. Many religious Americans never looked beyond Scripture. Those who wished to reduce the dogmatic content of faith never reached a consensus about how to interpret the Bible. An important debate about religion and miracle swept through American culture in the first part of the nineteenth century. Unitarians were the most liberal Christian denomination formed in the young American republic. They no longer believed in the innate depravity of human beings, in the damnation of unbaptized infants, or in predestination. None of those doctrines passed the test of reason or common sense. The very name Unitarian derived from their rejection of the doctrine of the Trinity, the mysterious three Gods-in one, that both Catholic and Protestants had made central to their faith. But if Unitarians did not think that Christ was exactly God, most of them in the early nineteenth century regarded him as a special emissary of God. He performed the miracles recounted in the books of the New Testament. They insisted on that belief as a link to historic Christianity. If Christ had not turned water into wine, then Christianity had no claim to think of itself as a better religion than Judaism, or Islam, or Hinduism.

The belief in biblical miracles did not turn American Unitarians into opponents of science. Joseph Priestley, the discoverer of oxygen, was a Unitarian. But the belief set limits on how far they dared go in liberalizing

Christian doctrine. They did not, for example, go as far as a group of historical-minded Christian revisionists in Germany who in the 1840s and 1850s subjected the Bible to "Higher Criticism." David Friedrich Strauss's *Life of Jesus*, published in 1846, exemplified their aims. They applied to the Bible the same principles of scientific and historical method that they applied to the interpretation of any other book. Miracle was not part of their vocabulary. Like J. F. Renan, a Frenchman whose *Life of Christ* appeared in 1863, Strauss argued bluntly that none of the gospel records that purported to tell the life of Jesus could be trusted. Neither Matthew, nor Mark, nor Luke, nor John was a reliable narrator. Higher critics aimed to separate fact from myth, a project that according to the first American Unitarians endangered the entire basis of Christian belief.

Unitarians in plotting a strategy that updated Christianity without throwing out the reality of biblical miracles faced a strong challenge from another group of well-educated Bostonians. Before Ralph Waldo Emerson helped to launch transcendentalism, he was a Unitarian chaplain. He quit his post because his fellow pastors in Massachusetts, even the liberal ones, spent too much time splitting doctrinal hairs. They clung to a bookish concept of miracle. Placing value on special providences that happened long ago, they were oblivious to the miracle of life that was everywhere around them. Their feelings toward nature were "corpse cold." People would understand miracle when they opened their senses to the wind and the blowing clover. Miracle lay not in what was exceptional but in what was ordinary. Knowing that, the keen observer read in the world of natural objects a symbol system that corresponded to the truths written in the human heart. Emerson reinterpreted Paley's idea of natural revelation so that his metaphor of the world was no longer a machine but a living organism. God's presence was all about.

Henry David Thoreau, who was Emerson's friend, wrote perhaps the most famous book associated with American transcendentalism. *Walden*, published in 1854, records the impressions of a naturalist with a keen appreciation for the natural world unspoiled by the artifice of human culture. Thoreau was not at all a modern biological researcher. He was not interested in how nature worked but in what nature revealed. Transcendentalism, however, represented one way to reconcile science and religion. It posited a religion without dogma, without priests, and without a community of believers organized into churches. Religion freed itself from history. What mattered was the investigation of the present moment.

Preparing for Darwin

Once again, the quarrels between transcendentalists and Unitarians suggested not a war between science and religion but a search for formulas to keep the two things harmonious. The notion of having to choose between one and the other occurred to no one. American colleges were just beginning to distinguish science as an organized form of investigating the world from other parts of the curriculum. On the eve of the American Civil War, donations established the Lawrence Scientific School at Harvard and the Sheffield Scientific School at Yale. The Massachusetts Institute of Technology opened its doors in 1865. In their first years, these were relatively marginal operations in the American academic community. No one affiliated with the programs represented science as a way of knowing the world that made belief in God unnecessary. If they had, they would quickly have lost their funding.

We are back to Darwin. In some significant ways, the publication of Darwin's *On the Origins of Species* shattered the foundation of projects that had maintained the harmony of science and religion. Earlier evolutionists, Jean Baptiste Lamarck and Darwin's own grandfather, Erasmus, had built providential purpose into evolutionary development. Giraffes developed long necks for a reason. Alfred Russell Wallace, the Englishman who hit upon the idea of evolution by natural selection at almost the same moment as Charles Darwin, saved his own conventional religious views by excepting human beings from the laws of evolution. Unlike the rest of the animal kingdom, human beings were special creations of God. In contrast, Darwin's evolutionary scheme, which worked by natural selection, was a record of chaos and aimlessness. Fossils told scientists about creatures that no longer walked the earth. They were God's mistakes. The emergence of human beings was a bit of chance luck, for they were no more divinely singled out for special creation than the apes from whom they had descended.

Theologians in England immediately sensed the problem. One of the most famous intellectual confrontations in nineteenth-century history was the debate in 1860 between Bishop Samuel Wilberforce and Thomas Henry Huxley. It took place at the University of Oxford Museum. By conventional accounts, Huxley's sharp retort to a bit of sarcasm from Wilberforce carried the day for evolution. Wilberforce asked Huxley whether it was through his grandfather or his grandmother that he claimed descent from a monkey. Huxley shot back that he was not ashamed to have a monkey for an ancestor but he would be ashamed to be connected to a man who used his great gifts to obscure the truth. He validated science as an enterprise unconcerned with whether it furthered the cause of true religion. Huxley called himself an agnostic, a new term that designated someone who could not on the basis of scientific evidence decide whether God existed. Since in his mind science was the only basis of certainty, Huxley devoted his life to "scientific" questions he could hope to answer.

Without question, the controversy over Darwinian evolution helped create an environment where educated men and women found it possible not merely to stop believing in Christianity but to stop believing in God as well. Up to that point atheism had scarcely existed as a possible intellectual stance. But by 1900 when the various natural sciences had established academic disciplines separate from philosophy, it was. Chauncey Wright, an American thinker based in Cambridge, Massachusetts, echoed Huxley. Darwinian evolutionary theory, he said, created an obligation in people who cared about truth to stop worrying about questions that haunted theologians. Human beings had no reliable way to claim that God existed or that there was life after death or that Jesus had risen from his tomb. Rather than being at the center of people's lives, religious questions ought to be put on hold. The secular was not merely the area of life that was apart from religion. It was an area of life that threw doubt on the claims of religion.

The emergence of atheism is an important story. But if American polling data at the beginning of the twenty-first century mean anything, the story unfolded very slowly. The Swiss-born naturalist Louis Agassiz was older than Chauncey Wright but a much more typical figure in setting the path taken by most Americans in reacting to Darwin. Agassiz came to Harvard in 1848 after a distinguished career in Europe. In the mid-nineteenth century he was the most famous scientist in the United States. He decided that Darwin was simply wrong. Rather than a gradual process of aimless development, evolution was punctuated by various catastrophes, directed by God. They explained the appearance of new species of plants and animals. During one of those catastrophes Noah had boarded his ark. Darwin's evidence, unlike the evidence Agassiz thought backed up the flood, was insufficient to sustain his theory. When Agassiz died in 1873, he remained a respected scientist whose strong defense of religion seemed unexceptional, even two decades after the appearance of Darwin's book. That was true even to scientists who accepted Darwin's theory. Asa Gray, a botanist who taught at Harvard, correctly predicted the triumph of Darwin's theory of natural selection. At the same time

Gray, who regularly attended church, saw nothing in Darwin that conflicted with Christian belief.

Ministers in late nineteenth-century America who paid attention to the controversy agreed with Gray. Henry Ward Beecher, whose career we traced earlier, hit upon a popular phrase that was supposed to calm fears. Darwin's God had designed the world by wholesale rather than by retail. Like many other popular phrases, Beecher's did not mean much. Many Protestant liberals took it as a way of saying that the details of creation were not very important. What mattered was that somehow human beings had gained a moral sense that made them different from other animals, that evolution was an ongoing process, and that God was in it somewhere. More conservative Christian ministers had an easier formula to cheer them. If Darwin's theory proved to be incompatible with Christianity, Americans would reject Darwin. By the time of the Scopes-Darwin trial, American fundamentalists had lost that confidence.

The Pecking Order of Knowledge

If American universities in the late nineteenth century were any indication, Christianity stood in no imminent danger of disappearing as the faith of most educated Americans. The idea of academic research based on scientific method, borrowed from the German university, transformed American colleges into different institutions. After the Civil War, they abandoned the classical curriculum and built graduate programs in a number of specialized disciplines. The task of institutions of higher learning was no longer to introduce young minds to the wisdom of the past. Nor was it to train mental faculties by rote discipline. Students "elected" courses. They asked questions. They sought instruction in a particular discipline. Most of them no longer intended to become ministers. People trained in religion disappeared from the faculty of Harvard and Yale and from the governing body of the universities. College presidents less commonly were ministers.

Nonetheless, American university students continued to attend compulsory chapel services. Very few of them declared for atheism. William Graham Sumner, a sociologist at Yale who took up the cause of Social Darwinism, was an exception. Social Darwinism taught that human societies advanced under conditions of free competition that permitted the fittest to survive. A number of Yale trustees expressed alarm at Sumner's indifference toward moral issues in teaching a course about human conduct. Sumner had earlier studied theology in Germany and was an ordained minister in the Episcopal Church. But Yale's trustees were right in thinking that his faith had fallen away. Although Social Darwinism suggested that government regulation of business was a bad idea, most businesspeople went to church and looked for a God-ordained law to justify their practices. Sumner kept his job and is generally rated as one of the most creative American social scientists during the late nineteenth century. However, in his agnosticism he was not a typical figure.

When John Rockefeller, a staunch Baptist, gave money to found the University of Chicago in the 1890s, he wanted to create a university in the very front ranks of research institutions. To a surprising degree he succeeded. Chicago's department of sociology ranked as the number one department in the country. It was almost entirely composed of men who were ministers or the sons of ministers. Its distinguished chairman, Albion Small, regarded sociology as the practical application of the ethical teachings of Jesus. His colleagues were practicing Protestant Christians who had close ties to men in Chicago's Divinity School, a division of the faculty that Rockefeller viewed as essential to his enterprise. Even at Cornell University, where Andrew Dickson White gathered material to write *The History of the Warfare Between Science and Theology*, most students were Protestant believers. Cornell's chapter of the YMCA was one of the most active in the country.

Twentieth-Century Changes

The nineteenth century had churched the majority of Americans. All of the major Protestant denominations had increased their membership and wealth. The American Catholic Church, despite the predictions that it could not survive in a democracy, had become the majority faith in many of America's largest cities. Jewish immigrants had organized themselves in religious communities. Important religious groups that had not existed one hundred years before were spread over the American landscape. This achievement did not come undone easily and would last well into the twentieth century.

Yet the twentieth century introduced enormous changes in the social and cultural lives of Americans. Many of them might make us wonder how organized religion remained as powerful as it did. The Protestant conservatives who took their stand at Dayton, Tennessee, and brought John Scopes to trial were not worried about nothing. Physics and chemistry made great leaps forward in explaining how the world worked. The inner world of the atom was a long way from the sort of nature where Emerson and Thoreau had found God. After two devastating world wars, science dominated the research agendas of America's leading universities. Theology was no longer queen of the sciences. In the twentieth century's hierarchy of knowledge, research science took its place at the top, uncoupled from the idea that science existed to unravel God's secrets. Social scientists, especially sociologists and anthropologists, differentiated the sacred and the secular. Their subject matter was often religion, but their way of understanding religion followed the rules of scientific observation. Emile Durkheim and Max Weber suggested that the secular was rapidly replacing the sacred as the primary producer of the meanings that explained human existence. They classified societies stuck in religious worldviews as "primitive."

Almost all religious leaders, whether they stood with the liberal or fundamentalist wings of their faith, recognized an erosion of the intellectual prestige of theology. While most of them did not attack science, they knew that science no longer looked much like the science that had nurtured Benjamin Silliman's religious faith. Liberals and conservatives had different ideas about what to do. The former called for adjustments in dogmatic theology so that people were not asked to believe in things that science had shown to be untenable. A group of theologians at the Yale Divinity School tried early in the twentieth century to turn religion into an empirical science. It was the only way, they thought, that religion could survive. Their efforts finally went nowhere. Other liberal theologians fell back on another strategy. While they could not make religious belief subject to the same laboratory tests as physics, they could make religious belief rational and credible. If religion were merely science, then people in the modern world had no need of it. Science could explain, but it could not give meaning to life.

At the other extreme from the Yale empiricists were the fundamentalists, who insisted that a faith claim always trumped a scientific claim. But they did not relish forcing believers to make a choice. To take such a stand against science was to turn against education and social advancement. It was to become the backward yokels that H. L. Mencken said peopled the town of Dayton, Tennessee. Religious conservatives did not want a watered-down religion, but most of them also wanted their children to be well educated. By the end of the twentieth century, people who identified themselves as fundamentalists or as born-again Christian evangelicals had roughly the same educational profile as other Americans. As we noted at the beginning of the chapter, they might reject Darwin but not with the intention of making a blanket rejection of twentieth-century science and mathematics.

The question that self-styled secularists posed to religious believers of all kinds was new. Simply put, that question was whether science left any room for religion. People found more than one way to answer that question. Religious thinkers who say yes have often quoted the views of important physicists who believe in God. But they know that one entirely respectable answer to the question is no, science does not leave room for religion. In 1850, this was not a respectable or even a possible answer. If most Americans today still answer the question yes, close to a majority of people in important European countries do not. Americans, for reasons peculiar to the development of organized religion in this country, might be a bit behind the curve but destined nonetheless to go the way of Europe. Who knows? One thing is absolutely clear. The anti-Darwinists cannot win. If conservative religious thinkers continue to make the test of faith a worldview that stands in conflict with Darwinian evolution, they will lose. They will be stuck with a religion of the flat earth.

One attractive twentieth-century compromise has placed a partition between sacred knowledge and secular knowledge. Each speaks to different human needs and to different ways that people can think of something as true. Most religious Americans can work in laboratories and go to church without the least sense of cognitive dissonance. Quite often very bright minds who are interested in whatever seems extraordinary or defies easy explanation regularly cross lines between sacred and secular without caring a fig about a possible distinction. Many of the people who grew up in the generation of the 1960s counterculture and enthusiasm for New Age religions went on to find their fortunes in cyberspace. Bill Gates and Steve Jobs developed computers while half estranged from the narrow rationalism they associated with western culture. Stewart Brand, once part of the Merry Pranksters who tripped on LSD, lived among American Indians, and founded *The Whole Earth Catalogue* in 1968, embraced computers almost as a drug substitute. They were a way to expand consciousness. If the 1960s showed us anything, it is what a protean word "mysticism" is. Something like the Yellow Brick Road links the New Age to Silicon Valley. Many of the wealthy wizards of Apple and Microsoft once waited with the Beat poet Lawrence Ferlinghetti for the world to wake up to a new birth of wonder.

To conservative Christians, none of this is particularly good news. Nor is it necessarily encouraging for them to learn that students in American colleges and universities are very interested in religion. More courses about religion fill university catalogs than at any time in the past. The problem for religious conservatives is pluralism. Students do not just study Christianity, although they can. They study with equal interest Judaism, Hinduism, Buddhism, and Islam. Comparative religion stands on a par with comparative literature and comparative history. It provides a critical means of understanding the cultures of the world without necessarily suggesting that one religion is better than another. Science courses, in contrast, provide answers or at least ways to choose one theory of explanation over another. One hundred years ago it was unthinkable for a Christian of any sort to say that another religion might be as good as Christianity. Now campus Christians must say that or appear to be intolerant.

Possibly, as some pundits argue, the prestige of science has declined in the past thirty years. That is in part because science has put the future of humankind in jeopardy. It is also because postmodern philosophers have placed the truth claims of any statement in doubt. Modern science was part of the great Enlightenment project that began in Europe and spread to the United States at the end of the eighteenth century. Its faith was that we could use reason to get to the bottom of things. Postmodernists regard this claim of the Enlightenment as untenable. Yet if critical relativism has in recent years hurt the truth claims of science, it is hard to see how it has helped religion.

The beginning of the twenty-first century, especially after September 11, 2001, is a poor time to make predictions. Things change too rapidly. With respect to the themes of this book, any prediction about the eminent demise of organized religion in the United States seems premature. If fewer American scientists believe in God today than in earlier epochs, other Americans in pretty much the same numbers as before regularly attend places of worship. And despite everything, they manage to adapt their religious beliefs to their endless willingness to consume whatever technology puts in the marketplace. As we have observed throughout this book, religion in America is always about much more than what happens in private places of worship. It fits into every nook and cranny of American culture.

Perhaps nothing better illustrates the way in which contemporary Americans mesh religion with science than their quest for health. That subject too has a long history, as we will see in the next chapter.

Chapter Eight

America's Therapeutic Culture:
The Quest for Wholeness

A s a young man L. Ron Hubbard enjoyed a reputation as a gifted writer of science fiction. Devotees of the genre put him in the same league as Robert Heinlein and A. E. Van Vogt. John Campbell Jr., Hubbard's close friend, was the editor of *Astounding Science Fiction*, one of the most significant journals of post–World War II American popular culture. In 1950, however, Hubbard published a different sort of book, one that rose quickly on the bestseller list. In subsequent decades it would sell millions of copies around the world. Titled *Dianetics: The Modern Science of Mental Health*, the book purported to teach Americans a new form of psychotherapy, one with its own language of "auditing," "reactive mind," "engrams," and "clears." The psychiatric establishment in the United States was not impressed. In a review for *The New York Times*, Rollo May wrote, "It so clearly illustrates the most common fallacy of our time in regard to psychological ills." The fallacy, which was also at the heart of the book's appeal to readers, boiled down to the belief that people using self-help techniques at home could think themselves into a state of mental health. *Dianetics* belonged squarely in a long tradition of attempts by Americans to cure disease using the powers of mind to make themselves whole.

The history of mind cure movements was filled with controversy, and Hubbard moved quickly to raise that level of controversy to new heights. At the end of a series of confusing events that followed the publication of *Dianetics*, Hubbard decided in 1954 to found a church. His many critics raised a cry of fraud. They were convinced that Hubbard decided to turn from pop psychiatry toward religion only after his Dianetic Research Foundation, which he organized in various cities to market his techniques of mental health, fell into a sea of debt. To them it seemed obvious that

Hubbard transformed his enterprises into the Church of Scientology for the sole purpose of gaining tax exemption. Religion was his ploy to throw government regulators off the trail of his embezzlements.

The critics had a pretty good case. Among other things, Hubbard was selling "E-meters," a form of skin galvanizer that supposedly allowed people to "audit," or assess, their mental state. They then could clear their minds of psychiatric blocs that stymied their human potential . . . or something like that. Critics were exasperated that anyone could credit E-meters with spiritual significance. Yet the law had no way to dismiss Hubbard's claims out of hand. In advertising techniques that allowed members to move to a higher plane of spiritual awareness, the Church of Scientology argued that it was doing nothing categorically different from what any number of tax-exempt Christian churches were doing. Oral Roberts, a dynamic product of American Pentecostalism, launched his national faith-healing crusade just a few years before Hubbard founded the Church of Scientology. Roberts also had many critics who said that he deluded his victims into making unwise medical decisions. But as long as Hubbard and Roberts pitched their product as bringing spiritual benefits, American law had to accord it a strong presumption that it was religion. Both of them tapped an American tradition of calling upon spiritual remedies to restore health.

Hubbard never quite solved the problem of marketing in a way that pleased the Internal Revenue Service. In 1986, at the end of his life, he was still fighting court battles. In the early 1960s the Food and Drug Administration seized E-meters from the building housing the Church of Scientology in Washington and charged the church with false advertising. In 1977 the Federal Bureau of Investigation broke into church offices and found evidence that Scientologists had been stealing government documents relevant to an ongoing investigation into Hubbard's activities. That raid resulted in the fining and jailing of several high church officials, including Hubbard's wife. Both the national and state governments refused to continue tax exemption for Scientology. Yet none of these actions destroyed Hubbard's church or quieted its demand for protection under the First Amendment. The Church of Scientology seemed to thrive on a diet of litigation. Every time critics wrote a book "exposing" church practices, Scientology pursued them with legal suits that even if the critics were right cost them dearly. The church filed hundreds of cases against government officials.

Finally in the early 1990s the United States government threw in the towel. The church gave the government some of the money it supposedly owed in back taxes, and the government gave the church tax exemption for most of its activities. Only a few years after that, President Bill Clinton openly defended Scientology. He urged European governments, especially the German government, to halt religious persecution of Hubbard's church. In the end, what saved Scientology in the United States is what has saved any religious movement presenting controversial claims—wealth, a growth in membership, and the insistence of prominent people, in this case mostly movie stars, that they reaped substantial benefits through membership in the church. Empirical verification of spiritually based health claims catches the attention of Americans who want to eat at McDonald's and live forever.

A Nation of Self-Healers

The Church of Scientology remains a puzzling example of American religious behavior because it poses hard questions about the motives of anyone who founds a new religious movement. What drives such hubris? Is it the voice of God? Or a quest for spiritual enlightenment? Or is it greed and the desire for power? New religious movements are especially vulnerable to the worst assumptions about motives. Being dead for a long time helps the reputation of religious prophets. L. Ron Hubbard has not been dead long enough. The fact that he taught a religion that promised mental health has not yet worked in his favor. Even so, there is something very American about his story.

The United States has always been a nation of autodidacts. Self-help manuals became a staple of the book trade early in the nineteenth century. They were part of the American passion for equality and an impatience with authority. Novelty received a curious look. American culture was lively, bustling, and innovative. Spiritual claims, as we have often seen in this book, mixed freely in the marketplace of culture with claims that promised to enrich people in material and physical ways. In many popular movements, the quest for mental and physical health was both a form of worship and a way to found an alternative system of medicine.

The first important example in the early American republic originated in Europe. Franz Mesmer was a significant figure of the French Enlightenment. Regarding himself as an opponent of Roman Catholicism and other religious superstitions, Mesmer sought natural explanations for powers attributed to a supernatural spirit world. He claimed to provide a physical demonstration of invisible forces that had been labeled mysterious simply because they could not be seen. According to Mesmer, invisible forces had useful applications. He posited the existence of universal magnetic currents that moved through human bodies. When these currents were in a proper state of equilibrium, human bodies were healthy. If not, humans became sick. A mesmerist, one skilled in the theories of Mesmer, could heal someone by passing his hands over the non-aligned parts of a sick body. His own magnetic power restored the equilibrium.

Mesmer presented his ideas as empirical science, pure and simple. But in the United States mesmerism immediately gained religious associations. Americans who were treated by mesmerists went into an unconscious state of trance during which they were insensible to normal stimulants. They often demonstrated clairvoyant powers. In 1836 Charles Poyen, a Frenchman who advertised himself as a professor of animal magnetism, toured New England. Poyen was not an enemy of religion and wrote a pamphlet about how to promote Christianity. Churched Americans joined unchurched Americans in turning out to attend Poyen's lectures. They gasped in amazement at the clairvoyant powers of the mesmerized (later called hypnotized) subjects.

In the previous chapter, we noted that to many Americans science carried hints of "Infinity and the Unknown." In the case of mesmerism it also promised to cure a variety of ailments from rheumatism, to back pain, to liver trouble. Andrew Jackson Davis, who became known as the "Poughkeepsie Seer," was among the most remarkable products of the antebellum popular cultural blend of religious and scientific claims. Davis discovered mesmerism when he was seventeen. In a trance he could read people's minds, discern their ailments, and prescribe cures. He joined the lecture circuit as a "clairvoyant healer." In the 1840s he also became interested in spiritualism and published several large volumes containing moral and philosophical teachings that he had received from his spirit voices. *The Principles of Nature, Her Divine Revelation, and a Voice to Mankind* appeared in 1847 and was followed in 1850 by an even thicker tome, the first volume of *The Great Harmonia*.

The number of readers who made their way through Davis's publications from cover to cover must have been very small. Yet the attention they received was a symptom of what passed the test of plausibility. Davis had little formal education, but George Bush, a professor of Hebrew language and literature at New York University, certified that Davis, when in one of his trances, could speak fluent Greek, Hebrew, Latin, and Sanskrit. Pentecost had come to upstate New York. Davis also had a discernible point of view that suggested he knew something about Emanuel Swedenborg, a Swedish philosopher of unquestioned scholarly and scientific attainments.

Swedenborg was dead long before Davis was born. The Swedish thinker was the son of a Lutheran bishop. His writings on the natural sciences made his reputation across Europe, although he finally concluded that the world at its deepest levels had to be known through intuition rather than through observation. After 1745, when he was approaching sixty, he began to receive revelations from the spirit world. A century later, the followers of Swedenborg in the United States established the Church of the New Jerusalem. It still survives in Pennsylvania. Swedenborg was also an important influence on the American transcendentalists, especially Ralph Waldo Emerson. Emerson's notion of correspondences between natural forms and truths written into the human heart closely resembled some of Swedenborg's teachings. Andrew Jackson Davis was not in the same intellectual league as the transcendentalists or the learned Swedenborg. But in a way that joined the systems, Davis's harmonial philosophy erased the boundaries between the physical and the spiritual. It pointed the way toward spiritual wholeness and health.

Health Crusaders

Mesmerists and Davis were only a small part of the health crusade of early America. The most famous health guru was Sylvester Graham. He was a stern Protestant with an insatiable appetite for reform. His appetite for anything that stimulated the senses was more restricted. Graham is doubtlessly best remembered in American history as the inventor of the graham cracker, a distant cousin of what is now marketed under that name. But Graham had not sprung from a line of ministers for nothing. He himself had been licensed to preach by the Presbyterian Church in 1826. For him, the pursuit of health was an act of worship that treated the human body as a creation of God. Practices that debilitated physical vigor (masturbation led the list) also diminished spiritual capacity. Eating meat was forbidden. Sexual activity was permitted only to married couples and then only in a moderation verging on abstinence. Graham called his crusade the Christian health movement. The men and women who heeded his requirements avoided a life of sin by praying and by eating a healthy diet. One of Graham's followers said, "It is our solemn and deliberate conviction, after faithfully studying the book much of the past year that, next to the Bible, Graham's *Lectures on the Science of Human Life* should be read and studied by every family and especially every minister and medical man."

Many early American prophets of health had "come out" of their churches. Their enthusiastic embrace of many reforms, everything from temperance to abolitionism, made them impatient with the inertia that seemed to be a property of all institutions, whether secular or religious. Many of them tried living in communal societies for a time, such as Brook Farm, the Northampton Society, Fruitlands. Their quest for spiritual awareness led to the invention of new religions or to health movements with strong religious undertones. Thus, Samuel Thompson moved about the United States carrying a message of medical self-help using botanical remedies. He was associated with Elias Smith, an innovative religious publisher who in turn was a close associate of Joshua Himes, the man who made William Miller, the prophet of Christ's second coming, a household name in antebellum America. Homeopathy, a medical movement founded by Samuel Hahnemann, traveled a similar path. It rose in the same era as hydropathy, a craze that sent many Americans in search of spas where they could cure themselves by bathing in naturally pure water. Appropriately, some of these movements have surged back into popularity in recent years in close association with New Age techniques of religious meditation.

Phineas Quimby, the mental healer who played a crucial role in the career of Mary Baker Eddy, got started in his own practice after working with Lucius Burkmar, who also diagnosed and healed diseases. Quimby discarded mesmerism, however. When he opened his own office in Portland, Maine, he decided that trance states were not important, either to the healer or to the patient. The problem of disease did not rest in unbalanced magnetic forces but in the mind. To achieve harmony, the condition of health, a person had to eliminate wrong mental ideas and focus on his or her spiritual nature. As we have seen, this came very close to the ideas later advanced by Mary Baker Eddy, even if she gave no credit to Quimby. Eddy's Christian Science characterized evil as an illusion, a mistaken idea of the mind. It caused terrible illness, but it was not physical. Learning to free the mind of illusion was the basis of the church that Eddy founded.

Quimby did not found a church. The people who came to him for healing were not looking for an alternative church but for a cure that their regular doctors had not provided. Since a germ theory of disease lay in the future, medical practitioners who worked in early America had little in their bags to cure anyone. Many of their treatments only added to the pain and suffering of the patient. Yet it was no accident that Eddy went from Quimby's care to found her own religion. Quimby, like all alternative medical practitioners, wanted their patients to understand that they had not fully developed their mental and spiritual powers. Antebellum health nostrums bristled with implications about God's allocation of good and evil in the world. They suggested that what people called spirit took tangible forms. Ellen Harmon White, as we saw in chapter 4, intertwined her invention of Seventh-Day Adventism with concerns about health. The strong stand that she took against the use of caffeine, alcohol, and tobacco was religiously intended to purify the body as a proper dwelling for God's spirit. Like Eddy, she incorporated health into a religious institution. Battle Creek, Michigan, aside from being the cradle of the breakfast food industry, was also the nation's most famous spa.

Even the nineteenth-century fascination with phrenology depended for its popularity on a program of moral improvement both for individuals and for American society. This point needs underlining because on the face of it, phrenology was steeped in materialist assumptions. Phrenologists never talked about the soul or about invisible currents that gave some special spiritual energy to human beings. They made maps of the human skull with a confidence that their cranial charts revealed innate character and personality traits. By feeling the bumps and other configurations of the skull of any individual, the trained phrenologist could say almost everything there was to know about a person's strengths and weaknesses. In the way they presumed to map the brain, phrenologists were not unlike neurologists who in our own time try to specify which area of the brain determines which bodily functions.

The difference, aside for the demonstrable value of the projects, was that in the nineteenth century the effort to map the brain was most definitely and explicitly a moral mission. All of the personality and character traits that supposedly resided in various parts of the brain related to human motives that were either morally good or morally bad. The hope of people undergoing a phrenological reading was that the parts of their skull associated with good traits had large bumps and that the parts associated with bad traits had none. A person whose bumps indicated a large degree of generosity could be pleased with the reading. A lump on the skull indicative of sloth was bad news. The person with this unhappy skull configuration had to work to overcome the handicap. Thousands of Americans paid money to have their skulls read. They wanted to be able to monitor their skills and learn to encourage inborn traits that boded success and to overcome traits that if left unchecked would surely get them into trouble. A phrenological reading provided what the E-meters used by Scientologists are supposed to provide—a way to master the brain and one's environment. In these cases the line between the promise of spiritual health and the promise of personal worldly success, including financial success, becomes very fine.

The Influence of the East

At the end of the nineteenth century mind cure movements in the United States were very much enriched by the discovery of Eastern religions. At the International Parliament of Religions, held on the grounds of the famous Columbian Exposition in Chicago in 1893, Americans got their first extensive exposure to the great religious traditions of Asia. Soyen Shaku came to Chicago from Japan representing the tradition of Rinzai Zen Buddhism. He introduced Americans to a practice of meditation that challenged the mind with riddles without answers (koans such as the famous "what is the sound of one hand clapping?"). The exercise was intended to lead the mind away from the concerns of ordinary consciousness to enlightenment or satori. Shaku's disciple, Daisetz Teitaro Suzuki, stayed in the United States until 1909. After returning to Japan he wrote many books in English about Buddhism. Later in his life he taught for a few years at Columbia University in New York City.

The enlightenment sought by Zen masters, as Western practitioners translated it, was neither a quest for health nor a search for salvation, not in any case as most Americans understood those terms. Even so, because it promised a release from the evils associated with normal thinking, many Americans seized upon it as a cure for nervous disorders and tension. That affected the trajectory of Zen Buddhism in the United States. As we have seen, Japanese American immigrants founded the American Buddhist Church. But quite aside from that institution, many well-educated American professionals in the twentieth century studied Eastern meditation. They sometimes used it in conjunction with Western psychoanalysis as a way to bring relief from the strains of their work. The American psychiatrist George Beard had defined American nervousness as a national disease already in the 1870s. He linked it to what many Americans regarded as their greatest national strength, a commitment to disciplined hard work. That rooted the disease firmly in the Protestant ethic. Logically, then, a cure lay in something that was radically different from Protestantism.

Eastern religion as it was introduced to non-Asians in the United States was not confined to Buddhism nor learned only from Asian teachers. Shortly before Soyen Shaku visited Chicago, the Russian-born Helen Blavatsky settled for a few years in New York City. She founded the Theosophical Society, a movement that became much more significant when Blavatsky moved the headquarters of her religion to Madras, India. Theosophy played a major role in twentieth-century India, both in informing Indian struggles against the British Raj and in the education of elite national figures such as Nehru. In the United States the influence of theosophy was more modest. Blavatsky was a bit bizarre for most American churchgoers. She smoked. She had a gruff manner. She dressed in flowing robes and turbans. Her claim to be in contact with Mahatmas, or "masters," who came to earth to introduce a New Age was no more unusual than that made by other religious leaders who claimed to be fonts of new revelation. But Blavatsky made too much of her "foreignness" and in any case was upstaged by Mary Baker Eddy. What remained important in Blavatsky's teachings was the notion that many health problems linked to American nervousness resulted from Western ways of thinking. Westerners had in the name of reason and logic cut themselves off from the creative potential of human consciousness.

The Question of Fraud

Health crusades in the late nineteenth century raised the question of whether free religious practice allowed Americans to label the claims of some religious teachers as fraudulent. The question became especially important after medical schools began to graduate people who actually knew something about curing disease. The American philosopher William James, who taught at Harvard until his death in 1910, was witness to more than one religious novelty in America. He was reluctant to see the law interfere with religiously founded health cures. He disapproved of efforts made by the state of Massachusetts to silence Mary Baker Eddy. To call her claims "outrageous" only meant to James that they lay outside the realm of most people's experience. For James that was precisely their value. The advance of human affairs depended absolutely on developing habits of mind that looked sympathetically on what seemed beyond normal experience. Novelty was no guarantee of positive results. But taking a "bizarre" opinion seriously sometimes led to a quantum leap forward in human consciousness. Since there was no way to tell in advance whether it would or would not do this, human beings, according to James, had best keep an open mind.

For that reason James was an avid backer of the American Society for Psychical Research, an organization that investigated a wide range of reported paranormal phenomena. James was especially interested in spiritualist mediums. He knew that many of them were frauds. But it took only one genuine medium to make a difference. James saw no reason to deny a priori that human minds interacted with other human minds even when separated by a great distance. A human mind, in fact, might have undeveloped channels that linked it to other worlds. If the mind were that powerful, then Mary Baker Eddy was surely right in thinking that it was implicated in the cause of many kinds of disease. James championed the variety of religious experience both inside and outside the Christian tradition. His relish for the novel extended to things his colleagues at Harvard regarded as kooky. James did not care. It was only through the exploration of what one generation called "abnormal" that humanity lifted itself out of the ruts created by comfortable but outmoded ideas and accomplished something that might reasonably be called progress.

Yet a religious claim might cause harm. Or it could be intentionally fraudulent. A fraudulent religious teaching about healing could take away someone's life and money. At the beginning of the twentieth century the American Congress, believing that people needed protection from unhealthy food products, passed the Pure Food and Drug Act. It also acted to restrict the practice of "false advertising" despite the fact that the same First Amendment to the Constitution that protects religion also protects speech. Advertisers could not say things that they knew were untrue. Perhaps Americans also needed protection from false religious prophets. If spiritual leaders collected money from people promising them better health, then did not the spiritual leader who made the promise need to prove the efficacy of the treatment? Even if courts decided not to interfere with adult Christian Scientists who refused to see doctors, should these adults be allowed to make life and death decisions about medical treatment for their children? These were tricky questions that came before American courts on more than one occasion.

Guy Ballard and his wife Eda were responsible for an especially interesting case that reached the American Supreme Court. Ballard created the "I Am" movement and claimed that an "ascended master" named Saint Germain had designated Ballard as his earthly messenger. Ballard claimed to have met Saint Germain on Mount Shasta, a claim that to most people already placed Ballard well inside the realm of the preposterous. But there was more. Ballard made many promises to his followers, including better health, and collected their money. Prosecutors finally believed that they had had enough. They charged Ballard with mail fraud and sought to put him in prison. Their case was based on what they thought was Ballard's clear insincerity. No one could honestly believe the things he said. He therefore must have made them up in order to extort money. The pretense of religion was an effort to help him slip by the law.

Ballard died before the 1941 trial in Los Angeles, but the prosecutors continued their case against Ballard's wife and other church leaders. From their perspective, Ballard's wife was even more brazen than her husband. She said that Jesus Christ had descended to earth to sit for a portrait owned by the "I Am" Church. In the trial court, the judge proceeded carefully. He instructed the jurors that they could not in deciding the issue of fraud consider whether the beliefs of the "I Am" movement were true or not, however improbable they might consider them. They could only consider the question of sincerity. If the jurors thought that the people on trial did not believe what they said, they were guilty. That is what the jury decided. It did not take an especially hostile reading of Guy Ballard to conclude that he was a small-time crook who switched his profession from selling questionable stock offerings to selling religious and medical hokum.

As the Ballard appeal worked its way toward the Supreme Court, legal scholars and judges remained divided. Some thought that if religious beliefs advanced health claims potentially harmful to gullible people, they ought to be restricted. Others who clung to absolute protection of religious beliefs argued that the jury should not have been allowed to consider whether the Ballards were sincere. They plausibly insisted that if a jury viewed a set of beliefs as malicious nonsense, they would have little difficulty deciding that the proponents of the belief were insincere. The sincerity question was a dodge to get around the First Amendment's protection of religious belief. Justice William Douglas, who in 1944 wrote the majority opinion for a divided Supreme Court, sided with the trial judge. True, the Constitution absolutely protected religious belief, making heresy, in Douglas's famous words, an unknown offense in the United States. Yet if the jury thought that Ballard and his wife did not believe in ascended masters, they ought to go to jail.

A related issue hovered around the Ballard case that was equally difficult to resolve. In the important *Reynolds* decision that in the nineteenth century upheld the federal law outlawing polygamy, the Supreme Court decided that the Constitution did not offer the same protection to religious practice that it gave to religious belief. Mormons might with impunity believe in plural marriage. But if they practiced it, they were ordinary lawbreakers. It was one thing to believe in a religion that prescribed human sacrifice but quite another thing to carve up a young child on an altar. Accepting the distinction between belief and practice did not make it easy to apply. Were religious groups ever permitted to do things in the pursuit of their faith that other people could not do? Could Jehovah's Witnesses, for example, proselytize in quiet neighborhoods on a Sunday morning when door-to-door vacuum cleaner salespeople could not? The issue raised by the Ballard case and by any other religious group making health claims went beyond the issue of sincerity. Even if the Ballards thought they had a faith-based cure for cancer, should they be allowed to advertise that claim and collect money in the process?

Plausible and Implausible in Today's World

All of these issues came together in the controversies that swirled around Scientology. Was Hubbard sincere? Did E-meters have the beneficial effects that many people said they did? If Scientologists could not advertise cures for physical ailments, then what could they advertise? In 1952, two years after Hubbard published *Dianetics*, Norman Vincent Peale published *The Power of Positive Thinking*. It became one of the largest nonfiction bestsellers published in the United States in the postwar years. Peale was a respected Protestant clergyman, the pastor of the Marble Collegiate Church in New York City. *The Power of Positive Thinking* was Peale's second best-selling book, and his kindly demeanor became a familiar image on American television during the 1950s. He never, in anything he said or did, had a problem with the law. Yet he was selling peace of mind, in the process enriching himself, with claims that from some perspectives were highly dubious. How was it that Peale could market a book that promised the reader a way to "become a more popular, esteemed and well-liked individual . . . a person of greater usefulness" who will "wield an expanded influence," but Hubbard faced trouble when he sold a device with putative health benefits? To be sure, Peale paid taxes on his royalties. But that is not the only issue. False advertising is always a tricky matter to settle but is especially complex when a religious claim is involved.

What finally distinguished Peale from Hubbard is that the former worked more acceptably within prevailing cultural norms. Peale addressed Christians, telling them how they could grow in their faith and at the same time channel the power of their belief to accomplish secular goals. He told them to repeat over and over to themselves a passage from Philippians 4:13, "I can do all things through Christ which strengtheneth me." Peale had invented a Christian mantra for busy Americans. His book was little more than a collection of anecdotes from satisfied customers, especially from businessmen who had overcome feelings of inferiority and despair to rise to success. They became better husbands and fathers, and better salesmen. Peale did not mention riches directly, but most of his stories ended with financial dividends along with peace of mind.

Peale, of course, had a host of critics who said that he cheapened the message of Christianity and made a mockery out of the doctrine of Christian salvation. Others simply called his message tacky, a symptom of the superficial culture of post–World War II American society. Happy thinking made for happy families and a prosperous nation. Yet nothing Peale said shocked anyone. A sunny optimism rooted in a pragmatic religious faith was too normal to permit Peale's critics grounds to charge him with fraud. What he offered his readers might not work for all of them, but his commonsensical advice would not harm them either.

In contemporary American life the Internal Revenue Service (IRS) has been as important as the courts in efforts to distinguish religious organizations—which like other not-for-profit charitable and educational institutions are tax exempt—from secular, profit-seeking enterprises that are taxed. In many cases the issue is not whether a particular church qualifies for tax exemption, but whether some of its activities and property holdings are taxable. Church buildings may not be on the tax rolls. But a hotel owned by a church is. In the case of Scientology, the IRS held for a long time that almost everything the church did had the sole purpose of making money and hence the income was taxable. Then suddenly in the 1990s the paradigm shifted and Scientology became "legitimate." Tax exemption followed. The case proved the central argument of this book: Because sacred and secular are so entwined, one can set and reset lines of division almost at will.

Yet sometimes lines need to be drawn. Clearly there ought to be rules that forbid churches from seeking tax exemption when they are running a "secular" business. Of course, we are dealing in legal fictions with different ways to read them. Tax rules state that if churches or church-related groups spend too much of their time promoting political action, they can lose their tax exemption. It is a good rule in a country that as a formal matter separates the state from religion. Yet it cannot define in a way that satisfies everyone what exactly is political activity or specify precisely when a church has gone too far down the path of political perdition. The Christian Coalition, when the very political Ralph Reed headed it, lost its tax exemption because the IRS decided that the "educational" information it distributed to voters was blatantly politically partisan. But the Christian Coalition was an easier target than churches. Many churches maintain lobbying offices in Washington. The IRS leaves them alone. It also leaves the Catholic Church alone even though the church spends large amounts of money to encourage legislation limiting women's rights to have an abortion. Are political efforts to pass legislation viewed by a particular church as moral part of its religious mission or not?

The Unification Church has not enjoyed a very good press. Its founder, the Reverend Sun Myung Moon, has almost as high a notoriety rating as L. Ron Hubbard. Although his church has gained a substantial following around the world, critics say that the "Moonies" represent a dangerous example of a religious cult. It "kidnaps" and then "brainwashes" vulnerable and lonely young people. It promises them happiness and peace of mind by separating them from everything that they are taught to think has poisoned their lives. "Kidnap" and "brainwash" are loaded terms. Opponents of the Unification Church know that the Moonies do not tie victims up, throw them in car trunks, and hold them blindfolded in the basement of an old farmhouse. Nor does "brainwashing" in this case mean anything more than a strong regimen of religious education, or more pejoratively, indoctrination. Members of the Unification Church do not see their practices as different from those of any tight religious community that tries to restrict contact between its members and the rest of the world. Why are they different from the Amish whose children are kept at home with the permission of the Supreme Court? Or from nineteenth-century ethnic Catholics who sent their children to parochial (indoctrinating) schools? Or from Japanese immigrants who formed the Buddhist Church of America in part to ward off the "dangers" of ethnic intermarriage?

Nonetheless, criticism of the Moonies has run deep, in part because social conservatives associate it with the cultural radicalism of the 1960s. Never mind the fact that Reverend Moon is conservative by almost any definition of the word. A more important reason for the hostility is simply that the Unification Church is new, founded in the same year as Scientology. In the case of religion, respectability comes with age. Newcomers on the religious landscape, and especially ones that make health claims, are almost never welcome. They are vulnerable to IRS inspection, as the Reverend Moon learned when he served time for tax evasion. A church cannot own a hotel in Manhattan, a newspaper in Washington, D.C., and a fleet of fishing boats without owing the United States government some money. Moon probably got what he deserved. Even so, the suggestion here is that "commercial property" is a difficult concept to define when a church is the owner. Older religious organizations have an easier time keeping property exempt from taxes than newer religious organizations.

A Basis for Discrimination?

One lesson from this observation might be that all churches need greater scrutiny. Sometimes that is hard to do. The Unification Church has many names and in its public solicitations for money it almost never uses the one that most people would recognize. Their solicitors who freely roam airports and railroad stations asking money for charitable and religious purposes might as well be anonymous. Not one traveler in a thousand would have a clear idea of who their sponsors are. Business companies, of course, also diversify their labels. If someone, for example, wants to boycott a company that uses child labor in South Asia, that person would have to consume hours trying to decide which companies to avoid. But businesses as profit maximizers are expected to behave badly and government at least has power to regulate what they do. The question is whether churches in today's world do not need more regulation than what the IRS provides. Given the difficulty of distinguishing the sacred from the secular in American society, why should churches be granted the presumption of sacred enterprise when so much of what they do is not clearly related to religious worship, or religious charity, or religious education?

Churches with therapeutic missions or ones that promise mental health raise the most contentious examples. A peace of mind that comes from being in tune with the infinite blends with a wide range of psychotherapies, making all but invisible the line that Hubbard crossed early in his career from secular to sacred. Sigmund Freud was a "secular" Jew who attributed many of the world's ills to organized religion. Carl Jung, on the other hand, had considerably more sympathy for the powerful religious symbols that he believed were almost universally present in human cultures. Like William James, Jung believed that human consciousness was neither finite nor bounded by sensory impressions. In the archetypal forms that were secreted in the inner layers of human consciousness, human beings found traces of the infinite. Organized religion was a construction of culture. The religious imagination was not. Human beings in the modern Western world were only beginning to rediscover the range of restorative power it brought to people in other societies.

In the nineteenth century, western New York state was known as the "burned-over district." New religious movements quickly took root there. But California has more recently been the hothouse nursery of religious innovation. As soon as Anglos started flooding into Southern California in the late nineteenth century, Los Angeles became a city of storefront churches and street-corner prophets. California today records one of the lowest rates of formal religious observance among the various states of the Union. But those numbers are deceptive. In place of thriving communities of Presbyterians or Methodists or Baptists, experimental religion or personal religious questing has boomed. Some of it has claimed the name of religion. Some of it has not.

For example, the Esalen Institute, founded in Big Sur California in 1962, is not classified as a religious organization. The product it sells is the development of "human potential." Aldous Huxley used the phrase in *The Doors of Perception*, his book about his experiments with mind-altering drugs. During the 1960s, Huxley's book became a beloved text of counter-culture seekers who saw no difference between the visions of a religious mystic and the visions of someone on an acid trip. In the early 1960s Richard Alpert, a young scientist at Harvard, conducted experiments on the psychological effects of LSD. Tripping apparently became his direct channel to God. Like the Beatles and the poet Alan Ginsburg, he went to India in search of enlightenment. In 1972 he re-created himself as Baba Ram Dass, a religious teacher.

The Esalen Institute is not as confused as that. It combines the techniques of psychotherapy with religious style mediation. The result, as its brochures announce, is a blend of East and West. Perhaps its "product" is best labeled secular because it focuses on how human consciousness might overcome whatever blocks its full development. The language of the New Age is ambiguous and eclectic. Many of those who are enthusiastic proponents of everything passing under that general rubric see little reason to distinguish the Hare Krishnas, classified as a religious organization, from the Rolf Institute, the Erhard Seminars, and the Institute for the Development of the Harmonious Human Being. The latter groups are not classified as religious movements but they are attracted to meditative practices of various Eastern religions. Whenever conversation turns toward the unrealized powers of the human mind, the vocabulary becomes indistinguishable from that used by many people to describe their "spiritual" journeys.

Marketing Zen Awareness

All of this has something to do with the baby boomer generation who during the 1960s and beyond discovered a lot wrong with American society and with Western styles of thinking. Altering consciousness was a release from the stresses of the Protestant work ethic and other mental traps that Western culture used to program its youth. The results were not nearly as revolutionary as they sounded. But for a time a generation of young college-bound students found some new heroes. They included a group of very serious religious seekers who even in the 1950s had pursued Zen

Buddhism as an alternative to Western materialism. Philip Kapleau, a New York businessman who almost died as a result of his pursuit of money, threw up his career and went to Japan. For years he sought enlightenment in a Zen monastery. He returned to Rochester to found the Center for the Study of Zen, a very serious place with serious discipline.

Meanwhile on the more relaxed West Coast, Alan Watts, a man deeply influenced by D. T. Suzuki, wrote a number of books seeking to popularize Zen among non-Asian Americans. His books found many casual readers. Were they serious about Buddhism? A raucous group of 1950s writers known as the Beat Generation might get hooked on a quest for Dharma, in between their bouts of drinking and incessant womanizing. But could Americans really take that as evidence that they were a religious people? Did Beat style "dropping out" have anything to do with the renunciation of the world once practiced by Christian ascetics?

Put that way, the answer to these questions was clearly no, even if Western history presented many examples of religious enthusiasts whose excessive behavior mocked the usual moral norms of organized religious groups. On the other hand, as we have seen, the religious seeking of the 1950s that found a large youthful audience in the 1960s and in subsequent decades was not exactly a new phenomenon. It was a manifestation of the long fascination that Americans had had with therapeutic religion. Young people were experimenting with different claims, without full commitments to any of them. They could smoke pot or drift into a group of Hare Krishnas or spend a month in a commune directed by some self-anointed guru. The advice to the lonely and bewildered and confused was to try anything. They were eager to find the peace of mind that their parents kept talking about but so clearly did not have.

Religious enthusiasms are easy to criticize as passing fads. It is true that yoga classes seemed in some areas to become a craze, rather like jogging. The Maharishi Mahesh Yogi, a charismatic religious figure whose ashram in India attracted the Beatles, introduced in 1959 the principles of transcendental mediation (TM). TM promised to lower blood pressure, relieve stress, and increase intelligence. Students who worried about their performance on exams were counseled to focus on a mantra for fifteen or twenty minutes two times a day. Doing this enabled them to get rid of their tension and to ace their exams. The commercially organized practice of TM offered expensive courses on weekends and evenings to busy Americans bent on success. How could that be religion? Yet if the testimony of educated and sensitive people means anything, TM is more serious than it sounds. The discipline may have seemed easy, but it took more time and attention than many churchgoers expended weekly on their faith.

Without question the Maharishi Mahesh Yogi was steeped in the tradition of Vedanta and had studied the classic religious texts of Hindu India. To the Maharishi it mattered little whether one called TM a religion or the "science of creative" intelligence. Although a United States Court of Appeals in 1979 decided that transcendental meditation was a religion, hence defeating an attempt by some of its proponents to make it part of the school curriculum, the disciples of the Maharishi in the United States organized nothing resembling a traditional church. Instead, they founded Maharishi International University in Fairfield, Iowa. Perhaps most of the people who tried TM for a while tired of the discipline and moved on to something else. That in no sense made them different from many Americans who moved in and out of religious movements during the whole of the nineteenth century. Moreover, the appeal of transcendental meditation is impossible to differentiate from the appeal of Norman Vincent Peale. If the superficiality of a religious commitment means that people are not really interested in religion, then Americans need to take a serious look at any statistical boast that they are the most religious people in the world. It is not the specifics of this or that religion that keep many Americans interested in religion. It is the way religion moves so easily through many areas of their lives. Religion is about something else.

In many settings, then, Americans wear their religious beliefs lightly and link them to other things that concern them. What at the beginning of the twenty-first century in the United States is marketed as New Age accentuates the general American tolerance for religious eclecticism. Even Southern Baptists read their horoscopes in the daily newspaper. The New Age has reinvented the notion of religion as harmonious living, of trying to find a way to stay in close touch with nature and with the transformative powers buried in human consciousness. It tries to keep alive, following the advice of William James, an interest in what normal science says cannot possibly be true—with the reality of flying saucers, the mystical powers of crystals, the phenomenon of channeling that puts human beings in touch with spirit masters. In a society where intelligent people often work one hundred hours a week to make money they have no leisure to spend it on, the promise of a New Age is something worth thinking about.

What Americans want is not an escape from everyday life but some way to purify it. New Agers can embrace a vegetarian diet, exercise, and organic gardening. Their hope is nothing new. Human beings have been since the time they were expelled from the Garden of Eden in conflict with their environment. Therapeutic religion seeks to restore harmony between human beings and the natural world. Healing marks the achievement of that harmony. Health is a sign that a person has attained purity. The identification of mental and physical health with spiritual enlightenment turns the environmental movement for many people into religion. Pollution of the environment will someday destroy human life on earth. That is a certainty but perhaps not the main point of environmentalism. Polluting the environment is religious desecration. It literally destroys health, and disease of any kind weakens the possibility of successful communication with God.

Sylvester Graham, were it not for the naturalness that New Agers assign to sex, might have been perfectly happy living today in Sedona, Arizona. He would surely notice that the cost of the tools for healthy living, the yoga mats, the meditation cushions, the vitamins, the macrobiotic cookware, cost a great deal more than a diet of graham crackers. Even peace of mind in contemporary America requires a family with two incomes. Yet Graham would be happy to see that Americans have kept alive the notion that spiritual perfection and bodily health were very close to the same thing.

This may not get them anywhere. Probably Americans are stuck with a religious culture that promotes a simple life but invents every conceivable form of self-help technique to defeat its realization. The zeal for simplicity creates the Type-A personality. If my neighbor jogs twenty miles a day, I can jog twenty-five. My smoke-free environment is better than your smoke-free environment. Purity becomes an exhausting contest. Americans seek harmony because it is the most difficult thing to achieve under the competitive terms laid down by American society. The quest can lead to romanticizing what never was and never can be. Consider some of the literature that now praises traditional American Indian culture as one filled with richness. It was, but affluent non-native Americans may be doing the wrong sort of imitation by spending a small fortune decorating their homes with Indian artifacts. Besides, it is not quite true that American Indians typically lived in full harmony with their environments, that they took from nature only what they needed and that hunting and gathering brought greater spiritual returns than the Presbyterian Church.

Americans are not likely to find the simplicity they might ascribe to American Indian life in Manhattan or even in two weeks of wilderness backpacking. But maybe that is not the point. What lies behind any spiritual quest worth pursuing is a wish to transform parts of a culture. Some of what is imagined may be fantasy, but it is not hypocrisy. Nor is it always useless fantasy. Imagining American culture modified by the religious insights of other cultures is a species of utopian thinking. What is imagined creates tension between what we have and what we ought to want. The tension permits space for social reform movements to come into being.

Religion, in its quest for personal health and material happiness, easily becomes politics. That also is a strength and a weakness of the American system. It accounts for an idealism that makes the United States look foolish and sometimes dangerous to the rest of the world. It is also part of a powerful dream that leads many people to seek sanctuary and a new life in the United States. Religious politics is appropriately the subject of our last chapter.

Chapter Nine

Evangelizing the World in This Generation: American Religious Triumphalism and the Turn Toward Politics

In 1900 the United States had only begun to act on a world stage. Many European states had by that time established colonies in Asia and Africa. But the Yankee empire was limited to Hawaii and the possessions that had fallen under America's control after the brief Spanish–American War in 1898. Despite the lack of an "official" empire, Americans throughout much of the nineteenth century had worked around the globe trying to establish trade networks. And wherever American traders went, missionaries went as well. Often men of the cloth preceded the commercial agents. Early in the twentieth century, foreign mission groups in the United States were outspending those in all other nations. Arguably the United States became the major missionary power in the world faster than it achieved clear dominance in any other area. Inevitably, links developed between twentieth-century Protestant missionary work and diplomatic goals to establish American-style democracy abroad. Efforts to Christianize the world and to Americanize the world became joint endeavors.

American religious triumphalism burst into spectacular view during the World's Parliament of Religions held in Chicago in 1893. This extravagant event was part of Chicago's great Columbian Exposition, a world's fair held to celebrate Western progress over the four hundred years since Columbus's first voyage to North America. An American press corps awed by the colorful dress worn by religious dignitaries from non-Christian parts of the globe made the Parliament famous. It was an invention of American liberal Protestantism. Judged against many less ecumenically minded religious leaders who boycotted the affair, John Henry Barrows, the Presbyterian who chaired the sessions, was a tolerant man. He and other American leaders were genuinely interested in learning about the other great religions of the world. They were thrilled to welcome in Chicago religious teachers from Asia, including Swami Vivekananda from India.

Yet the event was also part and parcel of a heady and aggressive movement within American Protestantism to "evangelize the world in this generation." Several years after Barrows had banged the final gavel closing the Parliament of Religions and had assumed the presidency of Oberlin College, he articulated the popular opinion that the United States, with all its wealth, bore the responsibility for world redemption. "I am almost persuaded," he wrote, " that within the area of a thousand square miles of America there is more of uprightness, moral purity, and true self-respecting manhood and womanhood than can be found in all Asia." He continued that "ours is the chief branch of the Anglo-Saxon race. . . . America's place in the Christianizing of the world is far ahead, in the very foremost ranks." President William McKinley, in trying to persuade Americans that they had a white man's burden to civilize the peoples of the Philippines, could not have put the matter in a more politically palatable way.

In the first three decades of the twentieth century, America's most famous missionary voice belonged to the remarkable John R. Mott. Mott was a Cornell graduate who turned the intercollegiate YMCA movement into a potent religious force on American campuses. In 1888 he founded the Student Volunteer Movement for Foreign Missions and pushed the Y into missionary work. It played a major role in American relief efforts in Europe during and after the Great War. Starting in 1914, the YMCA raised more than $150 million during the years of the conflict and served more than twenty million soldiers. Y workers sold themselves as agents of American goodwill that European prisoners of war would remember "as they set their faces toward home." According to instructions given to them, their disinterested but highly visible work in Greece, Rumania, Russia, Poland, and Czechoslovakia would in the end serve the interests of America. The Y's practical efforts to serve Christ, which exemplified the American "passion for uplift," were bound to change the oppressive religious and political systems of Europe.

Mott's prominence in international circles owed much to his political connections. He was a friend of President Woodrow Wilson and accepted diplomatic missions both in Mexico and in Russia. He also was close to Herbert Hoover, who was one of the people who nominated Mott for the Nobel Peace Prize that he won in 1946. By the standards of the time he was a cosmopolitan, an indefatigable and curious world traveler who found something to praise in every world culture. However, his relish for visiting other places did not turn him into a cultural relativist. The world needed Christianity, and it also needed American business and democracy. Mott instantly turned his face against the Russian Revolution. He declared to a group of Chicago businesspeople his "unqualifiedly uncompromising warfare" against the Bolsheviks. Both their economic theories of class warfare and their attempt to build a nation without religion threatened world peace.

To combat Bolshevism, Mott sold American missionary work. It was a sound investment to stimulate economic development. Speaking in Egypt in 1926, he linked the work of the YMCA with that of the World's Bankers Association, the World's Chamber of Commerce, and the World's Advertiser Clubs. "The world expansion of commerce, industry, and finance," he said, "constitutes another great force [in addition to Christianity] which should tell more and more for the stabilization, unification, and upbuilding of the world." Addressing a conference attended by President Calvin Coolidge and Secretary of State Charles Evans Hughes, Mott urged a closer cooperation between churches and American diplomacy. "The nearly thirty thousand missionaries whom we represent," he said, "should be regarded not only as ambassadors, but . . . interpreters and mediators between peoples and civilizations."

Christ and the Cold War

World War II interrupted efforts to export American freedom that, according to Mott, accounted both for America's economic success and the prosperity of its religious denominations. The onset of the Cold War, however, brought religion back into league with the State Department. In the war against godless communism, American religious groups became part of a national crusade. Protestant missionary groups led the way. John Foster Dulles, the American Secretary of State under President Eisenhower, had cut his teeth in working with groups committed to the expansion of Christianity. He was among the organizers of the World's Council of Churches in 1948. In his passionate belief in the ultimate superiority of Christianity to all other world faiths, Dulles had not moved one inch beyond the perspective of the American Protestants who had organized the World's Parliament of Religions. As Secretary of State he enlisted his faith to stop communism.

In 1947 delegates to the fifty-third annual meeting of the Foreign Missions Conference of North America supported strong efforts to push back the advances made by the "materialistic faith of Marxian philosophy." Its resolution pinpointed the danger of Stalin's "military conquests, political coercion and able propaganda" as forcefully as any statement issued by the U.S. State Department. A year later, at an assembly sponsored by the Foreign Missions Conference of North America, Dr. Ralph E. Diffendorfer, the executive secretary of Division of Foreign Missions of the Methodist Church, warned again of "Communist ideology." Echoing the famous Containment Doctrine advocated by George Kennan, he insisted that the communists "can be pushed back only by the forceful offensive of an idea and program that stops them in their tracks." The Foreign Missions Conference equated the Soviet takeover of Eastern Europe with the "spread of Islam from Arabia in the seventh and eighth century." Islam and communism were close to the same thing in showing Western democracies the danger of "fanatical zeal and political expansionism." This equation suggested just how much misunderstanding was later going to separate the United States from many Muslim countries.

Henry Luce, the powerful editor of *Time* and *Life*, predicted early in 1941, even before Pearl Harbor, that a military victory over Germany and Japan would introduce the American Century. American power would be unrivaled in the world. The United States would be obliged to take strong action to ensure its hegemony, but Luce was confident of the result. The American Century would bring prosperity and happiness not only to the American people but to people everywhere. As it turned out, one of the players in America's response to Soviet expansion was a man whose career Luce helped launch in the pages of his journals. That was Billy Graham, who also benefited from an order that William Randolph Hearst gave to the editors in his newspaper chain to "puff" Graham. The evangelist emerged as a poster boy in the campaign to identify the United States with moral goodness.

By the early 1950s Graham's revival crusades had reached millions of people in America's large cities. Graham was eager to work abroad. He challenged the leaders of the Soviet Union to allow him to preach the gospel there. The challenge pleased American policymakers. They had been somewhat slow to inject human rights, including religious freedom, into the rhetoric of the Cold War. Throughout the 1950s the United States had many allies that cared little about human rights. In addition, talking about human rights risked exposing America's own sorry record in denying civil rights to African Americans. Nonetheless, the Soviet habit of throwing Jehovah's Witnesses and Pentecostals into jail made religion a trump card worth playing.

Graham's petition to crusade for Christ in Moscow went unheeded for many years. Ironically, when he was finally allowed to preach in Russia in

1982, he traveled against the strong urging of President Ronald Reagan. American Cold Warriors of the 1980s no longer deemed Graham a reliable spokesman for anti-communism. Nonetheless, Graham had had a good run as a sponsor of Western religious freedom. His efforts during the 1950s and 1960s to work in Soviet-controlled countries were calculated to demarcate the differences between East and West. When Graham preached to large crowds in Berlin in 1960, he set up his microphones so that his voice carried into East Berlin. That was before the construction of the Berlin Wall, and Graham's campaign boasted that thousands of East Berliners crossed into West Berlin to hear the message of Christ. Graham's first visit to a communist country was to Yugoslavia in 1967, followed ten years later by visits to Hungary and Poland.

The Cold War ended although it was far from clear that the result guaranteed worldwide admiration for the American system. Freedom of religion as Americans understood that concept did not become the norm in any of the states delivered from communism. Islamic theocracies took over important areas of the world. Israel, one of America's closest democratic allies, remained a Jewish state where religious laws held sway in ways unthinkable in the United States. Democracies in Western Europe restricted religious practices deemed socially harmful with a much freer license than what American courts permitted. Italy under the present-day regime of Silvio Berlusconi has officially reaffirmed its Catholic heritage. Berlusconi and others are pressuring the European Parliament to acknowledge "God and our responsibility before God" in the European Constitution. Even Americans, confronted with mounting evidence that the world is a very dangerous place, have reopened debates about whether the state should sponsor more religion in the public sphere. Some vocal Americans argue that the country will be safer if it repairs the godlessness of its Constitution. In some ways, Americans are back to the debates of the nation's founders.

Efforts to Amend the Secular State

Perhaps it is more accurate to say that those debates have never ceased. In the early years of the republic, the most important argument about the meaning of a secular state arose over the unlikely issue of Sunday mail delivery. The Constitution requires the national Congress to establish a postal system. No one questioned the need for mail delivery. The issue was whether in carrying out this responsibility postmasters needed to pay attention to the biblical Fourth Commandment, "Remember the Sabbath

Day, to keep it holy." Most Americans assumed that God in mentioning the Sabbath was talking about Sundays.

Big battles often have small beginnings. The Sunday mail controversy started in 1809 in Washington, Pennsylvania, where Hugh Wylie, the town's postmaster, followed a common practice of keeping the post office open on Sunday. The custom allowed churchgoers from neighboring villages to pick up their mail. Wylie's own Presbyterian Church was not pleased. Though he was an elder, the church expunged his name from the membership roles. Gideon Granger, the postmaster general of the United States, moved to give Wylie and others legal protection. He persuaded Congress in 1810 to pass legislation requiring post offices to be open at least one hour every day. It also required postal workers to transport the mail daily. Granger argued that if Congress stopped its official business in order to gratify the wishes of religious groups that observed a Sunday Sabbath, it was not observing religious neutrality. Besides, clerics were not supposed to be telling government officials how to conduct their business.

The argument convinced some Christian groups but not all of them. Unpersuaded Christians started a petition campaign demanding that Congress repeal the 1810 law. It went on for the next twenty years. But proponents of Sunday mail delivery also had Christian advocates. Indiana was one of three states filing petitions to uphold the 1810 law. It argued "there are no doctrines or observances inculcated by the Christian religion which require the arm of civil power either to enforce or sustain them." Only a false Christianity required the state to prop it up.

Predictably many politicians tried to waffle on the issue. Few of them spoke as bluntly as Richard M. Johnson of Kentucky, chairman of the Senate Committee on the Post Office and Post Roads. A devout Baptist, he sharply rebuked the Sabbatarians for suggesting that the national "Legislature was a proper tribunal to determine what are the laws of God." Efforts to stop the mail represented a religious zeal that was dangerous not only to the state but to churches as well. Religious groups that called on government to enforce particular religious beliefs, however widespread they might be, brought calumny upon religion and threatened the nation with civil war. That to Johnson was the clear lesson of history. Johnson's opinion triumphed over the opposition. In 1836 he was elected the nation's vice president to serve under Martin Van Buren.

For all that, the practice of Sunday mail delivery did not survive. With the introduction of the railroad and the telegraph, news traveled faster and made the economic argument for seven-day postal delivery less compelling. By the 1850s the Sunday movement of mail had largely stopped.

The law permitted post offices to open on Sunday, but fewer and fewer postmasters found a reason to do that. Finally Protestant ministers persuaded them that they needed a day off. Clerics and postal workers joined forces and successfully lobbied Congress in 1912 to close all post offices on Sunday. It was not a victory won by Protestant fundamentalists but by progressive reformers. They would later switch roles. But in the early twentieth century Protestant liberals worked with other reformers to overcome what they viewed as a crisis of corruption threatening American democratic government. Giant corporations bought members of Congress with the same ease that they purchased raw materials, and the rot in public life extended from Washington down to every level of state and local government. Progressive crusaders warned voters about a decline in the nation's moral codes, and sold Sunday closing laws as a quick fix for the problem.

By 1912 when Congress repealed the 1810 law, the constitutional issue raised by postal closings no longer seemed very important. Defenders of the secular state could take heart in knowing that a much greater threat to their principles had failed. They had successfully beaten back efforts to add a Christian amendment to the Constitution. Even during the heat of the American Civil War when ministers argued that God was punishing the nation, efforts to rewrite the Constitution so that it recognized God's stewardship did not pass. The seceding states of the Confederacy perhaps served as a useful caution. They made God the author of their enterprise and the protector of their peculiar institution. They lost the war. Northern ministers who wanted God placed in the Constitution won some smaller victories. God made it onto American currency after the Civil War. In the early years of the Cold War, Congressional legislation wrote God into the Pledge of Allegiance. But a Christian amendment to the Constitution always failed.

On the Origin of Religious Politics

Preserving the godless language of the American Constitution was an important issue, but not the only issue. Nor was it the issue that caused the most contention among Americans. The most enduring divisive argument was over whether religion should ever be joined to politics. And if it was, what was the best way to do that? Over the course of the nineteenth and twentieth centuries, many elected officials have in the course of their duties talked about religion. Judges wrote opinions that referred to the United States as a Christian nation or to Americans as a religious people. Public officials may, of course, say anything they want. Their right to free speech is as protected as the same right for ordinary citizens. If politicians tell voters that they ask Jesus Christ about what legislation to pass, they are breaking no law. The question is whether it is a good idea. Does it violate the spirit of America's secular Constitution that separates human government from any responsibility to carry out God's will?

As we have seen, the men who wrote the Constitution premised the success of a democratic republic on the virtue of its citizens. Virtue in their minds rested on a religious base. The national government was required to remain religiously neutral. It could not allocate money to support religious institutions. But did separation of church and state by the terms of the First Amendment mean that politicians had no appropriate way to acknowledge the importance of religion? Was it wrong for them to suggest in their speeches that praising God was a good idea? Or that God was the ultimate judge of what nation states did? Could they not proclaim that the United States was a nation under God? Those are questions that Americans have never answered with one voice.

George Washington made some reasonable compromises. He believed in the secular state but also acknowledged the strong popular sentiment that God needed public recognition. Washington added a reference to God in the presidential oath of office. He swore the oath with his hand placed on a Bible. He evoked a nonspecific divinity in his inaugural address. These were practices imitated by every subsequent American president, no matter what their level of piety and no matter what strictness they brought to issues of church/state separation.

Much of the present-day controversy about religion and politics still looks back to Thomas Jefferson. What did he mean when he used the phrase "wall of separation" between church and state? He included it in a letter he wrote to Baptists in Danbury, Connecticut. They had supported Jefferson's statements about the need for government to stay out of the business of churches. According to most readers of the letter, Jefferson used the "wall of separation" metaphor to emphasize the strength of his position. In 1998 James Hutson, the chief of the manuscript division of the Library of Congress, suggested something else. He placed Jefferson's letter in an exhibition titled "Religion and the Founding of the American Republic" and agued that the famous phrase was more a political ploy than a carefully considered statement of principle.

Hutson's curiosity was aroused by passages in the draft that Jefferson had blotted out. What had they said? He placed the letter in the hands of the FBI laboratory, which was able to make almost the entire draft legible. Hutson noted that the unexpurgated version of the letter had stronger stuff in it than Jefferson included in the final text. In one deleted passage, he promised not to call national days of fasting and celebration. Hutson concluded that Jefferson had cut out this phrase to avoid needlessly alienating some potential political supporters. While he wanted to rebuke his Federalist opponents in New England who were vilifying him as a French infidel, Jefferson also wanted to appease a group of his New England supporters who saw no contradiction between the principle of church/state separation and the calling of national fast days. Conservative Protestant groups immediately saw political ammunition in Hutson's suggestion. If Jefferson's letter was a political document rather than a declaration of principle, American jurists ought not to pay much attention to it.

Poor Jefferson. Almost every move he made as president has been subjected to scrutiny for evidence of how he might stand on contemporary issues. Who knows what Jefferson would have decided about issues that were not before him? Even so, Jefferson had more on his mind than political opportunism when he wrote the phrase "wall of separation." Jefferson was a man of great learning. The issue of church/state separation was not new to political theory. In the American context it stretched back to the colonial period. The zealous Puritan divine Roger Williams, who wanted absolute protection of religion from state interference, spoke of a wall (he also said hedge) between the "garden of the church and the wilderness of the world." John Locke, England's great philosopher of liberalism, held that states had only worldly tasks. They were instituted to protect people's lives, liberty, and property. In his *Letter Concerning Toleration* he sought to "distinguish exactly the business of civil government from that of religion, and to settle the just bounds that lie between the one and the other." Even before there was an American Constitution, Jefferson had made clear the influence of Locke upon him. He and James Madison succeeded in a difficult political fight to get the Virginia legislature to adopt its "Statute for Religious Freedom." It reads in part, "Our civil rights have no dependence on our religious opinions, more than our opinions in physics or geometry."

"Wall of separation" was not a slip of Jefferson's pen. But Hutson was certainly right to suggest that even this strong metaphor cannot settle controversies about every practice where church and state might intersect. What perhaps most bothered Jefferson was the use of religion to attack a political opponent. Article Six of the American Constitution states that "no religious test shall ever be required as a qualification to any office of public trust under the United States." That had not stopped Jefferson's foes from declaring him unfit to be president because he was a "French infidel." Presumably some Christian ministers were sincere in expressing their fears. Constitution or no Constitution, they could not bring themselves to believe that someone who doubted the truth of Scripture could be trusted as president. Other opponents of Jefferson were simply opportunists. Alexander Hamilton, a man with almost no religion, regarded hypocrisy as a small sin if it helped him to defeat the Virginian. So he willingly let the presidential campaign of 1800 ring with cries that Jefferson was a "howling atheist."

Jefferson, as we have seen, believed in God. But that was no one's business. Christ was, according to Jefferson, "the greatest teacher of moral truths that ever lived." But he deemed his personal opinion about Christianity irrelevant to the question of whether he was qualified to hold office. Whether someone believed in one god or twenty gods or no god had no place in political argument. In running for office, Jefferson never talked about his religion, which his enemies deliberately misrepresented. But he held strong opinions about the people who attacked his religious views. When he wrote in a letter to his friend Benjamin Rush, "I have sworn upon the altar of God eternal hostility against every form of tyranny over the mind of man," he was referring to clerical tyranny. Ministers who tried to hold politicians to religious tests were a danger to the young republic. They were doing what European clerics had too often done in the past. They wanted to use religious dogma to close people's minds to the need for free and open debate. His sworn hostility to them is his political testament. It is carved into the memorial that Congress dedicated to Jefferson in 1943.

Jefferson's stand against religious politics did not end the matter. It was in fact only the beginning of a controversy that stretches to the present. But Jefferson's eloquent rhetoric set terms for future debate. No one wants to be associated with tyranny. Usually, the people who use religious appeals to achieve political goals try to avoid the semblance of sectarian dogmatism. Yet often in the case of morally charged issues that is very hard to do.

Fighting for God's Justice

In American history candidates from both ends of the political spectrum have used religion. One of the oldest forms of public address in America is the Jeremiad. Dating back to the seventeenth century, it was named for its attempt to echo the thunderous rhetoric of the Old Testament prophet. New England ministers regularly delivered sermons on election day. Their texts reviewed in detail all the sins committed by the colonists in their private and public life. They warned that unless they collectively atoned for their offenses against God, they would face a terrible judgment. Judgments came in the form of floods, shipwrecks, and Indian attacks. The Jeremiad tradition continued through the colonial period and into the early years of the new nation. Jefferson's enemies used it for partisan purposes. Elect Jefferson and the nation would collapse. Throughout subsequent American history the political right and the political left have mimicked the Jeremiad to push their various agendas. Without higher taxes or lower taxes, depending on the politician, the American ship of state will run aground.

Politicians have also promised Americans a glorious future. By the time of the American Revolution, religious rhetoric from pulpits set in contrast the virtue of the independent colonies against the corruption of the mother country. Americans were about to join forces as a redeemer nation. Politicians liked that theme a lot better than one about the imminence of God's displeasure. Again they reached back to colonial models, this time to John Winthrop's speech aboard the ship that carried the first Puritans to Massachusetts Bay. His "Model of Christian Charity" proposed that the New World would be a "city upon a hill." "The eyes of all people are upon us." The young American republic was already in 1790 setting its course toward the mission noted at the beginning of this chapter. It was destined to convert the world to its model of a virtuous republic. American foreign policy has never strayed very far from the theme.

Yet by the third decade of the nation's existence many Americans were worried about the ebbing of public virtue. Antebellum America became a hothouse of reform movements. All of them, whether they were about dietary habits, or prison reform, or the need to rid America of the demon rum, had religious themes. Many of them borrowed heavily from Christian millennial teachings. The United States, they said, was about to enter a new age that foreshadowed the second coming of Christ. Most reformers, although not all, saw the battle of Armageddon as a distant event. Millennial themes, however, gave their demands a sense of urgency. More urgent than any of the rest were the cries of the abolitionists. Slavery was an offense to God. Unless the nation cleansed itself immediately of complicity in the sins of slaveholders, it faced a terrible reckoning.

Abolitionism was religious politics, but of a kind unlike many of the examples that followed it. It remained aloof from political parties and all other political alliances. Its most radical proponents, including William Lloyd Garrison, who edited *The Liberator*, had "come out" of their churches because most American churches recorded only tepid objections to slavery.

They felt very strongly that all human institutions were corrupting. It was better to stand apart from them. Democratic politics was especially corrupting because it required compromise. Radical abolitionists refused to petition Congress to pass a law against slavery or in any other way to seek a legislative solution for their complaint. They did not join the Liberty Party formed by more moderate antislavery Protestants or support the campaigns of any candidate for office. They did not in fact vote. They aimed to change America by appealing to conscience.

If the slaveholders did not repent of their sins, abolitionists were prepared to leave them alone. They wanted to secede from the devil's compact that was the American Constitution. Its flaw was not its failure to mention God but its permitting slavery to continue. If they could not persuade other Americans to secede with them, then they would perfect themselves in small groups. How exactly the slave would benefit from this uncompromising earnestness was unclear. But the rhetoric of religious fervor was one factor that drove the nation into crisis. It serves as a prime example of a way religious politics can change a nation, and in a way that everyone now agrees was vitally important.

Partisan and Nonpartisan Politics

We saw in chapter 4 that women were involved in many nineteenth-century reform movements. Women's groups that were often organized by churches led the fight for temperance. They worked to better the conditions of families who lived in poverty. They found a voice in the antislavery crusade. Frances Willard in the last quarter of the nineteenth century turned the Woman's Christian Temperance Union into a nationally influential organization that lobbied for a wide range of progressive social laws. Like the abolitionist crusade, women's groups refused to let their agenda be absorbed by electoral politics. Indeed they could not, for women could not vote. In this case it was possible to make a virtue from a deficit. Religion was a moral force. Politics was not. Women's religious organizations reflected conventional gender distinctions that just happened to reinforce one important view about church/state separation. Women placed religion in the public sphere. They gave it a role in debates about national legislative agendas. At the same time they kept it clear of politicians who survived in electoral contests by cutting unholy deals with blackguards.

Aloofness from electoral politics was not the only model of religious politics. Black churches provided an important example of the uses of partisanship. Independent African American churches, first in the North and then after the Civil War in the South, were centers of black political action. Ministers took political stands. They ran for office. A careful regard for church/state separation was not an option for people who had few reliable institutions through which to pursue political and social equality. Where they were able to retain the vote, African Americans until the era of Franklin Roosevelt gave their overwhelming political support to Republican candidates. After the New Deal, they voted Democratic. Not very many white American politicians chose to address black audiences. But those who did were welcome speakers in black churches. We shall come to Martin Luther King Jr. But a long list of other African American political partisans—among them Adam Clayton Powell Jr., Jesse Jackson, and Al Sharpton—were also ministers.

The major religious denominations in the United States, whether Protestant, Catholic, or Jewish, often avoided politics altogether. When they did enter the fray, they usually stood at some midway position between ignoring elections and taking party stands. Denominations securely rooted in the white middle class have tried to sustain the American tradition of bipartisanship. In the late nineteenth century the most important example of nonpartisan church politics was the so-called Social Gospel movement. The movement represented a loose coalition of mostly Protestant clerics who worried about the grave social costs of rapid industrialization and urbanization. The period in American history from 1880 until the outbreak of the terrible European war in 1914 was marked by great entrepreneurial energy and economic growth. The human toll caused by social disruption was also great. Too many families lived in unsafe, crowded tenements. Too many men, women, and children had to take poorly paid, insecure jobs in unsafe workplaces. Too many people died from diseases that could have been controlled. Americans proclaimed equality but close to a majority of its citizens faced discriminatory barriers everywhere they turned.

The views of most of the religious leaders associated with the Social Gospel were mildly progressive but not radical. Only a few of them turned to socialism, and those few wanted a socialism that eschewed violence. Social Gospelers urged churches to increase their charitable activities among the poor. They cited the Salvation Army, an English invention successfully exported to the United States, as a useful example of an urban mission. They wanted Americans to apply the moral teachings of Jesus to social policy. They gave at best tepid support to trade unionism, but most of them supported legislative efforts to eliminate child labor, to regulate large corporations, and to improve safety standards, especially for women workers. They formed a political wing within the Federal Council of Churches that was organized in 1908. Over the course of the twentieth century, the council's brand of Social Gospel politics angered many conservatives, although it never ventured very far left of the political center. During the heyday of its influence, which lasted through the first half of the twentieth century, its leadership was as apt to vote Republican as Democratic. It pinned its hopes for progressive social change on the benevolent actions of Christian businesspeople.

Reinhold Niebuhr is one of the most powerful religious voices that emerged in twentieth-century America. He graduated from the Yale Divinity School just after World War I and took a pastorate in Detroit. There he saw the Social Gospel in action. He witnessed well-meaning ministers who tried to convince the men who ran automobile companies to treat their workers better. Clerics argued that workers needed higher wages and more secure jobs. They might even need trade unions. From Niebuhr's point of view, their appeals to conscience fell on absolutely deaf ears. The automakers, in fact, used their great wealth to silence the criticism of clerics. Christian businesspeople who supported churches had their own gospel to promote. They told ministers to stick to the business of saving souls and not to comment on economic issues. Detroit convinced Niebuhr that the Social Gospel brand of Christian politics was a useless exercise. He moved to the Union Theological Seminary and to the far left of the political spectrum.

Niebuhr talked about politics for the rest of his life, although after World War II he became more moderate. He was one of the founding members of the Americans for Democratic Action, a political action group within the Democratic Party. What was distinctive about Niebuhr was the secular basis of his religious politics. His experience in Detroit convinced him that the Christian law of love had no direct application to the world of human politics. It served only as a utopian perspective to remind humans of the inadequacies of any society they concocted. In that sense the Christian law of love was a spur to further social action. God did not permit men and women to give up in their efforts to ease the burdens of the poor and powerless. But love offered no concrete guide as to what should be done to eliminate injustice. Niebuhr reintroduced a strong notion of sin into his Neo-Orthodox theology and his progressive politics. The rich would always do whatever served to make them richer. They had to be stopped with force, violent force in extreme cases, and sharply worded legislation in a well-run democracy. Christians could try to live the law of love with their friends and families. But in politics they needed to be realists.

For Niebuhr the only effective Christian politics was partisan politics. It supported candidates who took the right stands. The Americans for Democratic Action lobbied for legislation favorable to trade unions and to civil rights for black Americans. Niebuhr did not expect most Christian churches in America to follow his lead. He was a twentieth-century "come outer," who like the nineteenth-century abolitionists believed that most churches were not prepared to witness boldly against the social evils that beset America. But unlike William Lloyd Garrison, Niebuhr abandoned the strategy of moral suasion as a useful way to reform America. Many of his political allies were neither Christian nor particularly religious. They thought of themselves as moral men and women, but they gave secular reasons for the policies they supported. Whether America was a Christian nation or even a religious nation was to them not an issue that belonged in the political sphere.

In retrospect it is clear that what Niebuhr did helped awaken many slumbering Christians who held different political views from his. Before the decade of the 1960s, they had not thought much about politics. Suddenly they decided that liberal politicians were destroying the country's moral fiber. Among others they blamed Niebuhr. A young African American student reacted in a different way to Niebuhr's work when he came across it while pursuing a doctorate degree at Boston University's School of Theology in the mid-1950s. Martin Luther King Jr. believed that the country's moral fiber had long been seriously damaged but not in the way imagined by many white fundamentalists. King thought that Niebuhr understood injustice much better than Christian conservatives, even better than some black religious leaders. But unlike Niebuhr he was not convinced that Christian political activism should give up on appeals to conscience. Politicians were useful, but they could not be trusted to change the direction of American society.

Civil Rights and the Christian Right

Contemporary American controversies about the place of religion in public life fall under the shadow of the civil rights movement of the 1950s and 1960s. Secularists argue that Martin Luther King's role in fighting for civil rights legislation should not be used as a model to legitimate the political activism of the Christian Coalition. A moral crusade for equality, they say, is different from a crusade to elect conservative Republicans who want to cut taxes. Ralph Reed does not agree. When he ran the Christian Coalition, he cited King as one of his primary inspirations. Reed might have been wrong, but he was not uninformed. He had among other things a doctorate degree in American history.

This chapter has tried to make clear that religion in American life has frequently been about politics. Quite often it has been about progressive politics. But religious politics have not come in a single variety. Historians who have studied elections in the United States have demonstrated a correlation between how people vote and their religious identification. Nineteenth-century Episcopalians voted for Whig candidates until the Whig party folded. Then they voted for Republicans. Catholics voted for Democrats. But these correlations were not dictated by religious doctrine. Nor were they determined by pastoral advice. They rather resulted from other factors that were also correlated with religious identification. Social class affected religious as well as political choices. So did the way one group perceived another group. Protestants voted one way because Catholics voted the other way. People's religion also influenced the level of their political involvement. For a long time, adherents of very conservative religious groups were less likely to be politically active than members of religious denominations that modernized their doctrines.

A number of ironies lurk in this last observation. For much of American history it was not just the Jeffersonians who protected the wall of separation. It was religious conservatives who carefully cordoned off church work from the howling wilderness of the world where politicians raked their muck. They wanted no advice from the state about what it meant to be a good Christian. Suspicions about the dangers of a strong state were precisely what drove Americans to separate church and state in the first place. Southern Protestants had particular reasons to resist political moves that might impose someone's moral standards on others. Casting themselves as the victims of abolitionism and other Yankee crusades, they were historically conditioned to treat religion as a private matter. Only in the 1890s did they show much interest in moral legislation. And they did so then because laws against gambling and alcohol and prostitution were seen as ways to control African Americans.

When Protestant fundamentalists first became militant in the early twentieth century, they reserved their militancy for issues within their churches. Aside from laws that forbade the teaching of Darwinian evolution, they did not expect much from government. Nor did they trust the state with religious instruction of their children. When the American Supreme Court struck down school prayer in 1962, the Southern Baptist Convention, the largest and among the most conservative Protestant denominations, supported the decision. Only after the turbulent decade of the 1960s did the convention change its mind.

Many conservative religious groups say that they were forced reluctantly into politics and to policies that relied on state intervention. The aggressive behavior of people they called secular humanists gave them no choice. Religious values, once a normal part of the background of American culture, suddenly vanished from public discussion. Schools not only stopped praying, but they stripped all references to God from the curriculum. Teachers were told not to point to the Ten Commandments as a source of ethical standards. Courts banned crosses and nativity scenes from public property. Meanwhile, popular culture in all of its forms ran with the message of the sexual revolution. From the standpoint of many religious Americans, popular singers, television characters, and movie actors all talked dirty. Every law that tried to protect moral standards was systematically cut down. Any suggestion that America was a Christian nation suddenly became a scurrilous remark.

In truth, at the beginning of the 1960s many white Christians who belonged to conservative denominations—just like many white Christians who belonged to liberal denominations—were racist. Their churches were segregated. They treated Martin Luther King with scorn. Yet it is some testament to King and to other civil rights groups that a large number of conservative white Christians changed their minds. Later, they were prepared to acknowledge, along with other Americans, that religious politics had their finest hour in the civil rights campaigns. It took some time, but by the 1980s Christian churches in both the North and the South embraced the doctrine of racial equality. What is more important, King had shown conservative Christians that the conscience of America could be altered. If they were going to save their country from moral perdition, they had to go public. They had, many of them said, to pay attention to politics.

Although conservative Christian groups accepted the justice of civil rights legislation, they reacted with disapproval to just about everything else that happened in the 1960s. They criticized churches for playing a major role in the moral protests aimed at American military involvement in Southeast Asia. Student-led demonstrations against the war in Vietnam offended their patriotism. A counterculture of pot-smoking hippies struck them as an odious resurgence of paganism. Five years after the introduction of the contraceptive pill, premarital sex had changed forever the dating practices of young adults. The only thing worse than the rising rate of divorce was the choice made by many young Americans that marriage was not necessary at all. The Supreme Court made abortion legal. Women moved into the workplace and gave their babies to day-care centers for tending. Feminists taught that if men wanted to lead, they could begin by doing the laundry. Homosexuals completed the sexual revolution by saying that no pattern of sexual behavior could be called normal. Social activists seemed to want laws that protected whatever people wanted to do. It did not matter how offensive those practices were to the majority.

Amazingly a lot of American churches were able to keep up with all of this. Those that did not looked for a political campaign to call their own. By 1980 Jerry Falwell was ready to launch the Moral Majority. Its agenda was political, and it focused on what conservative Christians called family values. The timing was fortuitous because the country's new president, Ronald Reagan, was sympathetic. It was odd. Reagan's predecessor, Jimmy Carter, was a Southern Baptist, a man of strong religious convictions, and a loyal spouse. Reagan was divorced, an indifferent father, a rare church-goer. But Falwell's followers liked Reagan. Perhaps they could not forgive Carter for telling *Playboy* magazine that he had lusted in his heart. Or maybe they had simply decided that in politics you had to side with whoever embraced your cause. Reagan did not practice family values, but he knew how to make them sound good. Effortlessly he made the moral issues of family life a bedrock part of his economic program. It called for lower taxes and less government spending in every area save the military.

Has the Christian Coalition Corrupted American Politics?

Falwell was never certain he had done the right thing. He spent the 1980s trying to organize a political campaign to reverse what he called moral decline. But the results disappointed him, and he went back to soul saving. He remained a vocal public figure who like many before him concluded that politicians were not reliable allies. They supported family values only when the issue won them votes. That sobering fact did not dampen the political energy of Pat Robertson and his lieutenant, Ralph Reed. Robertson was a convert to Pentecostalism and, as we have seen, something of a media genius. Reed is a political junkie who as a student of American history recognizes the power of religion to mobilize political energy. For him politics and religion are almost the same thing. He believes in family values and the benefits of a substantial income in promoting them. Both Robertson and Reed use religion to give legitimacy to conservative social programs.

Pundits argue about whether the Christian Coalition ever had a decisive effect on a national election. Clearly not all conservative Christian groups, whether labeled evangelical or fundamentalist, rallied to its call. It helped mobilize many conservative voters who went to church but were not otherwise deeply invested in their religious lives. Many of them were already Republican voters. Tapping their moral resentments helped get them to the polls but did not necessarily change their choices. The Christian Coalition seemed to work its political magic best in local elections and in primaries.

While political commentators argued about the long-range effectiveness of the Christian Coalition, many critics attacked it for encouraging opportunism. They had good reason to be concerned. Hypocrisy is always a danger in democratic politics. When politicians presume to sponsor religion, the danger of hypocrisy becomes major. Thomas Jefferson thought that politicians who wore their religion on their sleeves turned religion into a purely instrumental set of calculations aimed at self-advancement. He reminded voters that the Constitution removed religion as a test of public office. Candidates should not discuss their personal beliefs that had no bearing on issues. Yet in the presidential election of 2000 the major candidates all talked openly and constantly about their faith.

George Bush probably mentioned his faith in God and Christ a few more times than Al Gore. But neither of them outdid Gore's vice presidential candidate Joseph Lieberman. Lieberman was Jewish. In the past American Jews had been especially resistant to God-talk in the public sphere. They knew all the ways that public religion threatened to turn non-Christians into second-class citizens. Yet Lieberman not only testified to the influence of his faith on his public actions, but after losing the election, he also endorsed President Bush's initiative to give financial assistance to faith-based charities. That initiative may or may not survive court challenges. If it does, it will be the first time the federal government has doled out money to charities that make religious worship an integral part of the services they provide. The government will be in the position of deciding which religious claimants for federal largess are "legitimate."

There are reasons to worry about that. Americans who want to see a widened role for religion in public life, even at the risk of making it state-sponsored, insist that they wish to restore a balance that has been lost. They want to reverse a trend that they say has pushed faith out of public life. Another consideration weighs upon those who oppose these initiatives. They point out that in the past American politicians who talked about the importance of religion in public life had their own religion in mind. They stoked the fires of discrimination. Nativist groups tried to keep Catholics from holding public office. Christian political groups mobilized an effort to block President Woodrow Wilson from appointing Louis Brandeis, a Jew, to the Supreme Court. Congress found it easy to pass discriminatory legislation against Asian immigrants because they were not Christian. The recent war against terrorism has resulted in a massive suspension of due process in criminal cases against suspected detainees who are almost always Muslim. To be Islamic in America in these days is to be a suspect.

Interestingly, one important religious group in the United States with a conservative voting record and conservative views on almost all moral issues has been notably indifferent to any alliance with the Christian Coalition. The Church of Latter-Day Saints, or the Mormons, remember their history better than many religious groups. They remember that they were the targets of religious laws throughout the nineteenth century. Their political enemies chased them from New York, to Kirkland, Ohio, to Missouri, to Nauvoo. In that last community established when Illinois was still a territory, Joseph Smith decided to try some politics himself. He cut political deals in exchange for Mormon votes. In 1844 he announced that he was running for president. The strategy backfired. Smith and his brother were thrown in jail by their political enemies and then murdered.

The Mormons next went to the Salt Lake basin where they hoped to establish a religious kingdom. Instead, the area where they settled became a U.S. territory. The federal government passed laws against the practice of plural marriage. In 1878 the American Supreme Court upheld the statute. It was a foregone conclusion. Before the Civil War, opponents of polygamy attacked it as one of the "twin pillars of barbarism." The other was slavery. The United States government threw Mormon men in jail and placed the church in virtual receivership. Mormons finally threw in the towel. In the 1890s they renounced polygamy and joined the union. Religious politics had forced them to say that Joseph Smith was wrong.

Thereafter, Mormons have not been shy in proclaiming their faith. They have engineered an organization of proselytizers unmatched by any other religious group. They are now the sixth-largest denomination in America, well ahead of Presbyterians and Episcopalians, and have more members outside the United States than within it. Yet while Mormons in the states where they are numerous vote for other Mormons, they recognize that in the matter of religious politics they easily become the victims. When Mitt Romney ran for the Senate in Massachusetts in 1994, his opponent, the incumbent Senator Edward Kennedy, allowed his campaign to spread fears about the Mormon menace. That a Catholic, whose own brother had once had to defend his faith against the smear tactics of Protestants, was willing to do that speaks volumes about the dangers of political opportunism.

In the United States, where religion is about everything, where mega-churches provide worship along with health clubs, credit unions, and fast-food outlets, religious politics are inevitable. The majority of Americans think of religion as a vital public resource. That makes the application of the no-religious establishment clause of the First Amendment a con-tentious issue. Disagreement in a democratic society is a good thing. But because religion has touched on so many things, including perceptions about who is or is not a real American, to err on the side of strictness in applying the First Amendment is a wise course.

The wisdom of separating the state from most expressions of public religion derives from the fact that state-endorsed religion can act as an insidious form of exclusion and intimidation. To practice religion freely in an arena where government pays no attention to questions of faith is intimately connected to the freedom to be different. Ralph Ellison, the great black writer, decided that what made America work as a society was the permission it extended even to people far down the social totem pole to "cultural improvisation." Religious freedom, as a constitutionally priv-ileged form of dissent, gives men and women the right to claim an iden-tity that while separate from that of any purported majority has the same protection under the law. It is the beginning of improvisation. Someone may be Hindu, Muslim, Jew, Christian, Freethinker, and many other things in addition. The Constitution permits a free choice of religious identification but does not freeze anyone into that single profile. That in any case is how American freedom is supposed to work.

If Americans have not learned to treat religious beliefs as equal, then they are not likely to perfect equality in any other area of civic society. Because religion in America is a form of social capital, because it is suf-fused in so many areas of public life, public officials should never use reli-gious belief in a witch-hunt to secure partisan advantages. The United States will not reach its full potential as a democratic nation until Ameri-cans at long last catch up with Article Six of the Constitution: "No reli-gious test shall ever be required as a qualification to any office of public trust under the United States."

Index